Mark Elliott's CV is as straight as the Karakoram Highway. He's danced rain dances in a Gambian village, placated tribal Cameroonian kings with gifts of whisky and nibbled chocolate strawberries with two US presidents. He first visited South-East Asia in 1987 and has returned on numerous occasions. He travelled in boycott-era Vietnam when buses were still steam-powered, he's eaten pigs' brains with Borneo Dayaks and has thus far avoided Cambodian land mines (touch wood).

Other books for Trailblazer include *Azerbaijan with excursions to Georgia*, for which he spent many scintillating hours in KGB interrogation, and *Asia Overland* which he co-authored with sadly-missed colleague, Wil Klass, whose disappearance has yet to be explained by modern science.

While playing blues harmonica in a Turkmenistan club Mark met the lovely Danielle, with whom he now shares a happy suburban life in Belgium.

South-East Asia – The Graphic Guide
First edition 2003

Publisher
Trailblazer Publications
The Old Manse, Tower Rd, Hindhead, Surrey, GU26 6SU, UK
Fax (+44) 01428-607571
info@trailblazer-guides.com
www.trailblazer-guides.com

British Library Cataloguing in Publication Data
A catalogue record for this book is available from the British Library

ISBN 1-873756-67-4

Editor: Anna Jacomb-Hood
Series editor: Patricia Major
Layout: Anna Jacomb-Hood and Bryn Thomas
Index: Mark Elliott

Every effort has been made by the author and publisher to ensure that the
information contained herein is as accurate and up to date as possible. However,
they are unable to accept responsibility for any inconvenience, loss or injury
sustained by anyone as a result of the advice and information given in this guide.

Printed on chlorine-free paper from farmed forests by
Star Standard (☎ +65-6861 3866), Singapore

SOUTH-EAST
ASIA
THE GRAPHIC GUIDE

MARK ELLIOTT

TRAILBLAZER PUBLICATIONS

This book is dedicated with all my heart to
Dani Systermans and to my unbeatable parents.

Acknowledgements

Appreciation for help, inspiration, information, love and support (or otherwise!) to Jane, Tim, Paula & Zak, Anna Jacomb-Hood (plus family and Jaffa cakes), Bryn Thomas, the invisible spirit of Wil Klass, Chen Guiyang, Mr Nu and his Beer Hoi surprise, Tim Winter, Chen Yong Bo, Michael Ash, Harrie 'Blondkop', François Benta, Burmese friends who'd prefer to stay anonymous, Dixie Bramble (sorry to miss the weddings), 'Mr Zan' in Sapa, Cheng Tao, Claus Qvist Jessen, Tom Robbins and his funky outfitters, Ward van Heddeghem, Amala and Loon Dunc, Peter B and Gaby G, David Benton, 'the gang' in Muang Ngoi (hope you remembered to leave eventually!), Ray in KL, Steve Bradley, Jaz and Maz for tunes, the JET programme for dosh, Peter Field, Gavin Machell, Jackie G, Natasha P, Alison Abernathy, the ever-inspiring Paul Maiteny, Harumi Matsumoto, Tim 'free will' Morgan, Mr Guppy (of course) and to hundreds of fellow travellers and friendly helpers, many of whose names I never knew.

Update request

We've tried to ensure that this guide is as accurate and up to date as possible but things change quickly in this part of the world. If you notice any changes or omissions please email the author at **mark.elliott@trailblazer-guides.com** or write to him at Trailblazer (address on p2). A free copy of the next edition will be sent to persons making a significant contribution.

Updated information will shortly be available on the Internet at
www.trailblazer-guides.com

❏ **Philosophy of this book**
Ultra thrifty, but not cheap. It's better to spend $2 on a hotel and $20 on a cultural experience than spending $20 on a hotel and then gouging the poor locals for every last penny. Anyway, real cultural experiences are rarely expensive, if you have the time and generosity of spirit to make local friends.

CONTENTS

Map page references shown in **bold** in this contents list

THAILAND (cont'd)

LAOS

Introduction

Practical information

CAMBODIA

Introduction

Practical information

VIETNAM

Introduction

Practical information

YUNNAN (SOUTH-WEST CHINA)

Introduction

Practical information

BURMA (MYANMAR)

Introduction

Practical information

SINGAPORE

Introduction 188

Practical information

Map page references shown in **bold** in this contents list

INTRODUCTION

What on earth is all this?

Call this a guide book?

Well, sort of. More like a set of treasure maps.

This book aims unashamedly at the budget traveller who is relatively self confident and doesn't need to be cosseted at every turn. These days it's remarkably easy to travel on a whim in South-East Asia. Traveller cafés and backpacker ghettos are worth finding if only to collect up-to-date information and then escape. There are also useful tourist offices with plenty of colourful brochures offering details on all the local monuments, sites and cultural events. Your challenge is to work out which places are worth the bother, find transport to get you there, and locate the tourist office and/or a cheap hotel on arrival. This book does that for you at a glance with its plethora of schematic maps.

Using a standard guide book, travellers busy themselves reading between the lines to pick destinations that sound interesting. Then, fumbling with pen and paper they work out from a series of different 'getting there' chapters, whether there's time to visit anyway. After all the effort they find they've often chosen exactly the route that all the others chose using the same method! This book takes a different approach. It uses mostly maps, not talk – a great way to cram in much

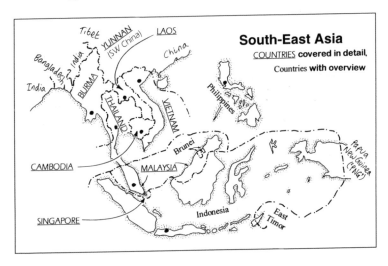

more information. The planning chapter gives general tactical help on where to cross borders, get visas and other such dull yet crucial issues. Then each country in mainland South-East Asia is divided into bite-sized chunks on schematic maps. Possible routes are shown with travel details (time taken, frequency, mode of transport etc); even the departure/arrival bus stations are indicated where confusion is possible. These may look confusing at first glance. But don't be put off! Like learning a new video game, you'll have to play a few times to get the hang of the style. It shouldn't take long ... and once you've got a feel for the short-hand and general miniaturization you'll find that each page contains as much condensed practical information as 10–20 pages of a standard guide book. And that means less weight in your backpack.

Note that I don't generally explain at length **why** to go somewhere. Instead there are very brief notes and 'site icons' designed to whet your appetite in a rather subjective way. The '*atmospheric*' icon (a square box with a cross inside) is generally a good sign that I liked a place and a star or two means it's something you really ought to see while you're in the area. For the full history, you'll usually find that the free or cheap pamphlets available locally are better than any commercial guide book (which probably took its information from that source anyway!). The hope is that you'll actually communicate with people en route rather than keeping your nose in a book. And that should make the trip more enjoyable in the long run.

NB This book focuses on 'mainland' South-East Asia ie Thailand, Burma (Myanmar), Vietnam, Cambodia, Laos, Singapore, and peninsular Malaysia plus Yunnan (south-western China). It also gives a basic overview of Indonesia, Brunei, East Timor and the Philippines.

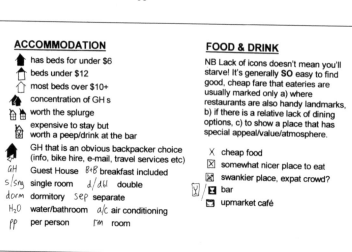

ACCOMMODATION

🛏 has beds for under $6
🏠 beds under $12
🏠 most beds over $10+
🏘 concentration of GH s
🏠 🏠 worth the splurge
🏚 expensive to stay but
     worth a peep/drink at the bar

🔨 GH that is an obvious backpacker choice
     (info, bike hire, e-mail, travel services etc)
GH Guest House   B+B breakfast included
s/sng single room   d/dbl double
dorm dormitory   sep separate
H₂O water/bathroom   a/c air conditioning
pp per person   rm room

FOOD & DRINK

NB Lack of icons doesn't mean you'll starve! It's generally **SO** easy to find good, cheap fare that eateries are usually marked only a) where restaurants are also handy landmarks, b) if there is a relative lack of dining options, c) to show a place that has special appeal/value/atmosphere.

X cheap food
⊠ somewhat nicer place to eat
⊠ swankier place, expat crowd?
Y/🍺 bar
☕ upmarket café

Key to symbols used in this guide

LINE TYPES

- Railway
- Metro/Suburban line station
- International border
- Crossing point open
- Crossing point closed
- Crossing point may open
- Road transport (bus, minibus etc)
- No public transport
- Roads
- Unpaved or pedestrianised road
- Walking path/Track
- Water/River
- Ferry
- Wall

TRANSPORT

- Main bus station
- Rail station
- Bus stand, stop or small station
- Airport
- Metro Station
- Jetty/Port
- Sleeper service
- moto Motorbike taxi
- Bicycle rental
- Motorbike rental
- p/u Pick up/bemo/songthaew/linega
- freq frequent/ sev several per day
- d/dep depart a./arr. arrive

DESCRIPTIONS

- PLACE 'Place' is interesting
- atmospheric, quaint, charming...
- recommended must see!
- English spoken (where rare)
- [POX] 'Pox' is unprepossessing - don't make a special trip to visit!

PRICES

- $ US$
- S$ Singapore $
- M$ Malaysian Ringgit
- ฿ Thai Baht
- Đ Vietnamese Dong
- K Lao Kip
- R/Rls Cambodian Rials
- Ky Burmese Kyat
- Y/元 Chinese Yuan
- P Philippine Pesos
- Rp Indonesian Rupiah
- B$ Brunei $

SHADING

- Park or green area
- Open area/car-park
- Market
- Enclosed market/shopping centre
- Travellers' area (GH s, bike rental, e-mail, cafés etc) or as described.
- Other 'area' (described)

RELIGIOUS BUILDINGS

- Temple/Pagoda
- Special temple
- Big Buddha
- reclining Buddha
- Indian temple
- Khmer Prasat
- Mosque
- Church

ATTRACTIONS

- Castle/Fort
- Palace
- Palace open as museum
- Classic Khmer temple
- Significant ruins
- Other ruins
- Museum
- Beach
- Cave
- Upmarket resort beach
- Scuba diving
- Attractive old houses
- Atmospheric (town, place etc)
- Backpacker centre
- Garden
- Viewpoint

AROUND TOWN

- Museum
- Bookshop
- Bike rental
- Motorbike rental
- Embassy/Consulate
- Cinema
- Bath-house/Hot spring
- Theatre
- Opera/Concert Hall
- TV Tower
- Post Office
- Telephone/Phone office
- E-mail/Internet café
- Info office (head here or to 'traveller area/GH' to get a map)
- Bank/Money changer
- Statue/Monument
- Gallery
- Stadium
- Hospital

Interpreting a schematic map

NOT TO SCALE!

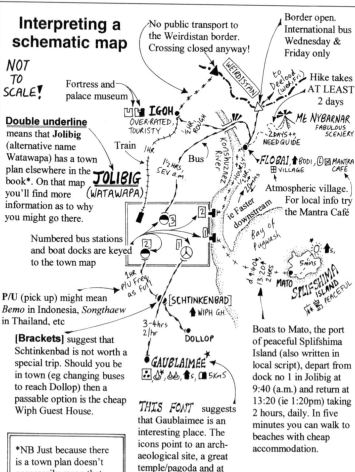

No public transport to the Weirdistan border. Crossing closed anyway!

Border open. International bus Wednesday & Friday only

Hike takes AT LEAST 2 days

Fortress and palace museum

IGOH OVER-RATED, TOURISTY

Mt NYBARNAR FABULOUS SCENERY

~2DAYS++ NEED GUIDE

Double underline means that Jolibig (alternative name Watawapa) has a town plan elsewhere in the book*. On that map you'll find more information as to why you might go there.

Train 1HR

Bus

JOLIBIG (WATAWAPA)

1½ HRS, SEV a.m.

Komshuznez River

FLOBAI ▲BODI, ☺⊠ MANTRA CAFÉ ⊞VILLAGE

Atmospheric village. For local info try the Mantra Café

ie Faster downstream

Bay of Pugwash

Numbered bus stations and boat docks are keyed to the town map

d 40m 13-20m 2HRS

MATO SPLIFSHIMA ISLAND PEACEFUL

5mins

P/U (pick up) might mean *Bemo* in Indonesia, *Songthaew* in Thailand, etc

1HR P/U Freq as Full

[SCHTINKENBAD] ▲WIPH GH.

3-4hrs 2/hr

DOLLOP

[Brackets] suggest that Schtinkenbad is not worth a special trip. Should you be in town (eg changing buses to reach Dollop) then a passable option is the cheap Wiph Guest House.

GAUBLAIMEE ☺🏊,♨♨,▲s,🏠5KmS

THIS FONT suggests that Gaublaimee is an interesting place. The icons point to an archaeological site, a great temple/pagoda and at least two more temples there, plus the availability of cheap accommodation. 5km to the south is a notable museum. (Most icons are listed in the general key plus there are some special ones for individual countries). Buses take 3 to 4 hours <u>from Jolibig</u> (ie between line ends) leaving twice an hour from bus station 1. Since it takes an hour from Jolibig to Schtinkenbad one can guess that Schtinkenbad to Gaublaimeee would take 2-3hours. A game-player mentality will help with these 'treasure maps'!

Boats to Mato, the port of peaceful Splifshima Island (also written in local script), depart from dock no 1 in Jolibig at 9:40 (a.m.) and return at 13:20 (ie 1:20pm) taking 2 hours, daily. In five minutes you can walk to beaches with cheap accommodation.

*NB Just because there is a town plan doesn't necessarily mean that the place depicted is especially interesting! Indeed, sometimes it's the drab big cities where you need bus station help and don't want to waste your time seeking out a tourist map.

Using this book

At first glance, much of this book may seem to be just a morass of squiggly lines and microscopic scrawl. Get your specs and I'll explain some key features.

THE MAPS
Schematic route planner maps (see sample map opposite)
The first few are route and strategy planners. These are a handy way to get an overview of the region before you choose your route.

● Schematic maps present the main regional transport possibilities to get you to and between places where you'll find information or something of interest, and preferably a bed for a few pennies.

● If a town/place is double underlined on 'real' or schematic maps, a basic plan of that town will appear somewhere in the book – usually within a page or two (if you can't find it, check the index and look for an underlined page number).

● Several towns appear not as a simple dot but as a box filled with curious, numbered circles. These represent the town's various bus stations, stops and pick-up points so you can see at a glance which departure point to use for which route. When numbered these correspond to similarly numbered points on the relevant town plan.

NB Schematic maps are not all to scale – spatial arrangements are merely suggested, but the idea is to show transport connections and key points.

Town maps (see sample map p15)
The information given is designed to:
i) be enough to get you between the train/bus station/port(s);
ii) get you to a bearable budget hotel – ideally with a 'traveller ambience'. That's not because we consider it a great idea to stick with other foreigners – au contraire. However, because such places can often give you the best tips and inside information, they can actually be the best launch pads from which to get the local and cultural tips you need to escape the 'circuit' – as long as you ask!!!
iii) show, if available, somewhere you can get a good (preferably free) city map;
iv) especially if neither ii) or iii) is available, show you how to reach the key attractions.

NB As with the schematic maps, I give somewhat disproportionate space to towns that I found relatively challenging, or those that don't appear in existing guide books. However, when English is widely spoken and/or information is easy to come by, I may leave you to get on with it, aided perhaps with cursory tips and suggestions for a guesthouse to aim for in case you don't find somewhere en route.

Again, icons and abbreviations are important. See key pp10–11.

Bus routes

Tourists prepared to pay $20+ a night can probably afford the taxi to get to their hotel. But for budget travellers it's very galling to pay $2 to get to a $1 crash pad. So in bigger places we'll show you the bus routes/metro stops to get you near enough to walk to key sights, accommodation and transport hubs (ports, stations etc).

MY CHOICES

Places to stay

Most accommodation suggested in this book is the cheapest available OK/back-packer-orientated place (or [just plain cheap] when in square brackets).

In some towns I simply mark the main traveller area where there are loads of similarly-priced hostels. In such zones I assume that you'll be able to find somewhere that suits you, but if you want more guidance you'll usually find a very comprehensive review of budget options on the relevant branch of 🖥 www.pass planet.com.

Where a more expensive hotel has particular charm, historical relevance etc I'll point it out too – you can often soak up the atmosphere by splurging a dollar or two at the bar without shelling out hundreds of dollars for a bed! The use of US dollars in the text isn't meant to suggest any sort of American imperialist ploy. It's just that dollars are the de facto reference currency in the region.

Places to eat

Unlike many guide books I make little or no attempt to suggest places to eat except where a café is either a landmark, a source of information, or is outstanding for atmosphere, view etc. In places where there seems to be a relative lack of eating possibilities, I sometimes mark local restaurants with an 'x' – for convenience more than for quality food. However, in most of the region, you'll always find cheap food in markets or at stalls nearby. Tips on local culinary specialties are baked into the text.

❏ **Pic'n'mix practical tips**

● Keep a mini notebook and pen/propelling pencil handy: write down the **name** of everyone you meet so you don't forget them later and seem rude. Repeating names in conversation helps you learn. If you aren't sure of your new friends' names after a couple of repetitions, get them to spell them in local script – it's fun to transliterate.

● Conspicuously write down the **registration number** of cars/taxis you ride in (pre-emptive safety) and of any motorbike you hire (saves embarrassment if you can't find it later!).

● Mark your rented bicycle or moped with a **coloured rag or ribbon** so you can find it amid a million parked others.

● Use your own **padlock** for cheap hotel rooms (especially in Thailand) and for rented bicycles.

● Don't be afraid of the **alphabets**.

Interpreting a town map

Key points

> **Road** and **river** names, and 'to' **directions** are written in *lower case*.
> **Other features** are in CAPITALS and SERIF STYLE when particularly interesting.
> **Icons** used are listed in the general key (though special icons may occur for individual maps or countries).
> Once you arrive in town head for (i) (tourist/info offices) or traveller areas to get a more complete map of the town.
> If (as below) there are **numbered bus/train stations**, **ports** etc these should correspond with one or more schematic maps which will give you the relevant transport information.

Sample map

(town maps are to scale)

The **Doobie** guest house upstairs near bus stand 3 has rooms in the US$6-12 range.

The '**traveller area**' north of Biggy St is your best bet for finding backpacker hostels, e-mail cafés, bicycle/motorbike rental, etc.

The **consulate** of Weirdistan is 1km west of Grand St on Biggy St. The office opens for visas 9:30am to 1pm Monday to Friday.

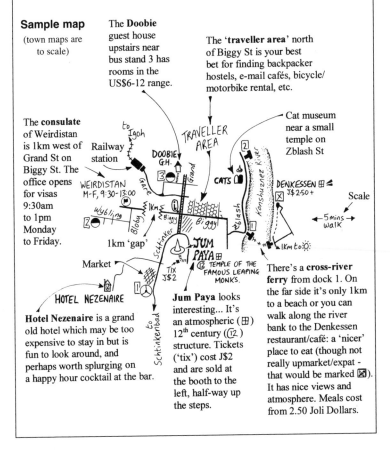

Cat museum near a small temple on Zblash St

Scale

There's a **cross-river ferry** from dock 1. On the far side it's only 1km to a beach or you can walk along the river bank to the Denkessen restaurant/café: a 'nicer' place to eat (though not really upmarket/expat - that would be marked ✉). It has nice views and atmosphere. Meals cost from 2.50 Joli Dollars.

Jum Paya looks interesting... It's an atmospheric (⊞) 12th century (⑫) structure. Tickets ('tix') cost J$2 and are sold at the booth to the left, half-way up the steps.

Hotel Nezenaire is a grand old hotel which may be too expensive to stay in but is fun to look around, and perhaps worth splurging on a happy hour cocktail at the bar.

Reading the signs

Many guide books condescendingly assume that learning the local alphabet is beyond the hopes of a casual tourist. However, while I don't attempt to teach you to read Lao, Thai, Chinese, Burmese or Khmer – I've tried to present those alphabets in a simplified version so that you can start to spot individual letters from maps and be aware of some of the characters' Jekyll and Hyde schizophrenics. The idea is that you'll at least be able to work out the destination board on a bus. Note that I have not had the space (nor in the case of Khmer, the patience!) to explain the full complexities of the vowel systems – but since these are often transliterated in very different ways, anyway – it's best to start with the consonants.

Once you've started, it's amazing to discover that the alphabets really aren't as hard as you may have thought and, best of all, local people with whom you can't communicate verbally seem delighted to help you sound out words on signs or maps. That can help you learn but more importantly it's a great way of making friendly relationships when you're linguistically out of your depth.

Meeting the locals

If you make no attempt to get to know the locals, travelling is little more than geographical stamp collecting. When you do make the effort, however, you'll find that this 'region of smiles' has all the 'soap opera' complexity of life anywhere, and that there are fascinating human dimensions to explore in any place you visit. In remote areas some folks may retain a fascination for your mere foreign-ness. But even where decades of tourism have jaded the population, you may be surprised by how much a little genuine background knowledge, interest and enthusiasm can open doors for future friendships.

Language is the most obvious barrier to making real friendships, along with cultural misapprehensions and distrust. But smiles and a real attempt to understand can bridge the gap. Getting to know local pop, tv, sports and film stars offers you easy 'conversation starters': if you can remember the names and spot the faces or songs you'll quickly get at least a little pub-talk for future encounters. If you share no common language, sounding out scripts can be a mutually hilarious way to pass the time with strangers and is the quickest way to learn, anyway. Politics and religion are obviously more sensitive and require more shared language. But it's worth understanding some of the history and the pressing local issues so that when you do meet the linguistically adept, you can ask something that's not going to sound hopelessly banal. Such random conversations are the essence of travel.

Of course you need to believe in people. Locals may not share your language nor (in their eyes) your fabulous wealth. But most are delightful, big-hearted individuals. Not taking advantage of their over-generosity can be more of a challenge than avoiding the few bad boys. Of course not absolutely everyone you meet is set on being nice all the time. But even life's less-appealing humans respond to genuine interest and respect. The few who're out to rip you off are just trying to make a living. Joke with them, enjoy their 'art' but get away before they win! Should you meet an axe-wielding psychopath anywhere in this life, you're very unlucky. But it's always worth complimenting him on his blade. He might have a sense of humour after all.

Preparing for the trip

WHAT YOU NEED TO PACK

Nothing.

Particularly if you arrive in Bangkok, you'll be able to buy absolutely everything you need for a fraction of the price you'd pay in the West.

Possible exceptions are hi-tech water filtration devices and other top camping equipment. However, neither is at all necessary for typical backpacking unless you are a mountaineer or serious trekker. The other consideration, if you plan to head way off the traveller circuit, is to bring a few **family photos** and small but '**typical**' **gifts** from your country.

There's no need to bring many clothes. It's almost always warm so laundry dries quickly (except in the rainy season when you'll be wet anyway!). You can often have washing done for you at backpacker guesthouses and it'll usually be ready within 12 hours for less than $1/kg. If you head for the mountains and are likely to be cold, you can get a cheap blanket in any market and give it away later. You can even buy second-hand boots, back-packs and day packs around Kao San Road, but this is not recommended. While some are sold by their genuinely impecunious traveller-owners before flying home, this trade can be dodgy encouraging theft from dormitories and cheap rooms (see the box on p46 about the key copy scam, and hence the padlock suggestions in guesthouses).

Once in Bangkok you can very easily buy:
● A **padlock** for your room door in cheap guesthouses.
● A light-weight **sarong** to double as beachwear, a towel and as a **bed sheet** (only under sheets are provided in cheap Thai hostels).
● **Second-hand guide books and novels** are cheaper bought direct from other travellers and cheaper still in Vietnam/Cambodia, though there you'll have less choice.
● **Malaria medication** costs a fortune in the West but on Kao San Road, Bangkok, an air-conditioned branch of Boots (yes! the reputable British pharmacist) has doxycycline at 3B/pill. You could get nearly a year's supply for the cost of a prescription in the UK.

NB Preventing mosquito bites is preferable to taking pills (which can have side-effects) and these days the high-risk areas are few and far between – they are worst in rural Cambodia and parts of eastern Indonesia.
● Boots on Kao San Road also has familiar **toiletries** and any **medicaments** you'll need (including Western birth-control pills, tampons, etc) at less than the marked

British price. In towns throughout the region you'll be able to buy mosquito coils/repellent and a good range of slightly less reliable medicines.

● Personally I find carrying a **mosquito net** an unnecessary burden, as most cheap hotels in problem areas have them already. But all you need is one bad malaria-mozzie night to justify the trouble (rural Cambodia, especially Mondulkiri, is that sort of place). Still, don't waste big bucks and shopping hassle getting one at home: in the Kao San Road area of Bangkok you can get DEET-impregnated nets for 90–130B (under $3) or second-hand from 50B (check for holes!).

MONEY

Travellers' cheques are recommended for safety and get a better rate than cash in Thailand, China and Malaysia.

US$ cash is more convenient in Vietnam, Laos, and notably in the Philippines where travellers' cheques are very awkward and pricey to cash. Rates for cash other than US$ are generally somewhat less competitive. Having some US$ cash is important in Cambodia (where the dollar is a de facto second currency) and virtually essential in Burma where travellers' cheques are a nightmare to exchange.

Useful **currency exchange websites** include 🖥 www.oanda.com/convert/classic and www.xe.net/currency/. However, almost all such converters are wrong for Burmese Kyat as they give inter-bank rates which in the case of Burma are some 200 times lower than the real rate for which people should consult 🖥 www.irrawaddy.org/.

Debit/credit cards are useful for cash advances and are accepted in many upmarket hotels/restaurants. However, particularly in Thailand, there is a significant risk of fraud. In Burma (where there is no MasterCard agent at present) paying by Visa card is possible in a few places and should be fine if your bill is denominated in US$. However, to pay local currency bills with a credit card would be self-bankrupting lunacy: your bank may well charge you at the 'official rate', some 60 times more than black-market cash value!

How much will I need?

South-East Asia is a bargain. While prices do vary significantly between countries you can survive in Thailand (just) on $3–5/day (cheapest dorm, basic market snacks, cheap bottled water, hitch-hiking). You'll do OK on $10/day (fan-cooled bus travel, entry fees, bicycle rental), and live in some comfort for $20/day (guesthouse room with en suite bathroom, eat decent local meals, travel in air-conditioned buses, drink a beer or two, have occasional local taxi hops).

The main additional expenses are flights (from £350 return London–Bangkok), visas (average $30 for China, $20 Cambodia, $30–70 Vietnam, $20–50 Laos), national park fees ($5 in Thailand) and other entry fees (under $1 in most of Thailand but $20–40 for Angkor, typically $5 a pop in Vietnam, very variable ($2–8) in Yunnan, cheap or non-existent in Laos. Malaysia and especially Singapore can be considerably more expensive, and a visit to Burma has to factor in the cost of a flight to get there (at least $120) as the land borders are closed.

You'll also have to spend $200 while there due to compulsory currency exchange rules. If you stay a month that's not a huge splurge.

GETTING INFORMATION

This book aims to give you information where it's otherwise awkward to find. Where it's easy to find all you need locally I'll simply indicate the fact and let you get on with it! Good **free sources** of help include:

Tourist information offices and free guides

Very varied. In **Thailand**, **Singapore** and **Malaysia** it's usually worth heading straight for the tourist information office. Virtually every town has extensive brochures often including long accommodation listings and maps. But you may need to ask very specifically for what you want. Ask for maps of neighbouring towns and districts too! Their free maps aren't always to scale but will show you where to find all the main sights, probably with photos and as much history as a standard guide book – that's why this guide tends to simply note personal favourite places – opinion is harder to find than fact! In Thailand, even when information offices are closed, the 'Tourist Police' will often have a map for you.

In **Burma**, Myanmar Tours and Travels (MTT) has brilliant free maps of the main sites but you'd be advised to grab them in Yangon as supply is limited or non existent elsewhere. The main attractions in **Cambodia** have free information pamphlets which are way better than even the best researched guide books. In **Vietnam** cheap maps and bootleg guide books are sold by hawkers in every tourist area. And everywhere except Burma, there's the internet.

Websites

You may be amazed to find just how easy it is to get cheap, convenient web access throughout South-East Asia (with the very pronounced exception of Burma). With powerful search engines such as 🖥 www.google.com, the web has the potential to revolutionize guide-book publishing. However, of the zillions of travel sites, surprisingly few offer detailed practical help. Indeed, especially in cranky slow-loading rural web-cafés you can easily waste hours to learn very little. Sites that are of real, specific help are included in the relevant chapters and on some maps. Below are the general gems – and they're free.

● 🖥 www.passplanet.com is hard to beat. You'll get an overview of each country covered (most of South-East Asia but not Vietnam). There are traveller 'ratings' on a variety of factors, but also very detailed, personal evaluations of hostels and guesthouses, bus trips (including times, frequencies and prices) etc all aimed squarely at the budget traveller. That a site as good as this can remain uncommercial is almost miraculous – do contribute your updates!

● 🖥 www.itisnet.com/english/e-top.htm is another great site with extensive practical information and photos as well as patchy (but often very useful and extensive) priced budget hotel listings.

❏ Which country?

It doesn't help you if I waffle on about how impossibly subjective the following generalizations are so I'll just get on and drop some 'E's:

	Exotic	Efficient	Easy	Expensive*	Enchanting/ friendly
Burma	★★★★★	★☆☆☆	★☆☆☆	★★★☆☆**	★★★★
Cambodia	★★★☆	★☆☆☆	★★★☆	★★☆☆	★★☆☆
Laos	★★★★☆	★☆☆☆	★☆☆☆	★☆☆☆	★★★★
Malaysia	★★☆☆	★★★★☆	★★★★☆	★★★☆☆	★★★☆☆
Singapore	★☆☆☆	★★★★★	★★★★★	★★★★☆	★☆☆☆
Thailand	★★★☆☆	★★★★☆	★★★★☆	★☆☆☆	★★★★☆
Vietnam	★☆☆☆	★☆☆☆	★★★☆	★★★☆	★☆☆☆
Yunnan	★★★☆	★★★★☆	★★☆☆	★☆☆☆	★★★☆☆

* Fewest dark stars is cheapest
** Living costs are low but there are high fixed costs to get there, $200 min exchange

Burma is unbeatably magical – ox-carts, slow river ferries, timeless villages and overpowering stupas giving a 'picture-book Asia' quality. **Thailand** is vastly more developed but has an unparalleled range of beaches, ruins and parks with great value for money in every price range.

Yunnan has the most gorgeous mountains and some little visited hill-tribe villages. **Laos** has delightful karst-riverine scenery and remains brilliantly laid back with bargain prices.

Cambodia is exciting to visit as it dashes headlong out of war-enforced isolation and Angkor is worth a very lengthy detour. Northern **Vietnam** has bays of jaw-dropping beauty and some great mountain hikes.

Multi-cultural **Malaysia** is rather more developed but its national parks maintain some of the oldest, most pristine rainforest anywhere, plus it has beaches that come into season when everywhere else is getting rained on. **Singapore** isn't really for budget travellers but is a model of order and trading wealth – perhaps this is what China would be like by now had Mao not made his little mistakes.

● 🖥 www.bootsnall.com has the great idea in putting you in touch with travel 'helper' volunteers, listed by country of expertise. You can email them with specific backpacker questions, though it's a hit and miss, personal service.

● Both 🖥 www.lonelyplanet.com and 🖥 http://travel.roughguides.com/ have an extraordinary wealth of travel information. Naturally as both companies are in the business of selling travel guide books, they don't give you much in the way of raw, practical hotel/transport details (that's the great strength of Passplanet, see p19). However, both have excellent forums on which you can ask (and answer) questions of other travellers: Lonely Planet's (LP's) Thorn Tree seems much more active than Rough Guide's (RG's) Travel Talk – don't forget to search the archives before asking a new question! Both sites also post travellers' reports: RG's

Community/Travel Journals tend to be better organized and more fact rich than LP's postcards. Check both though!

Other key starting points include:
- George Moore's 🖳 www.geocities.com/rectravel/khlavn/khlavn.htm for Laos, Cambodia and Vietnam.
- 🖳 http://talesofasia.com/ for Cambodia and (in less detail) Vietnam and Burma.
- 🖳 www.asiaphoto.de for great photo-journal trips to Burma, Laos and Cambodia.

Other travellers

Thirty years ago travellers in South-East Asia were so few and far between that meeting another Westerner was quite a thrill. Numbers increased dramatically in the '80s, travellers exchanged tips on information boards at the mushrooming backpacker guesthouses and the banana pancake was born.

Since the '90s the traveller influx has been quite overwhelming. The advantage of major backpacker hangouts is that everything you might need (to escape them!) is generally close at hand – maps, email, bike hire, travel agencies, dull but recognizable food, cheap accommodation and plenty of fellow travellers. Too many, you might well think!

Today, striking up random conversations in tourist area bars is as uncomfortable as it would be at any pub back home. Many 21st-century backpackers seem to sit silently for hours at internet cafés, semi oblivious to the fact that they have left home at all. The internet has all but obviated the use of Poste Restante mail services, and the Thorn Tree (🖳 www.lonelyplanet.com) has supplanted the once-useful traveller recommendation books. It's only in dormitory rooms, remote villages, or 'new' destinations that the old sense of backpacker camaraderie blooms anew. Of course, to find out where the 'new place' is you'll have to ask others: they are quite ephemeral.

Alternatively just buy a good phrase book, find a reliable mosquito repellent and strike out on your own.

When to go where

The chart on p23 gives a highly-simplified overview of the rainy season patterns for at-a-glance planning. Of course the reality is much more complex and even the heaviest rains may only last for part of each day interspersed with bright spells in which to enjoy photogenic emerald-green landscapes. Still, rain can make a mess of travel plans with shipping interrupted by typhoons, and roads (especially in Cambodia, Laos and Burma) transformed into rivers of mud.

Generally it's worth avoiding July and August altogether. Even though it rains across much of the region, there's still a certain tourist rush from those on northern hemisphere summer holidays.

December/January offers ideal weather in much of the region but with the Christmas tourist rush added to the long Australasian summer holidays, this is also very much the high season – beach hotels in particular can double their prices and still be full. There are some other important dates to take note of:

① Water Festival/Lunar New Year

South-East Asia's 'happy new year' goes by various names – *Songkran* in Thai, *Pi Mai* in Lao, *Chaul Chnam* in Khmer, *Thingyan* in Burmese, or the *return of Phya Wan!*'water splashing' festival in Yunnan. It comes at the peak of the hot season in mid-April (dates vary slightly according to the lunar calendar except in Yunnan where it's fixed for 13th–20th April, the 15th being the main day). Amid processions and gaiety the most visible sign is the water-throwing – expect to get very wet indeed: 'the wetter you get, the happier you'll be' according to a local saying. It's certainly fun as long as you stay put. Keep your bags in your room and valuables wrapped in plastic. After several days it can get a little tiresome if you have to travel – your backpack will get soaked, tuk-tuks and pick-ups become targets for bucket-loads of 'joy' as you pass by, and even on the specially tarted-up Thai buses you can get drenched through an open window. Forget travelling at all during this period in Burma when all transport either stops or is packed solid for days. In contrast, Laos seems to bring old buses out of hibernation making departures more frequent, though as stuffed full as ever.

Hotel rooms in key celebration towns (notably Louang Prabang in Laos, and Jing Hong in Xishuangbanna, Yunnan) will cost up to four times the normal rate if you can get a room at all. In Thailand locals head for Nong Khai (though backpacker hostels seem to remain fairly empty there) while the worst mayhem is often in the tourist zones with over-enthusiastic *farangs* (foreigners) on watery warpaths in Kao San Road. Head for north Yunnan, Malaysia or Vietnam if you want to avoid the whole thing.

❶ Chinese and Vietnamese New Year

Chinese *Chun Jie* and Vietnamese *Tet* New Years (both 1st February 2003, 22nd February 2004, 9th February 2005) are generally pretty bad times to visit Vietnam, most of Yunnan, and certain ethnic Chinese towns such as Taunggyi (Burma): everything closes down for up to 10 days of private family reunions with relatively little to see. In contrast Singapore, Penang and several Thai cities (where the festival is called *trut jiin*) celebrate with dragon dances and colourful festivities more like Occidental Chinatowns. Especially in China, hotels are booked solid, though backpacker places are less affected.

❷ Ramadan

Throughout the region there are Muslim communities, with particular concentrations in Malaysia, Brunei, south Philippines and most of Indonesia. Few are fundamentalist à la Talibaan, but it's worth being understanding that during the month of Ramadan the faithful are expected to fast during daylight hours. Ramadan is due to start 27th October 2003, 15th October 2004, 4th October 2005. The month finishes with the big Id Al Fatr feast which should be on 26th November 2003,

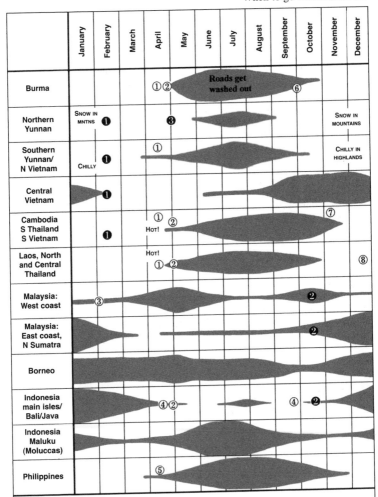

	January	February	March	April	May	June	July	August	September	October	November	December
Burma				①②		Roads get washed out				⑥		
Northern Yunnan	SNOW IN MNTNS ❶			❸							SNOW IN MOUNTAINS	
Southern Yunnan/ N Vietnam	CHILLY ❶			①							CHILLY IN HIGHLANDS	
Central Vietnam		❶									⑦	
Cambodia S Thailand S Vietnam	❶			① HOT!	②							
Laos, North and Central Thailand				HOT! ①②②②②								⑧
Malaysia: West coast	③								❷			
Malaysia: East coast, N Sumatra									❷			
Borneo												
Indonesia main isles/ Bali/Java				④②				④	❷			
Indonesia Maluku (Moluccas)												
Philippines				⑤								

When to go where

Likelihood of rain – more grey = more rain!

⑨ Major festival – worth special detour?

❾ Major event that you may want to avoid (see text for details)

14th November 2004, 3rd November 2005 providing that the new moon is spotted by the relevant authorities: by definition, not an easy task!

② Wesak/Waisak

Held to be simultaneously the Birth, Death and Enlightenment day of the Buddha, this is a great time to see candlelight processions and pious crowds visiting pagodas, wats and monasteries at dawn (eg Shwedagon in Yangon, Borobodur in Java). Doves and tortoises are often liberated to gain merit, even though they were nonsensically caught earlier specially for the purpose. Wesak dates vary according to the lunar calendar falling on a full moon night in April/May: 16th May 2003, 15th April 2004 and 24th April 2005.

③ Thaipusam

The most extraordinary Hindu festival in South-East Asia is Thaipusam (7th February 2003, 2004 and 2005 – check subsequent dates with tourist offices), in which incredible acts of masochistic self mutilation are supposed to bring devotees closer to the divine. Colourfully celebrated in Singapore and parts of Malaysia, most famously at the Batu Caves near Kuala Lumpur.

④

Bali's unique form of Hinduism makes almost every day into a festival somewhere, but the majority of special ones are held in mid-April and late September.

⑤ Easter

The Philippines is the only predominantly Christian country in the region and makes the most of it with dramatic holy week festivals, most famously the Moriones processions in Marinduque. On Good Friday in San Fernando (Luzon) volunteers are mock crucified in a way which is scarily realistic. Easter Sunday falls on April 20th 2003, April 11th 2004 and March 27th 2005.

❸ May Day

May 1st is a common holiday in many countries, but especially in China when the number of domestic tourists tends to peak, notably in Lijiang, making accommodation relatively hard to find.

⑥ Phaung Daw U

Boat races followed by a festival of light – despite the rain, accommodation is likely to be full for three weeks around Inle Lake (Burma) during this period (September/October).

⑦ Bon Om Tuk

Widely celebrated in Cambodia with boat races, the festival honours the reversal of water flow on Lake Tonle Sap. Held in early November though the date varies.

⑧ Elephant Round Up

On the third weekend in November you'll be lucky to find a hotel room within 50km of Surin (Thailand) where the pretty touristy Elephant fest occurs.

For the November full moon (also in Thailand) Loi Krathong/Yi Peng festivals see lotus-float candles sent on random journeys down the nation's rivers – supposedly the best place to see it is Chiang Mai.

Route planning

Choosing a regional route depends more than anything on planning visas and being aware which borders are open (the map on p26 gives an overview). Climate is also a major factor (23). The timings map on p27 gives a rough guide as to how long major route segments may take and all these factors are summarized in the Main Routes map on p29. An overview of boat and land hops across the islands of South-East Asia options is on p31. This book focuses on overland travel, but in some cases flights make sense. Those offering specially notable time savings and/or relatively good value are summarized on p32. Some key tips are:

VISAS AND VISA STRATEGY

More details are given in the country chapters and with reasonable accuracy on the website 🖳 www.worldtravelguide.net/ (click the country you want details on) but here's an overview:

● No visas are required for Malaysia, Thailand or Singapore. While any of these make good arrival points, Thailand is the handiest regional travel hub with its central position, bargain prices and cheap onward flights ex Bangkok.

● The Philippines and Indonesia are also visa free for almost everyone.

● Vietnamese visas generally take as long as a week to process and are not available in Yunnan but if you apply in Battambang or Sihanoukville (Cambodia) you can get them on the spot (or at least the same day). So going to Cambodia before Vietnam makes sense.

● Cambodian visas are available if arriving by air or at the main land borders with Thailand but not at those with Vietnam, so heading east requires less planning.

● Lao tourist visas are available arriving by air at Vientiane or Louang Prabang and on the Friendship Bridge (coming from Nong Khai, Thailand) but not at other borders.

Note that Israelis are generally excluded from Indonesia and Malaysia, Portuguese citizens need a visa for Indonesia. Several nationalities require visas for Brunei.

BORDERS   [See map, p26]

● Most borders close in the evening (Singapore–Malaysia is an exception), and some as early as 4pm.

● The Laos–Cambodia border has now opened but is awkward and the regulations for crossing remain fluid. Allow plenty of time if attempting this.

● There are only two Laos–Vietnam border crossings. However, a handy new flight links Dien Bien Phu in north Vietnam with Louang Prabang (LP) in Laos for only $58, three times a week. Lao visas are available on arrival in LP.

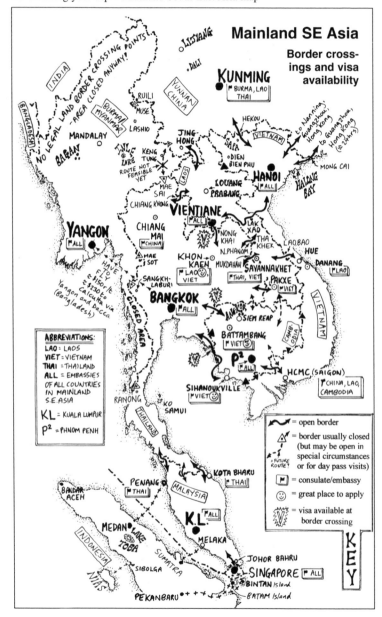

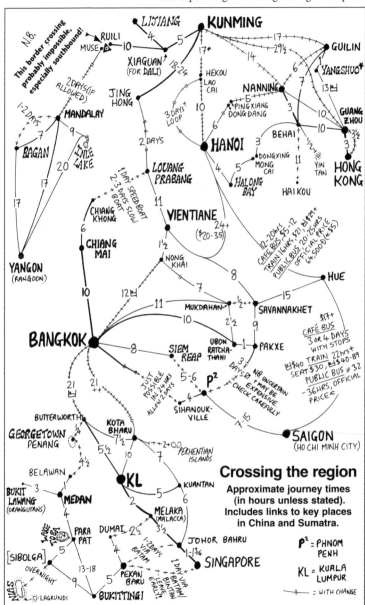

Crossing the region

Approximate journey times
(in hours unless stated).
Includes links to key places
in China and Sumatra.

P² = PHNOM PENH

KL = KUALA LUMPUR

–‖– = WITH CHANGE

● Burma also has many internal travel restrictions and its land borders are usually closed (except for one-day jaunts where you leave your passport in Thailand). Thus you'll probably have to fly in and out. If you're coming from/going to India, the cheapest way to do this is as a stopover with Bangladesh Biman Airlines (Calcutta–Dacca–Yangon–Bangkok). Tickets cost more to/from Dacca! There are also flights to Burma from Kunming (Yunnan) and Chiang Mai (Thailand).

ROAD TRAVEL

Road transport is particularly easy in Thailand, peninsular Malaysia, China and Singapore. In Indonesia and the Philippines roads are OK too, but frequent ferry trips can slow you down. Vietnam has some pretty poor roads but in Burma and Laos most are atrocious.

At the time of writing, Cambodia's roads are the worst of all but with a major reconstruction project already underway that should change very rapidly.

RAIL TRAVEL

Train travel is comfortable if not especially fast in Malaysia and China, handy if slightly less plush in Thailand and Vietnam but downright awful in most of Burma where delays can be interminable. Cambodia's two lines are pitifully slow but riding those trains is no longer a form of Russian roulette as it was in the Khmer Rouge insurgency days. In Burma and Vietnam trains are artificially expensive thanks to hefty foreigner surcharges.

While trains **to** Singapore from Malaysia are a reasonable deal, coming **from** Singapore fares are considerably higher for no extra service: cross the border before buying the ticket. A couple of useful through trains cross the Malaysia–Thailand border without big mark-ups. Although a weekly through train runs between China and Vietnam it's cheaper (and very easy) to go to the border, cross on foot, then pick up another train.

MAIN OVERLAND ROUTES   [See map opposite]

① **China–Burma at Muse** Generally the border is closed but if you have a chance at any Burmese border (see pp162–3) it's at this one. You'll probably have to pay up to $100 guide-fee for the privilege.

② **Vietnam–Yunnan–Laos** This is easier anti-clockwise as Lao visas are available in Yunnan but Vietnamese ones aren't. Going from Hanoi to Louang Prabang this way could be done in four to five days but allow at least three weeks to see Sapa, some of Yunnan and the Nam Ou river en route.

③ **Louang Prabang (Laos)–north Thailand** You can generally make it to Chiang Mai in a day and a half if you're prepared to endure/risk the Mekong speedboats (see p27 and 77–8). It's much nicer to take slower boats at least some of the way.

Note that contrary to common rumour, there is no Lao consulate in Chiang Khong (Thai border town) though some **guesthouses can get a Lao visa** for you simply by sending a delivery boy to Khon Kaen!

④ **Thailand–Vientiane (Laos)– Vietnam** Eastbound you can get a Lao visa on arrival, but not westbound. However, eastbound, the direct Hanoi–Vientiane buses miss the nicest scenery while westbound the best views are during daylight sections.

Theoretically it would be possible to get from Bangkok to Hanoi in two very long days and nights. However, that's easier to manage westbound. The other way you might have to wait a day or so to find a seat for the Hanoi bus and may prefer to break the trip in Lak Xao anyway (see p119).

⑤ **Thailand–Savannakhet (Laos) –Vietnam** A direct bus from Savannakhet to Hue (see p119) goes six days a week and takes all day. Doing hops will take substantially longer

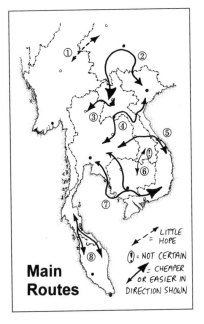

Main Routes

↗ LITTLE
= HOPE

🛈 = NOT CERTAIN

↗ = CHEAPER
OR EASIER IN
DIRECTION SHOWN

and may not save any money. Boats across the Mekong at Savannakhet are easy enough to find but unhurried and stop early.

⑥ **Laos–Cambodia** This route requires sufficient water for the ferries to run to Stung Treng. You may need to charter transport on the Lao side of the border. And there's likely to be tips to pay at the frontier points. At the time of research all this could add up to some $60 to go from Phnom Penh to Pakse. However, by the time you read this, the route will have become more 'worn' and probably transport will regularize and prices drop. See p27 and p90.

⑦ **Thailand–Cambodia–Vietnam** A few years ago Thailand–Cambodia overland routes were suicidal. Now you can drive quite comfortably from Bangkok to Angkor and other roads are being improved. See p107 and p109 for my snapshot of the present state of play but expect further changes. By either route, heading east makes sense because you can get Cambodian visas on the Thai border and cheap, instant Vietnamese visas in Battambang or Sihanoukville en route. If you are heading the other way getting visas is much more time-consuming.

⑧ **Thailand–Malaysia** Very easy. Direct buses run all the way from Bangkok to Singapore in less than two days.

BOAT TRAVEL

Within mainland South-East Asia, river boats offer anything from meditative daw-
dles to white-knuckle speed-boat rides. Such services are diminishing as roads
improve but in Cambodia, Burma and Laos the rivers still form veritable aquatic
highways. Vietnam also has a wide variety of water-born options, both in the
Mekong Delta and in the island-studded coasts in the north.

LINKS TO AUSTRALIA AND ISLAND SOUTH-EAST ASIA

In the island nations of Indonesia and Philippines, a veritable flotilla link all the
main islands. However, boat links between nations are relatively few and far
between and there is no passenger ferry between Australia and Indonesia. Sadly
cargo boats will not take backpackers and the cheapest flight is between Kupang
(West Timor) and Darwin on Merpati Airlines. There are flights to newly-inde-
pendent East Timor but onward travel into Indonesia is easier from Kupang.

If you want to get out of the Philippines without flying there are only two
(legal) options:

❶ **To Sulawesi (Indonesia)** EPA Shipping (☎ 083-380 3591) in General Santos
has a boat to Bitung, currently leaving at 9am on Fridays (check carefully!) and
returning to General Santos at 3pm on Wednesdays. This is predominantly a cargo
service so bring a thick sleeping mat and a good book for the 36-hour journey.

❷ **To Sabah (East Malaysia)** The Aleson Lines (🖳 www.alesonshipping.com/)
ship *Mary Joy II* now leaves Zamboanga on Monday (having started in Cebu) and
Wednesday. It returns from Sandakan on Tuesday and Thursday (continuing to
Pulauan/Dipolog on Friday, then to Dumaguete and back to Cebu). Beware – this
timetable changes frequently. It actually starts from Dagumete on Monday, calls
in at Zamboanga on Tuesday, then returns from Sandakan (where the agent is
Timmarine) on Thursday. Another much less pleasant boat, run by Sampaguita
Lines, leaves Zamboanga on Thursday and returns on Saturday. Prices start at
M$88.

An overview of the main options for crossing the south-east Asian islands
towards Australia are depicted on the map opposite. Brief details on the countries
in between are covered from p209 onwards.

FLIGHTS

Budget travellers generally shun internal flights, on the reasonable assumption
that flying you'll miss the scenery yet pay more for the privilege. However, there
are a few regional flights which do make a lot of sense given closed or awkward
borders and a few where the flight is not significantly more expensive than travelling by road. The most attractive such propositions are depicted on p32.

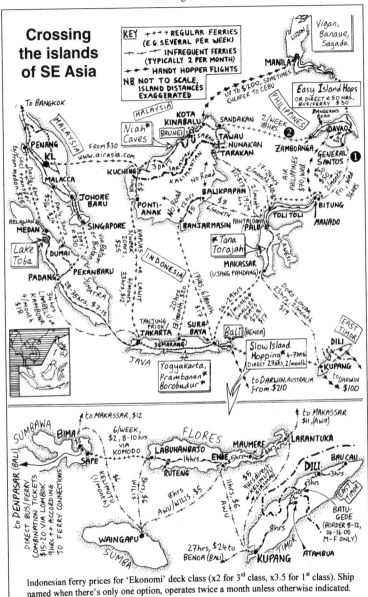

Crossing the islands of SE Asia

KEY ++++ REGULAR FERRIES (E.G. SEVERAL PER WEEK)
—+— INFREQUENT FERRIES (TYPICALLY 2 PER MONTH)
➤➤➤ HANDY HOPPER FLIGHTS
N.B. NOT TO SCALE, ISLAND DISTANCES EXAGGERATED

Vigan, Banaue, Sagada

LUZON
MANILA
PHILIPPINES

UP TO $200, SOMETIMES CHEAPER TO CEBU

Easy Island Hops OR DIRECT £50/US$30 BUS/FERRY $30

To BANGKOK
MALAYSIA
KOTA KINABALU
SANDAKAN
2/WEEK 18HRS
DANGEROUS ROAD
DAVAO

Niah Caves
BRUNEI
SABAH
TAWAU
NUNAKAN
TARAKAN
ZAMBOANGA
GENERAL SANTOS ❶

PENANG
KL
MALAYSIA
KUCHING
SARAWAK
3 DAYS
No Road
KALIMANTAN
17-24HRS 2/month
AIR PHILIPPINES $70, WEEK
Fri, Wed 2/month
36HRS ❷

MALACCA
JOHORE BARU
PONTIANAK
No Road
12HRS
$5
BALIKPAPAN
$8 6/MONTH
PANTALOAN PALU
TOLI TOLI
BITUNG
MANADO

BELAWAN
MEDAN
SINGAPORE
via Batam or Bintan
20HRS $25
KAPUAS 3/WEEK
BANJARMASIN
SULAWESI
FROM $30 www.airasia.com

Lake Toba
DUMAI
PEKANBARU
28-35HRS $7-15
INDONESIA
★ Tana Torajah
MAKASSAR (UJANG PANDANG)
23HRS 2/month
Doro Londa 2/month $19

PADANG
SUMATRA
LAMBELU & KAMBUNA 4/month $18
34HRS
LAWIT 4/month 33HRS $12
13/month $20
20HRS $20
14-29HRS $20 smaller boats $9
EAST TIMOR
DILI

TANJUNG PRIOK JAKARTA
SURABAYA
Bali (BENOA)
17HRS 6/month
KUPANG
toDARWIN $100

SEMARANG
JAVA
Yogyakarta, Prambanan★ Borobudur★
Slow Island Hopping 4-7DAYS DIRECT 27HRS, 2/month
to DARWIN, AUSTRALIA from $210

---

to MAKASSAR, $12
SUMBAWA
BIMA
FLORES
MAUMERE
LARANTUKA
to MAKASSAR $11 (AWU)

6/WEEK, $2, 8-10HRS VIA KOMODO
LABUHANBAJO
ENDE 3HRS
14HRS
BAUCAU
DILI 3HrS
3hrs

SAPE
RUTENG
8HRS AWU
11HRS $6 AWU
9HRS AWU or KELIMUTU SIRIMAU
EAST TIMOR
BATUGEDE (BORDER 8-12, 14-16:00 M-F ONLY)

to DENPASAR (BALI)
DIRECT BUS/FERRY COMBINATION TICKETS $15-20 VIA LOMBOK 9HRS ++ ACCORDING TO FERRY CONNECTIONS
KELIMUTU (1/month)
WILIS
$6
$6 AWU/WILIS $5
$6
8HrS
TIMOR
8hrs
ATAMBUA

WAINGAPU
SUMBA
27hrs, $24 to BENOA (BALI)
KUPANG

Indonesian ferry prices for 'Ekonomi' deck class (x2 for 3rd class, x3.5 for 1st class). Ship named when there's only one option, operates twice a month unless otherwise indicated.

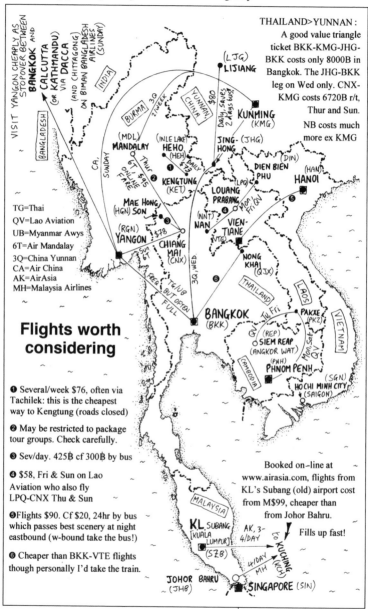

THAILAND>YUNNAN :
A good value triangle
ticket BKK-KMG-JHG-
BKK costs only 8000B in
Bangkok. The JHG-BKK
leg on Wed only. CNX-
KMG costs 6720B r/t,
Thur and Sun.

NB costs much
more ex KMG

VISIT YANGON CHEAPLY AS STOPOVER BETWEEN BANGKOK AND CALCUTTA (OR KATHMANDU) via DACCA (AND CHITTAGONG) on BIMAN BANGLADESH AIRLINES (SUNDAY)

BANGLADESH

INDIA

(LJG) LIJIANG

BURMA 3Q 2/WEEK

YUNNAN CHINA

$80 DAILY, SAVES 2 DAYS BUS

KUNMING (KMG)

(MDL) MANDALAY

(INLE LAKE) HEHO (HEH) ❶ $45

JING-HONG (JHG)

(DIN) DIEN BIEN PHU

(HAN) HANOI

6T ONLINE FARE Thur

KENGTUNG (KET) ❷

(LPQ) LOUANG PRABANG

MON, FRI QV

❺

CA. SUNDAY

MAE HONG (HGN) SON ❸

(NNT) NAN

❹ VIENTIANE (VTE)

TG=Thai
QV=Lao Aviation
UB=Myanmar Awys
6T=Air Mandalay
3Q=China Yunnan
CA=Air China
AK=AirAsia
MH=Malaysia Airlines

(RGN) YANGON $78

CHIANG MAI (CNX)

NONG KHAI (QJX)

Sun 6T

FREQ TG/UB BUT OFTEN FULL

3Q WED.

❻

THAILAND

LAOS

**Flights worth
considering**

BANGKOK (BKK)

QV TU, FRI

PAKSE (PKZ)

(REP) SIEM REAP (ANGKOR WAT)

MON-SAT QV

VIETNAM

❶ Several/week $76, often via
Tachilek: this is the cheapest
way to Kengtung (roads closed)

(PNH) PHNOM PENH

(SGN) HO CHI MINH CITY (SAIGON)

❷ May be restricted to package
tour groups. Check carefully.

CAMBODIA

❸ Sev/day. 425฿ cf 300฿ by bus

❹ $58, Fri & Sun on Lao
Aviation who also fly
LPQ-CNX Thu & Sun

Booked on-line at
www.airasia.com, flights from
KL's Subang (old) airport cost
from M$99, cheaper than
from Johor Bahru.

❺Flights $90. Cf $20, 24hr by bus
which passes best scenery at night
eastbound (w-bound take the bus!)

MALAYSIA

KL SUBANG [KUALA LUMPUR] (SZB)

AK, 3-4/DAY to KUCHING (KCH)

Fills up fast!

❻ Cheaper than BKK-VTE flights
though personally I'd take the train.

4/DAY MH

JOHOR BAHRU (JHB)

SINGAPORE (SIN)

So where's nice?

BEACHES

Thailand has dozens of choices in almost every price bracket and is generally the best value in the region (see p47 for options).

Malaysia has some beautiful islands but many are resorts that are beyond backpacker budgets: Langkawi has gone upmarket and the Muslim mores don't suit everyone. Still the Perhentian Islands, Cherating and Tioman offer sunny budget options when the rest of the region is suffering the rainy season.

Vietnam has lots of beaches, many relatively unexploited, but the main choice, Nha Trang, has had many reports of scams and thefts. Better to head for Phu Quoc Island, or find your own beach along the endless coastline.

Cambodia has only one real resort town – Sihanoukville – which I found much nicer than negative reports had suggested. However, there are no 'on the beach' huts à la Thailand, and to pay less than $10/dbl you'll need to stay on the hill above town. If you have a tent you can get a boat to drop you on magnificent uninhabited bays and isles.

Burma has some great beaches but most are off limits and only Chaungtha offers any choice of budget accommodation.

Indonesia's main budget choices are Lovina in Bali (dolphin watching), and the Gili Isles (off Lombok) but there are a myriad of others.

Similarly the Philippines' top spots, Boracay, Malapascua, Puerto Galera etc, are just the start.

SCUBA DIVING

The warm seas of South-East Asia make it ideal for diving though the combined effects of dynamite fishing, tourism and El Niño weather has wrought havoc to many of the once-beautiful coral reefs.

Resorts in Thailand and the Philippines are probably the best places to go to learn – the number of competing operators brings down prices and means there's a course about to start whenever you turn up.

The best diving tends to be in the most remote places: Phu Quoc Island in Vietnam, Palawan in the Philippines, the Similan Islands off Thailand (very expensive), islands in the far south of Burma (usually out of bounds or by special cruise from Ranong, Thailand), Sipidan in Malaysian Borneo (expensive and raided by hostage-taking Philippine rebels in 2000).

Incidentally, my top spot of all is beyond the spectacularly beautiful Rock Islands in the little-known Republic of Palau (Micronesia), a $200 one-way flight east from Manila (no visa is required and the double dives are well worth the $110 tag; you can snorkel in a jellyfish lake too!).

❏ HIGHLIGHTS

My personal recommendations, in no particular order, are:

Spectacular settings: Deqin (Y), Lijiang (Y), Sapa (V), Muang Ngoi (L), Nang Kio (L), Vang Vieng (L)

Charming old towns: Lijiang (Y), Louang Prabang (L), Hoi An (V), Taungoo (B), [Vigan (Ph)]

Old towns with more bustle: Jianshui (Y), Dali (Y), Georgetown (Penang, M), Melaka/Malacca (M), Siem Reap (C), Hanoi (V)

Special small-town appeal: Phimai (Th), That Phanom (Th), Chiang Khan (Th), Nyaung Shwe (B), Hsipaw (B), Kampot (C), [Ubud (I)]

Chill-outs: Muang Ngoi (L), Ko Chang 2 (Th)

Individual structures: Petronas Towers (Kuala Lumpur, M), Shwedagon (Yangon, B), [Prambanan (nr Yogyakarta, I)]

Classic ruins: Angkor (C), Bagan (B), Si Sachanalai (Th), Phnom Rung (Th), Kampaeng Phet (Th), Sukhothai (Th), Ayutthaya (Th), [Prambanan (I), Borobudur (I)]

Great stupas: Shwedagon (Yangon, B), Golden Rock (B), Shwesandaw (Pyay, B), Mahazedi and Shwemawdaw (Bago, B), Mingun (B), Wat Arun (Bangkok, Th), That Phanom (Th), Nakhon Pathom (Th), Vientiane (L)

Big Buddhas: World's biggest is at Leshan, China (train north from Kunming (Y); Thanbodhhay (nr Monywa, B) – Titanic hill-top figure, reclining; Bago (55m reclining, B); Wat Khao Kong (nr Narathiwat, Th) – 24m seated; Wat Hat Yai Nai (nr Hat Yai, Th) – 35m reclining; Roi Et (standing, like a stick figure, Th); Wat Traimit (nr Hualamphong station, Bangkok, Th) – only 3m high but solid gold!

Other great religious sites: Golden Rock (B); Cao Dai Cathedral, Tay Ninh (V); Ubidiah Mosque, Kuala Kangsar (M); Batu Caves (M); almost anywhere in Burma or [Bali, I].

Palaces: Phnom Penh (C), Bangkok (Th), Kuala Kangsar (M), Louang Prabang (L), Lijiang (Y), [Yogyakarta (I), Bandar Seri Bagawan (Brunei)]

Modern buildings: Petronas Towers in KL (M) – the world's tallest according to some calculations, the Skyscraper panorama in Singapore   *(cont'd opposite)*

HILL TRIBES

Throughout South-East Asia there are numerous tribal communities who, to varying extents, wear colourful traditional clothes, and in certain rare, impoverished cases still live in communal long houses. Hiking through their villages has become a major tourist draw particularly around Pai and Mae Hon Song (north-west Thailand) plus around Muang Sing/Luang Namtha (Laos), Kalaw/Inle Lake (Burma), Xishuangbanna (Yunnan – mainly for Chinese tourists) and Sapa (Vietnam). Fewer tourists visit similar villages in north Luzon (the Philippines), the various Borneo Dayak villages (Malaysia/Indonesia) and isolated mountain tribes of New Guinea.

HIGHLIGHTS (cont'd)
Colonial architecture: **Areas of town**: Louang Prabang (L), Champasak (L), Hoi An (V), Siem Reap (C), Battambang (C), Pyin U Lwin (B), Ipoh (M), Melaka/Malacca (M), Georgetown, Penang (M), Merdeka Sq in KL (M), [Vigan (Ph)]. **Upmarket classic hotels**: Old Smokehouse, Cameron Highlands (M), E&O, Georgetown (M); Raffles (S); Le Royal, Phnom Penh (C), Grand Hotel d'Angkor (C); Auberge Calao, Louang Prabang (L); The Strand, Yangon (B); The Pansea in Yangon (B) is new but feels timeless. **Affordable colonial hotels (under $30)**: Marco Polo, Kampot (C); Candacraig*, Pyin U Lwin (B), Kalaw Hotel, Kalaw (B); Auberge du Paradis, Savannakhet (L), several in Louang Prabang (L), Champasak Palace Hotel, Pakxe (L); several cool Chinese-colonial places in Melaka (M).

Other original accommodation: Stilt and floating hostels at Kanchanaburi (Th) – from $2; 'Crazy House' in Dalat (V) from $5 for a bed in a dorm (check the internet for a picture of Crazy House!); stilt hotels on Inle Lake (B) from $35 for a double.

Spectacular rice terraces: Yuanyang (Y), north of Chong Zuang on the Hekou–Kaiyuan railway (Y), Lao Cai to Sapa road (V), [central Bali (I), south-east of Ruteng, West Flores (I), Batad nr Banaue (Ph)].

Karst scenery: [ie abruptly jutting limestone peaks and pillars such as the classics at Guilin/Yangshuo, China] Halong and Baitulong Bay (V), around Ninh Binh (V), Phang Nga Bay (Th), Thong Pha Phum area (Th), Mahaxai (L), Vang Vieng (L), Shilin (Y).

Rainforest: Taman Negara (M), Khao Sok National Park (Th), [West Papua (I)].

If I had to choose my overall top 10 would be:
Lijiang old town (Y), Shwedagon viewed from the east (Yangon, B), the markets around Inle Lake (B), sunrise over Bagan (B), Angkor (C), Halong Bay on a clear day (V), mountain hikes around Sapa (V), Nam Ou river (L), dawn at Mt Bromo [I], Ko Phi Phi without the tourists (Th). Plus eating in Thailand and meeting local people anywhere.

KEY: B = Burma, C = Cambodia, L = Laos, M = Malaysia, S = Singapore, Th = Thailand, V = Vietnam, Y = Yunnan, [ ] for Indonesia (I), Philippines (Ph) and Brunei covered in less detail by this book.   * = run down   ** = over-renovated

Organizing such a trip is easiest in north-west Thailand or Sapa (Vietnam). Sapa also offers the most colourful costumes and most spectacular scenery, Yunnan villages around Mengla have the most attractively solid houses (as the people are richer) while the sometimes distressingly poor villages of northern Laos are most likely to allow you a blow on the opium pipe. But before you go, ask yourself how you would feel about groups of foreign tourists tramping through your garden every day, smoking opium with your ne'er-do-well cousin and giving your kids sweets that encourage them to beg and skip school. Would you really be pleased to receive a handful of dubiously effective old medicaments in return for having gangs of strangers snooping around in your home and pointing their zoom lenses at you?

❏ Hill tribes – who's who and where to meet them

The multifarious tribes and clans go by different names in different languages but you'll start noticing similarities between many:

Dai/Tai are related to the modern Thais of Thailand. Traditional Dai villages especially in Xishuangbanna retain their traditional wooden stilt houses and the fruity Dai cookery is one of the region's finest.

Hani (6,000,000) is a general term for a group of Tibeto-Burman tribes that include the **Hmong** (**Miao/Meo**). In China the term Miao is actually derogatory (it means 'barbarian') and is applied by some people to mean hill tribes in general. Deep indigo Hmong aprons and skimpy leggings sell for a pittance in Sapa and look most attractive, though they quickly stain your skin blue and seem utterly inappropriate for the cold mountain climate: 🖳 www.hmong.org/ is the website of the 60,000 strong Hmong community in Minnesota. Women of the related **Akha** (**Aini**, **Kaw** or **Ikaw**) tribe (approx 100,000) still commonly wear distinctive dark head-dresses with multiple silver baubles affixed, notably in northern Laos,

Yao are also known in China as **Mien/Mun** and in Vietnam as **Dao** ('**Zao**'). Widely spread throughout the region, they form various very distinct groups. Most dramatic are the '**Red Yao**'/**Hong Yao** – traditionally-dressed women wear scarlet trapezoidal turbans adorned with pompoms and often their posture and shaved eyebrows seem to lend them a rather noble if not haughty air. Meet them at the Saturday market in Sapa. In the Yuanyang area of Yunnan, Yao women's turbans tend to be gaudy multicoloured towels. The **Landian Yao** (literally 'blue trouser Yao') are at first sight rather similar to the Hani. Most of the 4,200,000 population now live in the Guanxi province of China.

Yi (**Lolo**) is a very general 'family' of tribes mostly in southern China with a total population approaching 6,000,000. This includes the **Lisu** whose language has its own alphabet, the **Naxi** (300,000) whose blue-clad women scuttle through Lijiang every morning before the tourists awake, and the **Bai/Pai/Pé** (approx 1,600,000) from the Dali/Erhai Lake region of Yunnan. Traditional costume has largely been relegated to ceremonial use, though you'll see modern stylised red-pink and white versions complete with cumbersome head-dress worn by the hostesses on certain luxury buses on the Xiaguan–Lijiang route.

Lahu (300,000) are linguistically similar to the Yi. The group includes many sub-groups in northern Thailand/Laos (also Musur), around Lai Chao in Vietnam, and Honghe in Yunnan: look for women wearing black turbans. In Burma the group is called Muhso.

Wa (**Kawa**, 360,000), known as the 'last headhunters', live mostly in Burma (Kayah and Shan states) where they effectively run their own mini-state funded by narcotics/amphetamine production.

Karen (**Kayah/Kayen/Kayenni**) is a large family of mostly Burmese tribes, though many have recently spilled into northern Thailand in the wake of rumbling civil war. The group includes the **Pa O/Taungthu** (around Lake Inle), the **Palaung** (near Kalaw), and the confusingly similar-sounding **Padaung** (notably around Loikaw), the famous long-necked 'giraffe women'. The Padaung are not blind to their photogenic appeal and have turned their improbable spirals of gold neck-hoop to their commercial advantage – charging tourists for snap shots or, around Mae Hon Song in northern Thailand, levying an entry fee to their villages.

Market days offer opportunities to mingle under slightly less voyeuristic circumstances. Despite the camera-toting temptations, it is basic good manners to buy something: converse and laugh with the vendors before simply asking to snap their portrait. It also helps to understand a little about the 'families' of tribes.

SEX AND DRUGS AND ROCK'n'ROLL

South-East Asia is pretty liberal towards tourists who see sex as a commercial commodity. Though slightly less 'in your face' than in Thai hot spots such as Pattaya, Patong (Phuket), Patpong (Bangkok), Cambodia has been rapidly emerging as the new sex centre of the region.

The attitude towards narcotics ranges wildly from the laissez-faire villages in Laos (where opium and ultra-powerful grass are smoked with gay abandon), to the incredibly strict regimes of Malaysia and Singapore which regularly execute drug offenders. In Thailand there is a much discussed 'scene' on Ko Phangan, but you'll need to be very discreet. Cambodia's 'Happy Pizza' is served openly and if you order it 'very happy' you may lose a day of your trip enjoying the consequences. However, that doesn't mean that dope is legal.

Illicit music (ie bootleg CDs) is commonly available particularly in travellers' centres. Although Thailand has clamped down, the best deals have always been in Vietnam where a vast range of Western albums sell (unboxed) at under $1.

CRAFTS AND SOUVENIRS

Burma offers by far the best-value handicrafts (notably laquerware, silverware, paintings etc), with some remarkable bargains, though you'll find a vast discrepancy between prices according to where you shop. Thailand is also good value, but often the best deals are Burmese imports! Toraja in Sulawesi (Indonesia) is also full of colourful, good value if somewhat scrappier souvenirs, generally carved from low grade balsa-style wood.

The textiles of many regions are great value (particularly colourful and easy to procure at sensible prices in Sapa, Vietnam, if you're happy to be stained blue wearing them!). The minimal cost of tailoring in Yunnan makes it a great place to have a pair of trousers made up.

Hats make great souvenirs, though they can get bulky – the gigantic parasol fisherman-hats of Banjarmasin (Indonesia) are as big as cruise liners. They may seem a bargain till you realise you can't hope to get one on a bus, in a bemo or do anything other than float down a river in one.

Throughout the region treat 'antiques' with scepticism unless you are a professional. Many (in fact most) ancient-looking items are skilfully artificially aged. Even if you really did get an ancient artefact it may well be subject to export restrictions. Gem stones' speculation is an even surer way to lose money and in Bangkok it can sometimes be hard to prevent a tuk tuk driver from taking you to a showroom or two, wherever you really wanted to go!

THAILAND

Introduction

Easy, friendly, central and generally visa free, Thailand makes an ideal starting point for visits to South-East Asia. With great food and a first-world infrastructure it is in itself a brilliant holiday destination and despite the influx of package tourists there remains a wealth of traveller-priced options.

It is still quite possible to escape the over-developed beach resorts (Pattaya, Phuket et al) by heading to less developed islands (notably Ko Chang 1, Ko Lanta and other smaller isles). And you can find dramatic ancient ruins such as Phimai or Kamphaeng Phet which are much less commercialized than world-famous Ayutthaya or Sukhothai. The cheap availability of motorbike rental means that you can explore any area 'properly', and really 'go local' if you're so inclined.

HIGHLIGHTS

The night markets/food stalls, random motorbike exploration, beautiful great value beaches (see p47 and p67), the craggy karst scenery around Phang Nga, the ancient cities (for example Kamphaeng Phet and Si Satchanalai), and Bangkok khlong trips are some of the highlights.

Escaping from the tourist trail

To get away from the main tourist horde try Thong Pha Phum on the 'Burma Road' or almost anywhere in Isaan (north-east Thailand). Few tourists visit the latter region largely because the scenery is mostly flat and subtle (OK dull) but the

---

❏ **Country ratings – Thailand**

● **Expense $$$** Inexpensive, but the constant temptations can make money go dangerously fast.

● **Value for money** ★★★★★ Excellent value, especially in backpacker areas. The flat 200B fee for each national park can seem excessive when, as en route to Kaoh Pra Wihaan, you simply drive through.

● **Getting around** ★★★★★ Roads paved and well maintained. Buses frequent and good value. Trains cheap but sleepers should be booked well in advance. Mopeds, easy and cheap to rent (150–250B/day in any traveller centre), are ideal for seeing the back roads.

● **English spoken** ★★★★☆ Throughout tourist areas English is widespread but in the north-east communication is very much tougher.

● **Woman alone** ★★★★★ Solo women travellers are common. Beware of certain bars in Ko Phangan which are notorious for drink-drugging molesters.

● **For vegetarians** ★★★★☆ Many tasty options, especially if you eat seafood.

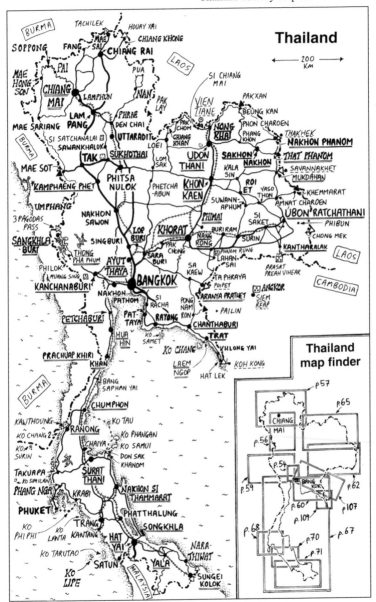

❏ **Essential information for travellers – Thailand**
- **Visa** At least 30 days visa free for most Western nationalities.
- **Currency** Baht. US$1=43.5B
- **Time zone** 7 hours ahead of GMT (same as Indochina; 1hr behind Malaysia and China; ½hr ahead of Burma).
- **Religious tone** 97% Theravada Buddhist. Every Buddhist male becomes a monk at some point in his life. Temples are everywhere. The far south is Muslim.
- **Health factors** Malaria exists but is not a widespread problem. The tap water is unsafe to drink.
- **Special dangers** No real worries. Some tourist scams. Flooding possible in the rainy season.

❏ **Geo-political information – Thailand**
Population: 61.8 million
Area: 514,000 sq km
Capital: Bangkok (6.5 million, 7.9m including satellite cities).
Other major cities: Udon Thani (230,000), Nakhon Ratchasima/Khorat (210,000), Hat Yai, Chonburi (190,000), Chiang Mai (170,000), Khon Kaen, Si Racha (145,000), Nakhon Pathom, Nakhon Si Thammarat (125,000), Surat Thani (117,000), Rayong, Ubon Ratchathani (110,000).
GNP per capita: $6700 (2000)
Currency history: Baht/US$1 – Apr 2002: 43.5B, Feb 1998: 47.2B, Lost value in 1997 South-East Asian economic crash, July 1996: 25.4B, Oct 1993: 25.33B.
Major exports/economy: Rice, textiles, tourism, electronics, mixed economy
Ethnic mix: Thai (75%), Chinese (14%), Malay, Khmer, Mon and hill tribes.
Official language: Thai. Also spoken are Min-Chinese, Yawi (old Malay dialect in the far south) and many hill-tribe languages (in the north-west).
Religious mix: Buddhist (95%), Muslim (4% mostly in the far south)
Landmarks of national history: **1220**: Sukothai founded, following Thai invasion which superseded a previously Khmer dynasty. **1350s**: Ayutthaya became dominant. **1569–87**: Burmese domination ended by Thai hero Prince Naresuan. **1767**: Ayutthaya sacked by the Burmese. **1688**: Contacts with foreigners legally restricted to prevent European colonial incursions. **1782**: Capital moved to Bangkok under King Rama I. **1867**: Gave Cambodia to France in return for guarantee of independence. **1893** Gave away Laos, too! **1896**: Recognized as a neutral buffer state by Britain and France. **1932**: Absolute monarchy became a constitutional one following a coup d'état. **1939**: Changed name from Siam. **1940** With France occupied, Thailand invaded Cambodia and parts of Laos. **1941–5** Japanese invasion, construction of the 'Death Railway' including River Kwai bridge (Kanchanaburi) by PoWs. **1960s**: Became major base for US troops in Vietnam war, creating the seeds of the tourism and sex industries. **1980–90s**: Rapid growth as an Asian 'economic Tiger'. **1997**: South-East Asia economic crisis: many building projects remain half finished.
Leaders: King Rama IX constitutional monarch (generally referred to as King Bhumibol and overwhelmingly adored). Prime Minister Thaksin Shinawata since 2001, leading a major political clean-up campaign, though only survived a corruption case himself by an 8:7 vote in the constitutional court.
Pressing political issues: Burmese border skirmishes, crack downs on drug use and the sex industry, AIDS, slow corporate debt restructuring, Bangkok's urban planning mess, anti-corruption campaign.

❏ **Sex and drugs and ...**

Thailand's prime minister, Thaksin Shinawata, is slowly trying to clean up the country's sex-tourism image. For now, however, obvious brothels, girly (and boy) bars and lurid sex shows are still commonplace notably in Bangkok (Patpong, Nana soi etc), Pattaya (South Pattaya 'village') and Phuket (Patong).

Many a 'gogo' bar offers cheapish drinks and the spectacle of sad-eyed village girls whooping with contrived excitement as they mechanically caress dancing poles with naked thighs and calculate how many 'customers' they need before they can send money home to treat a sick or impoverished family.

These days there's a major clamp down on the wicked weed. Buying grass was always a little dicey in Bangkok and nowadays police make random checks in the Kao San Road area. If you're found with as little as half a joint, you may be given the 'chance' of paying an instant fine, say 50,000B. You'd be advised to head straight for the nearest ATM and pay up – or risk facing a rather unpleasant time in jail.

In the '80s Ko Samui beach restaurants offered magic mushroom omelettes on almost every menu. These days mushroom shakes and marijuana are still widely available on Ko Phangan, famed for its full moon parties, but even here the police are tightening up and unless you are pretty discreet you can expect trouble eventually. Ironically it can be safer to smoke as a group in a café than to subtly wander off alone onto the beach where you may be followed. All in all, don't get blasé about smoking in Thailand. It is illegal and there's a fair chance you'll get caught.

people are friendly and the food is great. In this area you'll be largely 'on your own' to seek out the odd little Khmer ruin or family encounter. Unlike the rest of Thailand, relatively few people speak English in Isaan, buses are often marked only in Thai characters and even the maps seem less reliable.

This chapter's relatively disproportionate attention to Isaan towns such as Ubon Ratchathani and Udon Thani should not be taken as a great recommendation for the towns themselves – it's exactly because you'll want to get out of those cities quickly to the region beyond that you'll need help more help navigating between their multifarious bus stations.

WHEN TO GO

Thailand is hot and humid most of the time. High season is October to February; during these months it's very warm and relatively dry in Bangkok and cool at night in the mountains, though a modest sweater is sufficient. March to May is sweltering and sticky, with temperatures over 35°C for weeks at a time. This can be almost unbearable if your cheap Bangkok dormitory lacks air conditioning.

Summer (July/August) is the rainy season; the uncertain weather keeps the southern beaches refreshingly free of tourists till the end of September. Clouds gather in the afternoons but mornings can be clear and sunny.

At **weekends**, country getaways such as Erawan National Park (near Kanchanaburi) and Khao Yai Park (South Isaan) get swamped by local tourists from Bangkok, so it's bye bye tranquillity. However, if you don't mind the crowds, hitch-hiking within these parks becomes easier with the increased traffic flow.

Practical information

VISAS AND FORMALITIES

Most Westerners can stay for 30 days without a visa. Hop across the border to Malaysia, Cambodia or Laos then you get another 30 days on return to Thailand. And again. And again!!! Alternatively for longer stays, a two-month visa is readily granted at Thai embassies (usually US$30) which allows up to two one-month extensions. For those extensions apply at Soi Suanphlu, Sathon Tai Rd, Bangkok, or the Immigration Office in any provincial capital (500B per extension). If you need just a day or two extra, it's cheaper to pay the 200B/day overstay 'fine' on departure.

Scandinavians, South Koreans and New Zealanders get three months stay without a visa. Note that many (especially smaller and East European) countries which enjoyed visa-free entry till January 2002 may find that they now need a visa. Check carefully!

Technically you are supposed to be in possession of 'sufficient funds' and a return or onward ticket when entering Thailand. In over a dozen visits, I've never had such details checked. However, since a 2002 clampdown, you may find that onward/ return tickets are indeed being examined. To play safe, if arriving on a one-way/long-stay ticket, it might be wise to get yourself a visa before setting off.

MONEY

All major currencies are exchangeable in large cities/resorts. Even including the 23B commission (most of that *per cheque*), the rate for travellers' cheques is still usually better than for cash. Credit card advances are easy and often commission free. ATM cash machines are available in almost any town. Especially if you use your credit card for shopping or leave it in a hotel safe, do have someone at home survey your bill as card-fraud is particularly bad in Thailand.

TRANSPORT

Bus

Thailand's extensive, efficient long-distance bus system makes it easier to cross the country than to cross Bangkok. Buses leave on time and usually pre-assign seat numbers (though some will fill up en route). And even the smallest towns generally have at least one nightly service to Bangkok. The price of a ticket varies considerably according to the quality of bus. Cheapest are the open-window 'ordinary/fan' buses which can get pretty full and sweaty and are relatively slow as they stop to pick up passengers at most road junctions en route.

For nearly double the price you can take an air-conditioned bus on all but the most local routes. You'll usually be assured an assigned seat and a faster journey, though they'll pick up en route when not full. For an additional 20–30% the 24-seat, air-conditioned, VIP buses are something of a bargain – the extra money usually gets you a much more comfortable seat, and waitress service of drinks and the odd free biscuit. Note that in some towns air-conditioned and ordinary fan-cooled buses leave from different terminals. Also, in some places, terminals for different destinations may be quite far apart. However, in the last few years many cities have created big new all-destination terminals, and most buses will drop by even if starting from an outlying office or minor bus station.

On certain routes of backpacker interest there are special tourist minibuses, notably from Kao San Road (Bangkok) to Ko Chang, Chiang Mai, Kanchanaburi and Angkor Wat (Cambodia). While these often sound like a good deal and save the hassle of reaching the bus stations from central Bangkok, the ride is often less comfortable than the public air-conditioned buses, while the Angkor bus is a scamming minefield (see notes p98).

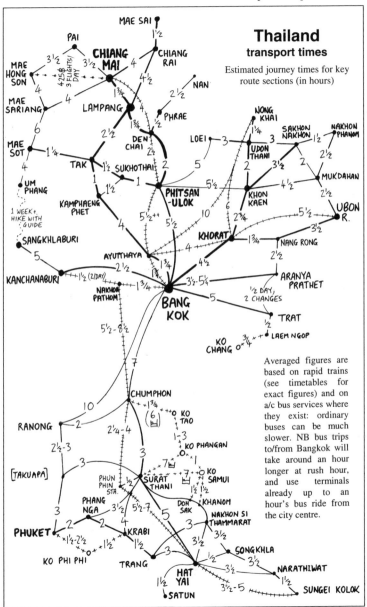

Thailand
transport times

Estimated journey times for key route sections (in hours)

Averaged figures are based on rapid trains (see timetables for exact figures) and on a/c bus services where they exist: ordinary buses can be much slower. NB bus trips to/from Bangkok will take around an hour longer at rush hour, and use terminals already up to an hour's bus ride from the city centre.

❏ **Bangkok Airport – insider's tips**

● Use the helpful Tourism Authority of Thailand (TAT) information booth. Ask specifically not just for Bangkok city and canal-route maps but also for maps/brochures of other places you plan to visit.

● *To* **Kao San Road** (the traveller area) The A2 air-conditioned minibus gets you there for 100B in 45 minutes if there's little traffic (dream on!). For only 3.5B use the No 59 (blue sign only!, rare, extremely slow), or the No 29 then No 3 bus combination (frequent, 7B, slow, see route map pp52 and 54).

● *From* **Kao San Road** Guesthouse minibus services (60–80B) are better deals than the A2 and pick you up at your hostel but may trundle around making pick-ups for nearly an hour before setting off – don't panic if it's not on time! **Always leave loads of time**.

● Do you really want to slog through the Bangkok traffic to the city? The airport's train station has direct services to the north and north-east of Thailand, and by using the bus No 29/No 145 combination (see map p54) you can hop very cheaply from the airport to Mochit bus station (for services to northern, north-eastern and eastern cities including Trat for Cambodia) without going downtown at all. Incoming buses from the same destinations can drop you right in front of the airport if you're alert and ready to jump out!

● The airport is well equipped but the in-terminal internet place is dreadfully pricey. For vastly cheaper email/web access and local food take the lift marked for the Amari Hotel, cross the central footbridge across the rail line and descend to your right where there's a selection of market stalls, food vendors and a 20B/hour internet shop.

● From the same point, a 30B tuk-tuk ride will take you the 2.5km to 'We-Train' hostel where there are dorm beds (165B) for arriving sleepy-heads unable to face trudging all the way to the city centre. It's best to book and print off the Thai directions from their website 🖳 www.we-train.linethai.co.th/.

Especially in the far south, **share taxis** are a good alternative to buses, for only about twice the price. Generally they leave from near the relevant bus terminal.

Motorbikes

These are easy to rent in any large city or tourist area (from 150B/day) and are a superb way to tour the country routes, but terrifying on busy major roads. Your licence is not usually inspected.

Hitchhiking

Hitching is pretty good once you get out of the large cities and can generally be relied upon in the few places (eg Khao Yai National Park) where public transport doesn't go. Rides are usually free but offering the equivalent of the bus fare would be a polite gesture.

Trains

The train can be the cheapest way to travel but, especially on short hops, beware of the fixed 40B surcharge on 'rapid' (RAP) trains, 60B on 'expresses' (EX) and 80B in SP 'special expresses'. To pay the bargain 'normal fare', take Ord (Ordinary) or local trains.

Departures are patchy with many services leaving close together then long gaps before the next, thus I've included several timetables to make the railway easier to use. These were correct as of 2002 but are worth checking on the official Thai Railways website 🖳 www.srt.motc.go.th/httpEng/index .html.

Trains are particularly handy for overnight journeys but sleepers must be booked a day or two before departure, and weeks ahead in the holiday season. You can do this online with 🖳 www.asia-discovery.com/train.htm for a 200B service charge and free delivery within Bangkok. I find the slightly cheaper upper berths every bit as comfortable as the lower ones.

All main rail lines converge on Bangkok but if you want to avoid the city you can switch between the Southern and Kanchanaburi lines at Nakhon Pathom, or between the North and Isaan lines at Ayutthaya – both interesting places in themselves.

Air

Domestic flights can be surprisingly affordable. Chiang Mai to Nan or Mae Hong Son by air costs little more than the bus fare. Bangkok Airlines offers seasonal deals (eg Chiang Mai–Sukhothai 700B) which are often available for on the spot departures.

Bangkok is the cheapest place in South-East Asia from which to find international flights. Prices obviously fluctuate considerably but, for a rough guide, here are some discount prices (one-way unless specified) as of 2002, from Bangkok to:

- Bali (DPS) 6150B
- Brunei 7765B return
- Ho Chi Minh/Saigon (SGN) 4050B
- Hong Kong (HK) 3900B, via Manila with a stopover 7500B on PIA
- Kunming (KMG) 4500B single (or 8000B triangle return fare with a stop in Jing Hong, Yunnan)
- Manila (MNL) 5500B single (or 7600B return on Egypt Air, Wednesday and Saturday. That flight continues on to Tokyo (one way with a stop in Manila costs 11,000B)
- Phnom Penh (PHN) 3050B
- Singapore (SIN) 2500B (compared to 1250B by bus)
- Vientiane (VTE) 2350B (but it's cheaper to take a train or internal flight to Nong Khai then hop across the border)
- Yangon (RGN) 2450B (visa plus return deals available but flights are often full).

Flights to Europe start from around 10,000B though 15,000B is more realistic with 19–25,000B for a return. These can be booked solid around New Year and between February and April when the season starts to sweat.

ACCOMMODATION

Ultra-budget dorms are available in most places of tourist interest for 50–80B and tiny coffin-single rooms (no window, grubby hardboard walls) for 60+B (mostly 100+B in Bangkok). Generally these are passable but very basic and you will need your own over-sheet (I use a cheap sarong). You may need to ask specifically if you want a fresh under-sheet. If you have the money, 300–500B rooms are much better and can offer surprising levels of luxury for barely $10. Curiously backpackers accept lower standards than most Thai people so when you get off the traveller circuit, accommodation is likely to cost more not less. Or be particularly grimy.

On the tropical islands the best value accommodation (and often the least spoilt beaches) are generally on the opposite end of the island from where the boat drops you off.

Before renting a cheap room, inspect it for peepholes and alternate ways in. Use your own padlock to secure the door.

Camping or government-run guesthouses are often the only choices within national parks: advance booking through the **Royal Forestry Department** (☎ 02-579 0529), National Parks Division, Phaholyothin Rd, Bangkhen, Bangkok, may be necessary and is recommended. A tent allows a greater choice of do-it-yourself treks in the mountains, but can often be rented nearby – don't forget insect repellent.

FOOD AND DRINK

If you can cope with its jangling chilli heat, there's little to match the rich spectrum of Thai flavours. Lime, lemon grass, and coconut milk add zest to dozens of unique dishes, easily sampled initially from smaller family restaurants where everything is pre-prepared and clearly displayed so you can see what you're getting.

Pad tai is the ubiquitous fried noodle standby but more interesting specialities include *tom yam* (spicy lemongrass soup), *som tam* (spicy unripe papaya salad) and *matsaman mangsawirat* (a vegetable curry flavoured with pineapple and coconut). On a menu *plaa* is fish, *plaa meuk* is squid, *moo* is pork and *kai* (chicken) is confusingly similar to *khai* (egg). Beware that *pet* is duck while

❑ Banglampoo and Kao San Road [See map p52]

Banglampoo is an area of Bangkok not a Jungle Book character. For cheap-skates and first timers in Bangkok, the place to head is Banglampoo's architecturally repulsive **Kao San Road** (KSR as it's commonly abbreviated). KSR is cacophonously crushed with street restaurants, sweaty second-hand book shops, noisy bars, and shoebox-sized travel agents offering cheapish flights, unnecessary tours and handy visa procurement services. Particularly at night the pavements heave with trinket stands, fake student-card makers, tie-dye costumiers and street food ranging from sculpted pineapples to squid on a stick via pad thai noodles so cheap that you couldn't really imagine they'd be any good. And they aren't. All this is interspersed with mercifully air-conditioned 7-11 shops and a branch of Boots the Chemists which makes Brits feel they've taken a tardis home. Till early morning, cafés blare videos so loud that 'round the world in 80 burgers' student types don't need to bother with conversation between checking their emails and calling home on the internet phones.

Alex Garland accurately describes Kao San Road in *The Beach* as a portal between Europe and Thailand through which most travellers pass. But forget the novel's outdated claim that you'll smell spliffs at every corner – the police are very hard on smokers these days and on a couple of occasions I've been stopped and politely searched at random. Although much vilified even by those who return regularly, KSR remains the cheapest, most central and convenient base in Bangkok for exploring the city and from which to launch your travels. A helpful Tourist Police office and tourist information booth dispenses free city maps, bus information etc so the rest of Bangkok becomes easily accessible from a KSR base. And you don't have to walk more than a few blocks to find the meditative Chana Songkram monastery grounds, the relative riverside calm of Tammasat University, the trendy cafés on Pra Athit Road or the traditional canal-side neighbourhood around Bamboo Guest House.

There are a myriad of hostels. The cheapest charge from 50B for a bed in a dorm and from 100B for a coffin single, though most budget rooms are in the 190–500B range. There are many quieter places in alleys off KSR proper and throughout the area, with marginally more expensive rooms on the vastly more appealing tree-lined Soi Rambutri (behind the monastery). Rooms are especially hard to find in that area between December and February so you should take whatever you can get the first day then look for somewhere nicer, arriving at your selected target before the daily mass check-out around 11:30am. There are so many choices that my map simply shows the main guesthouse areas plus a square dot for each hotel/hostel beyond. The less 'central' accommodations tend to fill more slowly in the peak season. If you're absolutely unable to find a bed, several bars and internet places stay open all night.

NB Down-and-out traveller thieves are known to copy the room keys of cheap hotels then return to pilfer from incoming residents. Next day you may find your own backpack and belongings for sale in the street outside! Protect yourself by using your own padlock in the metal 'eyes' provided.

phet means hot: any dish can be spicy, but if it's *phet* it'll blow out your sinuses.

To satisfy more xenophobic palates Kentucky Fried Chicken outlets have sprung up in most towns and ubiquitous 7-11 stores sell packaged sandwiches. Backpacker cafés are all too keen to stoke you up with muesli, toast and banana pancakes.

Ice is never 100% safe but in Thailand is fairly trustworthy adding appeal to chilled fruit milk shakes and fresh fruit juices. Beer is relatively expensive though the drinkable Beer Chang is cheaper than the better known Singha which offers skull-pounding hangovers. Mekong rice-whisky is a cheaper source of unnecessary headaches.

STAYING IN TOUCH

Post is reasonably fast, reliable and sensibly priced.

International **telephone calls** are relatively inexpensive and only 20B/min to Europe/US from internet phones around Kao San Road with call backs possible on better lines for a small fee. The access code is 001. International country code: +66. Bangkok: 02, Chiang Mai: 053, Hat Yai: 074. Local calls are only 1B/3mins from coin boxes.

Internet access is very easy and only 20B/hour in places that locals use (but 40–60B/hour in tourist areas). You'll pay much more from small rural outposts where the phone charges become significant.

SHOPPING

Stylish, increasingly exclusive boutiques and shopping malls rub shoulders with markets in which 'Rolexx' watches and 'Ray Bun' sunglasses sell for a few Baht. Kao San Road peddlers still sell fake student and press ID cards and, until a clamp down in spring 2001, sold pirated CDs at around $4 (much cheaper in Vietnam). Clothes, from executive suits to t-shirts, remain quite a bargain.

Bangkok has a selection of handicrafts from all over Thailand, with the weekend Chakuchak market some people's preferred haunt. However, the Chiang Mai night market is more enjoyable and many of the best crafts actually come from Burma where you'll find prices considerably lower.

Unless you know exactly what you're doing don't even look at the gem stores which try a plethora of scams to get you in and persuade you to 'invest' in pretty useless specks of glittery rock.

ACTIVITIES
Hiking/trekking

There is certainly better mountain trekking elsewhere but the semi-forested agricultural landscapes in the north-west can prove charming and offer easy access for those who like sticking their noses into hill-tribe villages.

Although many agencies work out of Chiang Mai and Chiang Rai, treks are generally more personal (and often less expensive) when organized from smaller towns such as Pai or Mae Hon Song, and often more interesting from Umphang or any random smaller village.

It is possible to hike independently if you have a good map and take your own tent and food, though beware of wandering too near the Burmese border. Further south, the Khao Sok National Park offers tempting forest hikes and equipment/guides are easy to arrange from guesthouses at the park entrance. Perhaps the best scenery is in Khao Yai National Park, though trails are over manicured for some tastes. The park gets busier at weekends but that also makes it more accessible by hitch-hiking.

Rock climbing

The karst cliffs around Phang Nga and Ao Nang (near Krabi) offer spectacularly scenic opportunities to drive yourself up the wall.

Water sports

The average cost for a four-day open-water scuba-diving course is under $250 and in popular dive resorts, such as Ko Tao, Ko Phi Phi, Pattaya, Phuket, you can generally find a course starting within a day or two of arriving. Other centres such as Ko Chang and Ko Lipe have fewer options.

Much of the formerly spectacular coral around Ko Tao has been damaged by the temperature fluctuations of El Niño, and much of the best diving is now a considerable boat ride from the nearest resorts.

The brilliant, pristine waters of the Similan Isles probably offer Thailand's best dives but access is awkward without a highly expensive live-aboard cruise tour (five days, $450++).

The biggest tourist resorts (Phuket, Pattaya, Hua Hin, Chumphon) have windsurfers and jet skis for hire and also offer water skiing. Sea kayaking is popular in the bays around Krabi and Phang Nga.

Beaches

(See South Thailand Beaches and Islands map, p67). If you just want to relax on a beautiful beach the sheer enormity of choice is the biggest problem, though getting a place to stay can be a bit hit and miss in the high season (December to February).

Ko Chang 1* (near Trat), Ko Phangan and Ko Lanta are the **backpacker beach islands**, beautiful but with a good range of basic, budget accommodation. Ko Chang has the added attraction of a mountainous jungle interior, though there's a slight malaria risk. Ko Phangan's Hat Rin is only attractive for **nightlife** lovers. With bars, raves and a certain drug scene it is full to bursting point during the famous full moon parties.

If you want things really quiet and are more interested in **seclusion** than perfect sand, try Ko Pu (Ko Jam), rocky Ko Wai, silty Ko Chang 2*, investigate the manatees on Ko Libong, or find your own! Talk to other travellers in Trang, Satun, Ko Lanta etc for ideas. There are a sprinkling of cheap and mid-market guesthouses on the mainland coast around Bang Saphan Yai, but these tend to be pretty spread out. If you have a tent and a motorbike there are some great, untouched beaches that you can have virtually to yourself within the Khao Sam Roi Yot National Park, stretching south from Hua Hin.

For more luxury and **stunning settings** it's hard to beat Ao Nang and Railea beaches, both of which are reached from the backpacker centre of Krabi. Accommodation on the main beaches is going upmarket but you can stay in the less fashionable areas and still be within walking/ boat hop distance of the loveliest vistas. Although generally castigated

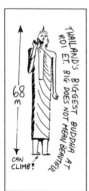

by backpackers as being horribly over developed, there's no doubt that Chaweng Beach in Ko Samui is beautiful (and the hotels are tastefully low rise), nor that the gorgeous, roadless Ko Phi Phi is a holiday maker's dream: full tourist facilities yet the image of a desert island. Both are pricey by Thai standards (and in peak season you'll be

hard pressed to find a space), but nice beach bungalows in the $10–20 range are a bargain by most global measures. And on both there are just a few budget huts on the far fringes of the tourist zones.

If you're looking for a **quick beach escape from Bangkok**, Cha-am and Hua Hin are popular local favourites and nicer than Si Racha. Ko Samet is much nicer than either and there is some budget accommodation notably on Ao Hin Khok, south of the main Hat Sai Kaew beach. It's difficult to imagine any reason to visit overpriced, towerblock-lined Pattaya beach unless you've been given free accommodation as part of a package tour, prostitute included.

With so many better places to choose from **Phuket is also worth avoiding**. Not that it's unpleasant – Karon beach is delightful – but the development is simply too overwhelming, and Patong is another mini Pattaya. Use Phuket town as a travel hub but hurry on.

* **Note**: There are two islands called Ko Chang so I have arbitrarily labelled them Ko Chang 1 and Ko Chang 2.

Meditation retreats

One of the many possibilities is 10 days of mostly silence, with some instruction in English eg at Wat Kow Tahm on Ko Phangan (book ahead via ⌨ watkowtahm@watkowtahm.org): you'll need to show up in the morning on the last day of the month to sign up.

Work

Any native English speaker marginally enthusiastic about teaching their language should be able to find a job in Thailand.

The pay, averaging $5 an hour, has fallen somewhat in recent years and isn't likely to make you rich. Bangkok seems the best place to arrange a job though many schools there have branches all around Thailand. *The Bangkok Post* has a few advertisements but talking with other teachers is the best way to find contacts and get a feel for the current teaching situation. Ask around eg at Gypsy Guest House near KSR.

Several go-go bars hire dancers by the day with pay inversely proportional to how much you wear: 200B in costume, 300B topless, and 400+B wearing slightly less.

There is a lot of money to be made through telephone soliciting work, but beware that in 2001 several dozen traveller-workers were arrested for selling fraudulent financial products.

Many tourist cafés hire travellers on the spot as waiters/bar staff though the pay is only enough to tempt those whose aim is to subsist in situ: food, drink (not alcohol) and 100B for eight hours' work.

FURTHER INFORMATION
Information and traveller centres

TAT (the Tourism Authority of Thailand) offers free maps, detailed information brochures and has useful offices in almost every town to help you orientate yourself. It helps to ask very specifically for particular information. Also, while not every office stocks maps of every other destination, it's worth enquiring for your next destination.

Then there are the guesthouses which make things particularly easy especially in Bangkok, the south-central beach areas and north-west hill-tribe areas. There's rarely any need for a guide book in these regions – for the local low-down first find the travellers' area (guesthouse suggestions are given on maps where things aren't obvious), collect maps, first-hand travel reports and a motorbike, then head out on your own to explore. A handy mantra: 'Backpacker ghetto; get a map and get out!'

You'll find major traveller enclaves in Bangkok (see KSR p53), Kanchanaburi, Pai, Mae Hong Song, Chiang Mai, Ko Chang, Ko Lanta, Krabi, Phang Nga, Ko Tau, Ko Phanghan and elsewhere.

In the north-east (Isaan), such places are fewer and further between – though ironically that makes those that you do find that much friendlier/more helpful (eg Phimai, and individual guesthouses in various Mekong villages, such as That Phanom, Sangkhoum, Si Chiang Mai, Nong Khai).

Books and maps

A remarkable range of new and used books covering almost every aspect of Thai life and culture is available in the country. The Silom and Patpong areas of Bangkok have the largest selection of bookstores for **new books** eg White Lotus Books (☎ 662-311 2177), 11/2 Soi 58 Sukhumvit Rd. The often excellent DK Books has branches across the country.

The Kao San Road area of Bangkok has a constant supply of **second-hand guide books** for all countries of the region both new (at higher than UK prices) and used ($12+ for recent editions): the better deals are from roadside stands rather than shops.

The Thailand guide in the normally reliable Lonely Planet series has some annoying quirks with successive editions continuing to repeat mapping errors, notably the same scale disparities that also show up on most free tourist maps, particularly in Isaan towns. The Rough Guide is often more accurate, but has fewer town plans anyway.

TAT offers a free map of Thailand but the Nelles map is more detailed and is widely available in bookshops. Buying a Bangkok bus map is very sensible if you're spending much time in the city.

Map reading tips Colloquially longer names are often shortened (eg Ubon = Ubon Ratchathani), spellings can vary greatly according to the transliteration system (thus Ubon = Ubol = Ubor). Yet some very similar names indicate very different places – ie Rayong (an industro-chemical city near Pattaya) is not Ranong (an intriguing town on the Burmese border with some Chinese architecture). Archaic written forms often don't accurately reflect the pronunciation, thus Sri is pronounced Si, while some cities go by popular nicknames which are utterly different (Nakhon Ratchasima = Khorat).

Generally it's the full, formal name that appears on locally-made maps. Note, however, that on regional maps the main city within its eponymous province (eg Buriram town on a map of Buriram province) is commonly marked not with its name but with the term *Amphoe Muang* which translates as something like 'county town'. In Thai, Bangkok is written and pronounced Krung Thep.

❏ Meeting the locals

● **The people** Thailand is a Buddhist country and normal Buddhist conventions apply (see p74). Thais are laidback people who are also very forgiving of foreigners' foibles – visitors are traditionally viewed as being sent from God. Nonetheless consistent faux pas (such as wearing shorts in monasteries) have made tourists, especially backpackers, appear rude and uncaring of the local traditions. If the reason you are in Thailand is to get to know the country, you will have an uphill struggle proving your sincerity. Those who do make it are uniformly delighted by the gentle and hospitable culture they find.

Thais take their royal family seriously; offending the King (even indirectly or jokingly) will not go down well and could theoretically land you in jail. At 6pm you may hear the national anthem blaring out on a public address system. Local people will generally respect you if, like them, you stand still and to attention for the duration of the music.

The *wei*, the Thai greeting of holding hands prayer-like at the chest, can mean 'really good to see you', 'good bye', 'sincere thanks', or be a sign of respect. It is polite to gesture back a *wei* when gestured to, or give a pre-emptive *wei* yourself.

● **Some phrases in Thai**:

    Welcome/hello – *sah-bai-dee*
    Thank you – *khorp-kun-kahp* (male speaking); *khorp-kun kah* (female).
    Excuse me – *khor thot*
    How much – *tow rie*
    Very expensive – *pan pai*
    Never mind (or 'It's OK') – *mai pen rai*
    <u>Very</u> delicious – *ah-roy <u>marg</u>*
    Not too spicy, please – *kor mai phet*

Useful websites

🖵 www.welcomethai.com/ gives plenty of tips on travel to and in Thailand including easy to read rail timetables (click Transportation).

🖵 www.tat.or.th is the official tourist information site. It includes the dates of upcoming festivals and a list of jail sentences for various sex crimes.

🖵 www.nectec.or.th/thailand/index.html has the self-described 'Big Picture'.

For motorbiking information, try the Golden Triangle Rider homepage at 🖵 www.gt-rider.com/.

🖵 www.trangonline.com/ for information on the up and coming beaches in the far south.

🖵 www.chiangmai-online.com for guess where.

❏ The Thai alphabet

Much of the country is very tourist friendly and you may never need to learn the Thai alphabet. However, especially in Isaan (the north-east) many bus stations have destination boards and timetables completely lacking any Latin characters so a basic ability to decipher town names can be a distinct advantage. Thai script looks somewhat similar to Lao but is rather more difficult to read accurately thanks to very different transliteration systems and because, for historical reasons, many names aren't spelt phonetically (like in English where Leicester is actually pronounced Lester). A big additional confusion is the startling difference between different fonts/typefaces. An increasingly prevalent bold/modern Thai font has many letters that are reminiscent of Latin characters, while the same letters in the spindly, almost botanical traditional lettering, appear to be blowing bubbles. I have included both in the chart below.

Two key deciphering tips: firstly at the end of a syllable 'B' becomes 'P', 'D'>'T', 'G'>'K' and 'L'/'R'>'N'. Secondly, without a vowel marker squiggle an 'open' syllable (da, ka, ma etc) is pronounced with an 'a' vowel. However, a similarly unmarked 'closed' syllable (dod, kot, man etc) takes an 'o'.

These days Western numerals are almost always used in commerce and you don't really need to learn the Thai equivalents. Nonetheless, you'll see them on bank notes and knowing them will surprise your local friends!

1 2 3 4 5 6 7 8 9 10

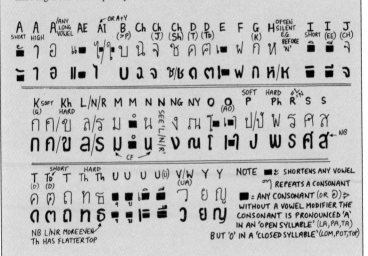

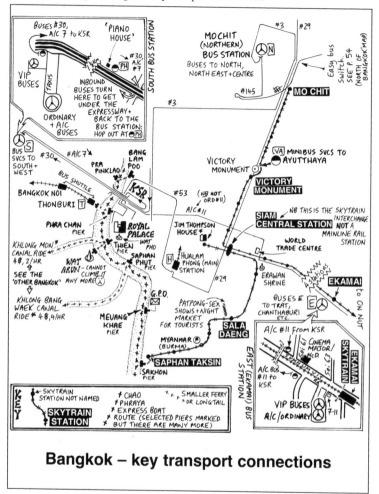

Bangkok – key transport connections

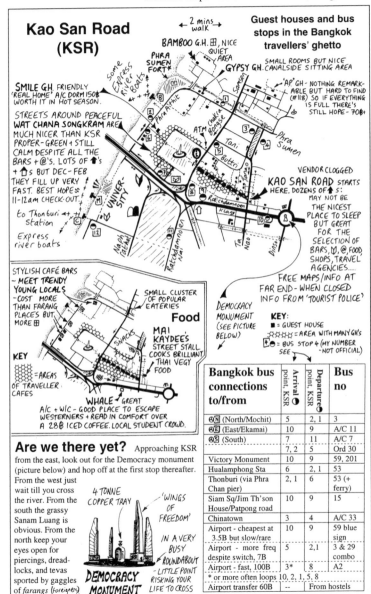

Kao San Road (KSR)

Guest houses and bus stops in the Bangkok travellers' ghetto

← 2 mins walk →

BAMBOO G.H. ⊞, NICE QUIET AREA

PHRA SUMEN FORT

GYPSY G.H. CANALSIDE SITTING AREA

SMALL ROOMS BUT NICE

'AP' GH - NOTHING REMARKABLE BUT HARD TO FIND (#118) SO IF EVERYTHING IS FULL THERE'S STILL HOPE - 70B+

SMILE G.H. FRIENDLY 'REAL HOME' A/C DORM 150B WORTH IT IN HOT SEASON.

STREETS AROUND PEACEFUL **WAT CHANA SONGKRAM** ARE MUCH NICER THAN KSR PROPER - GREEN + STILL CALM DESPITE ALL THE BARS + @'s. LOTS OF ⬆'s + ⬆s BUT DEC-FEB THEY FILL UP VERY FAST. BEST HOPE 11-12am CHECK-OUT.

to Thonburi Station

Express river boats

Some Express River Boats

Phra Athit

Chakra Bongse

ATM

Tani

Rambutri

Phra Sumen

Soi Ram...

VENDOR CLOGGED **KAO SAN ROAD** STARTS HERE. DOZENS OF ⬆s: MAY NOT BE THE NICEST PLACE TO SLEEP BUT GREAT FOR THE SELECTION OF BARS, ♥, @, FOOD, SHOPS, TRAVEL AGENCIES....

Ratchdamnoen Klang

UNIVERSITY

Naph Rathai

Ratchdamnoen Nai

Ta Nao

Din So

FREE MAPS/INFO AT FAR END - WHEN CLOSED INFO FROM 'TOURIST POLICE'

STYLISH CAFÉ BARS - MEET TRENDY YOUNG LOCALS - COST MORE THAN FARANG PLACES BUT MORE ⊞

SMALL CLUSTER OF POPULAR EATERIES

Food

SNACKS

MAI KAYDEE's STREET STALL COOKS BRILLIANT THAI VEGY FOOD

DEMOCRACY MONUMENT (SEE PICTURE BELOW)

KEY:
- ■ = GUEST HOUSE
- ✶✶✶ = AREA WITH MANY GH's
- ⬆❹ = BUS STOP 4 (MY NUMBER SEE → - NOT OFFICIAL)

KEY
- ✶✶✶ = AREAS OF TRAVELLER CAFES

WHALE - GREAT A/C + W/C - GOOD PLACE TO ESCAPE WESTERNERS + READ IN COMFORT OVER A 28B ICED COFFEE. LOCAL STUDENT CROWD.

Are we there yet?

Approaching KSR from the east, look out for the Democracy monument (picture below) and hop off at the first stop thereafter. From the west just wait till you cross the river. From the south the grassy Sanam Luang is obvious. From the north keep your eyes open for piercings, dreadlocks, and tevas sported by gaggles of *farangs* (foreigners)

4 TONNE COPPER TRAY

'WINGS OF FREEDOM'

IN A VERY BUSY ROUNDABOUT - LITTLE POINT RISKING YOUR LIFE TO CROSS

DEMOCRACY MONUMENT

Bangkok bus connections to/from	Arrival point, KSR ❶	Departure point, KSR ❶	Bus no
⊕Ⓝ (North/Mochit)	5	2, 1	3
⊕Ⓔ (East/Ekamai)	10	9	A/C 11
⊕Ⓢ (South)	7	11	A/C 7
	7, 2	5	Ord 30
Victory Monument	10	9	59, 201
Hualamphong Sta	6	2, 1	53
Thonburi (via Phra Chan pier)	2, 1	6	53 (+ ferry)
Siam Sq/Jim Th'son House/Patpong road	10	9	15
Chinatown	3	4	A/C 33
Airport - cheapest at 3.5B but slow/rare	10	9	59 blue sign
Airport - more freq despite switch, 7B	5	2,1	3 & 29 combo
Airport - fast, 100B	3*	8	A2
* or more often loops 10, 2, 1, 5, 8			
Airport transfer 60B	--	From hostels	

North of Bangkok

to Chiang Mai timetable p.55

MONKEYS

TAT

ลพบุรี
LOPBURI KHMER RUINS, MONKEYS + GROTTY HOTELS

Buses to Chiang Mai via Tak, Kamp. Phet.

2 HRS BETTER BY TRAIN

1-1½ HRS see T.T.

to Chiang Mai via Kamp. Phet 6,7. 7:30, 9:30,11, 13:30.

to Nong Khai, Udon, Ubon + NE: Timetables p. 66

อยุธยา
AYUTTHAYA

MAJOR RUINS WITH TRAVELLER-FRIENDLY GH's.

Wing's see map for exact route.

15-20 mins see T.T.

2 HR 35 mins

1-3 HR 41฿ BUS

บางปะอิน
BANG PA IN
ROYAL PALACE + CHALET. FREE CABLE-WAY ACROSS RIVER TO CHURCH SHAPED WAT.
50฿, 8:30–15:30

2 KM

45 mins—BY ANY AY↔BPI TRAIN

180฿ Express Boat 8 a.m, Sun only

MINIBUS FREQ AS FULL 45฿

1-2 HR

BKK AIR PORT

50 mins

BANGKOK

Bus departures table

Departures in **bold** are on rap/ex trains with surcharges

LOPBURI

04:40,	05:20,	06:05,		**09:34**,
07:19,	08:52,	09:10,		
11:18,	**11:55**,	**12:44**,		
14:34,	17:10,	**17:55**,		
21:12,	**01:02**→>>			
	05:49,	08:59,		
10:25,	13:00,	14:40,		
15:50,	**16:44**,	18:15,		
18:28,	19:04,	**19:45**,		
22:23,	23:46,>>			

AYUTTHAYA

02:46,	05:25,	05:40,	05:54,
08:31,	09:47,	10:46,	12:42,
13:11,	**14:00**,	14:50,	16:16,
17:41,	18:28,	20:06>>	
05:34,	06,	42,	08:39>>,
10:12,	10:33,	12:47,	13:13,
14:27,	15:36,	16:59,	18:01,
18:15,	18:28,	18:50,	18:59,
19:38,	20:55,	22:10,	00:54

BANG PA IN

BANGKOK

VICTORY MONUMENT

MINIBUS TO AYUTTHAYA +5฿

FUJI

Rachawithi Rd.

MINIBUS TO THE FUTURE PARK MALL (PASSES AIRPORT, 20฿)

VICTORY MONUMENT SKYTRAIN STATION

KFC AND MISTER DONUT

Phaya Thai Rd.

7-11

DON MUANG (BANGKOK AIRPORT) STATION.

#29 FREQ
#59 (BLUE) FEW

#3

MOCHIT (NORTH) BUS STA

#145

KEY BUS ROUTES (NORTH)

KSR

N & BLUE SIGNBOARD ONLY

#3

#59

SOUTH BOUND
NORTH

#53

MAHARAT PIER

#29

HUALAMPHONG (MAIN) STATION

SIAM CENTRE

#29 FREQ

SKYTRAIN

to Airport

Change from the #29 (ex airport) to #3 for Kao San Rd or to #145 for North Bus Sta.

CENTRAL PLAZA

Wiphawadi Rangsit Rd.

#29 turns

COMPLEX INTER-SECTION. LONG WAIT AT LIGHTS.

CHATUCHAK
HUGE WEEKEND MARKET

Phahon Yothin Rd.

#3 BUS Stops. Change to #29 for airport.

MO CHIT SKYTRAIN STATION

ELEVATED EXPRESSWAY

Ayutthaya

Ayutthaya - great ruins best seen by bicycle, big backpacker-friendly town, free maps widely available. Heading north/north-east? - See the train timetables below and p54/61/66. Many long-distance buses don't bother with ⊕4 - so arriving from the north you may well be dumped at the daunting Rte 32 junction ⊖5. Once you get across the road, it's a 5 min walk to the #5 bus route for the city centre (5B, runs 5:00-20:00). Or pay a moto direct (50B+, drivers wait all night at the shelters).

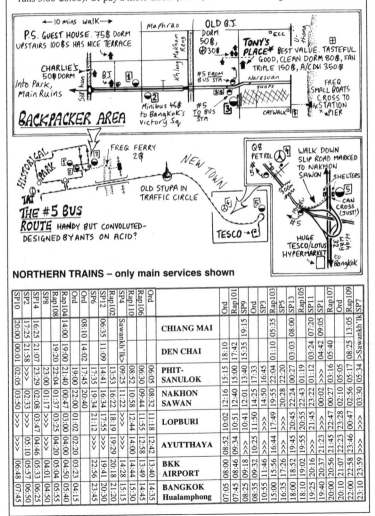

NORTHERN TRAINS – only main services shown

SP10	SP2	SP14	SP8	Rap108	Rap104	Ord	Ord	SP6	SP12	SP4	Rap102	Rap110	Ord		Ord	Rap101	SP9	Ord	SP3	Rap103	SP5	SP13	Rap105	SP11	SP1	Rap107	Ord	Rap109	SP7
20:00	17:25	16:25		14:00		08:10		06:35		Sawankh'lk				**CHIANG MAI**			19:15			05:35		08:00		07:20	09:05			13:05	>Sawankh'lk
00:01	21:07	21:01		19:20		14:02		11:09						**DEN CHAI**	18:10	17:42	15:35		01:10	03:03		03:24	04:42	05:40				08:25	
02:05	>>>	23:00		21:40		19:00		13:53	14:41	09:25			06:05	**PHIT-SANULOK**	15:15	15:00	13:40	17:33	16:45	22:04	22:20	00:27	01:19	01:12		03:16	05:05	05:17	05:34
03:50	02:33	02:08	01:17	00:47	22:00	20:40		17:35	16:34	11:22			08:32	**NAKHON SAWAN**	12:16	12:40	12:01		14:50	19:55	20:28	22:24	22:43	23:22	00:27	02:10	02:56	03:30	
>>>	>>>	03:47	03:25	03:00	01:02	22:20		>>>	>>>	12:44			10:58	**LOPBURI**	10:02	10:51	10:41	11:50	>>>	11:55	17:49	18:19	20:45	>>>	20:55	21:45	23:28	22:47	00:47
>>>	>>>	05:10	04:46	04:20	02:20	01:25	00:00	>>>	>>>	14:00	14:00	13:40	12:42	**AYUTTHAYA**	08:52	09:34	>>>	10:25	>>>	>>>	16:44	17:45	19:45	19:55	21:23	21:45	22:23	23:46	23:59
>>>	05:10	05:33	05:04	03:23	04:14	22:56	00:18	>>>	>>>	14:44	14:44	14:28	13:40	**BKK AIRPORT**	08:00	08:46	09:18		11:46	11:46	15:56	16:35	18:52	19:02	20:37	20:56	21:07	22:58	23:59
06:48	05:57	06:25	05:33	04:01	04:50	03:23	04:15			15:15	15:30	14:45	14:35	**BANGKOK Hualamphong**	07:05	07:45	08:25	08:35	10:50	10:55	15:00	16:35	18:00	18:10	19:25	19:40	20:00	22:00	23:10

Central Thailand
The great ruined cities

To **Mae Hong Song**
7, 9, 10:30
12:30, VIA
PAI + SOPPONG.
CONSIDER
FLYING-3/DAY,
ONLY 425฿!

(ex Chiang Mai) 6HRS to Nan (every 1-1½ HRS) d. 6:15-17:00 + 22:30♭

CHIANG MAI

ลำพูน LAMPHUN
COMPACT FORMER
ROYAL CITY. SECTIONS OF
MOAT, & HARIPHUNCHAI
HOLDS WORLD'S BIGGEST
BRONZE GONG.
& KUKUT, ▣.

3/4hr   1¼

฿ PHRAE
FREQ P/U ½HR

1½-2 HRS

LAM PANG ลำปาง

DEN CHAI

A/C 139฿ d. 5,10,11:30♭ OR VIA LAMPANG

≈1hr

BIG, BUSTLING CITY. & CHEDI SAO 6KM.

Dozens of buses but most for Bangkok dep C.M. 7-10:30 or 19:30-21

อุตรดิตถ์ UTTARADIT ▣ CULTURE CENTRE

NO REAL CHANCE TO GO to Mawlamyine, Thaton

BURMA

8-16:00
฿ OLD SI SATCHANALAI
(ASK BUS DRIVER FOR MEUANG KAO)
⑬-⑮ ANCIENT CITY. RUINS LESS TOURISTY THAN SUKHOTHAI.

NEW SI SATCHAN-ALAI. ♠ KRUCHUNG.
10 Km

⊕ AT BUS STOP. RENT BIKE AS SITE TOO SPREAD OUT TO WALK IN HEAT. NO♠s

CHA LIANG
22

MYA-WADI

FIGHTING IN 2001

RIM MOEI
แม่สอด MAE SOT
MODERN TOWN. BORDER TROUBLE
♠ #4 G.H.

SUKHOTHAI AIRPORT
ENDEARINGLY SMALL, MIDDLE OF NOWHERE!

อุทยานประวัติศาสตร์ สุโขทัย

*OLD SUKHOTHAI
⑬-⑭ CITY RUINS. STUPAS + OLD BUDDHAS STREWN ACROSS VAST AREA. ENTRY 150฿ (ALL) OR 40฿/ZONE. 'CLOSED'/FREE AFTER 18:00. RENT BIKE ON SITE OR COME BY ๗ FROM NEW SUKHOTHAI.

9,30,11:30 50฿
15 Km

9,20,11:30♭
10,12:00
10:30 40฿
Few in p.m.
LAST 15:30
+16:30

1½HR,1HR

สังคโลก SAWANKHALOK
3/4HR 8:00-11:00 ONLY

ตาก TAK
1½HRS

4-5HRS LOVELY SCENERY

BURMA

1 HRS 2/4HR

พิษณุโลก PHITSANULOK
('P-LOK')
& WAT YAI

WAT YAI
⑭ BUS#1

2/HR, 1HR

ุ่มผาง UMPHANG
SMALL, RELATIVELY 'UNDISCOVERED' TREKKING BASE
♠s VEERA, PHU DOI ETC...

2-3/HR + MORE VIA PLOK + 5HRS. 6:30-16:00

20 MINS

P/U

NOT TO SCALE

BUS#4
BUD-DHA FOUNDRY
Y.H.

Main bus route to Bangkok via Ayutthaya 1/HR TILL 19:00 (EX. K.PH.) + 23:30 ≈ 5½-6 HRS

1½HRS ≈ 1/HR TILL 14:00 + 16:20♭

สุโขทัย
NEW SUKHOTHAI

BEST BUDGET TRAV-ELLER BASE FOR VISITING CENTRAL THAILAND.

MORE RUINS
CITY P/U ROUTE
OLD CITY*
NEW TOWN
≈ 1KM

กำแพงเพชร KAMPHAENG PHET UNESCO RUINS

NEW BUS STA. PINK + PURPLE P/U TO TOWN 4฿ P.P. RARE.
(SINCE 2001)

BOGGY FIELDS ✕ No Path
♠ #4 G.H. 150-180฿ ♥ CUTE
99 G.H. 80฿ DORM
Charod with fong
HANDY IF UNSPECTACULAR TRAVELLERS' AREA
BEST CHOICE IS BANTHAIGH -POPULAR CAFÉ, ▣, FREE MAPS INCL OLD CITY.
CALTEX

Rte 101
14km to OLD CITY
300m
7-11

NICE GARDEN J+J G.H. 80฿ DORM, 120 s
THAI FARMERS' BANK
CENTRE
SUKH. TRAVEL SVC (#20)
FOR BAN THAI GET OFF P/U AT BRIDGE TO AVOID G/H COMMISSION
50฿ DORM, 100฿s

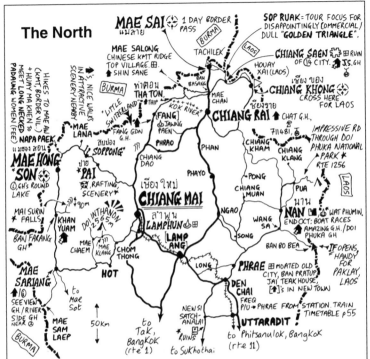

The North

MOTOR BIKING Northernmost Thailand is an excellent place to ride into the sunset on a rented motorbike. Roads are surfaced yet mostly quiet, good maps are available locally (especially in Chiang Mai) and David Unkovich's moto-touring guides to the region will hold your hand if you are nervous just heading out at random. See http://www.gt-rider.com/ For the best scenery consider route 1256 from Pua (near Nan), the Mae Salong to Fang road or almost anywhere along the Mae Hong Song loop, [eg the Soppong area]. Motorbike's also the best way to see the gently attractive golden triangle villages while avoiding the main tourist hordes. Bring a jacket as warm days turn suddenly cold at dusk. The top traveller hubs are at Chiang Mai (around Tha Phae gate), Pai, Soppong, Mae Hong Son, Chiang Khong and the riverside area of Mae Sai. Nan is starting to develop too. But think twice before being bullied into doing a trek.

HILL-TRIBE TREKS Even if you're happy with the voyeuristic, commercial nature of tramping through poor, jaded villages, led by an unsympathetic guide, Northern Thailand is rarely the best place to start. Around Sapa (Vietnam) people wear more colourful costumes and the scenery is more dramatic, Burma's Shan state markets are more photogenic, Yunnan's Dai villages are architecturally more interesting and N Laos is safer if you insist on smoking opium. If you do choose a N Thai trek, find an out-of-the-way starting point for an experience more personal and slightly more 'authentic' than most of the Chiang Mai outfits can offer. (eg Fang Garden GH off the main rte 107 (w side) 12km S of Fang, tel 534 53220 ask for Amala)

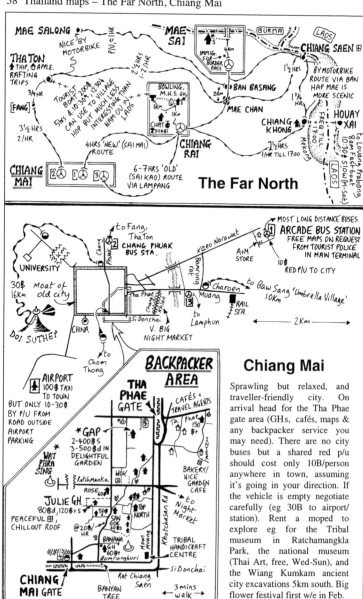

The Far North

MAE SALONG ● ● NICE BY MOTORBIKE P/U ½HR

MAE SAI

BURMA

LAOS

CHIANG SAEN ⊞

THA TON ↑ THIP, ●APPLE. RAFTING TRIPS

IMMIG. FOR BORDER PASS 4KM S

BAN BASANG 2KM

1½ HRS

BY MOTORBIKE ROUTE VIA BAN HAP MAE IS MORE SCENIC

HOUAY XAI

TOURIST BOAT 200฿ 5hrs d. 10-30 & 12-30. CAN USE TO VILLAGE HOP BUT MUCH LESS INTERESTING THAN NAM-OU IN X LAOS

3¼ HR

[FANG]

BOWLING, M.H.S. GH. 1km ↑ 1km CHAT ↑ 114฿

MAE CHAN

CHIANG KHONG ↑

1¼ HR

to Louang Prabang 8am fast-boat 10-30 & slow (M-Sat)

3½ HRS 2/HR

4HRS 'NEW' (SAI MAI) ROUTE

CHIANG MAI ② ① ③

CHIANG RAI

6-7HRS 'OLD' (SAI KAO) ROUTE VIA LAMPANG

1½ HRS 1/HR TILL 17.00

FREE TILL 10-30?

Mekong

LAOS

Chiang Mai

to Fang, Tha Ton

CHANG PHUAK BUS STA.

Kaeo Narawat

MOST LONG DISTANCE BUSES
ARCADE BUS STATION FREE MAPS ON REQUEST FROM TOURIST POLICE IN MAIN TERMINAL

UNIVERSITY

A+M STORE

10฿ RED P/U TO CITY

30฿ 16KM

Moat of old city

Tha Phae

Charoen 'Muang

RAIL STA.

to Baw Sang 'Umbrella Village' 10KM

DOI SUTHEP

CHINA

Si Donchai

V. BIG NIGHT MARKET

to Lamphun

← 2 Km →

to Chom Thong

↑ **AIRPORT** 100฿ TAXI TO TOWN BUT ONLY 10-30฿ BY P/U FROM ROAD OUTSIDE AIRPORT PARKING

BACKPACKER AREA

THA PHAE GATE

CAFÉS + TRAVEL AGENTS

Ta Phae

WAT PHRA SING

★ **GAP** 2-400฿ s 3-500฿ d IN DELIGHTFUL GARDEN

HOK

Ratchmanka

ROSE 60฿

JULIE GH. 80฿ d, 120฿ + s PEACEFUL ⊞, CHILLOUT ROOF

@20฿/HR

SAN GOK 80฿ s

BANANA GH. 60฿ Bumrungburi

BAKERY/ NICE GARDEN CAFE

TOP NORTH

to Night Market

Khotchasan Rd

Moon Muang

TRIBAL HANDICRAFT CENTRE

Si Donchai

CHIANG MAI GATE

BANYAN TREE

Rat Chiang Saen

3 mins walk

Sprawling but relaxed, and traveller-friendly city. On arrival head for the Tha Phae gate area (GHs, cafés, maps & any backpacker service you may need). There are no city buses but a shared red p/u should cost only 10B/person anywhere in town, assuming it's going in your direction. If the vehicle is empty negotiate carefully (eg 30B to airport/ station). Rent a moped to explore eg for the Tribal museum in Ratchamangkla Park, the national museum (Thai Art, free, Wed-Sun), and the Wiang Kumkam ancient city excavations 5km south. Big flower festival first w/e in Feb.

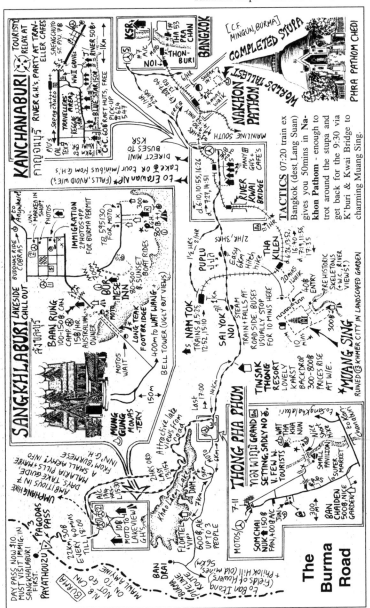

The Burma Road

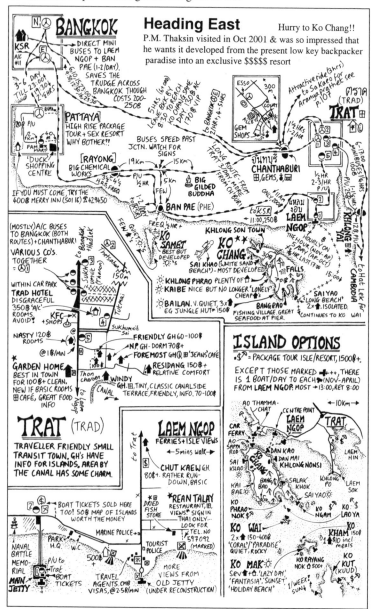

BANGKOK

KSR
A/C #11

→ DIRECT MINI BUSES TO LAEM NGOP + BAN PAE (1-2/DAY). SAVES THE TRUDGE ACROSS BANGKOK THOUGH COSTS 200-250B

3-6 DAY
6.10, 9.30, 23.30+
TILL 19.30+
23.30
2 HRS

BUPA

200B P/U
FAM MART

PATTAYA
HIGH RISE PACKAGE TOUR & SEX RESORT WHY BOTHER!!

'DUCK' SHOPPING CENTRE

IF YOU MUST COME, TRY THE 400B MERRY INN (SOI 16) ☎429450

[RAYONG]
BIG CHEMICAL WORKS

19Km   15Km

P/U ½ HR   5Km   BIG GILDED BUDDHA
4½-2-4½ FREQ   FEW   1-2 HRS

Heading East
P.M. Thaksin visited in Oct 2001 & was so impressed that he wants it developed from the present low key backpacker paradise into an exclusive $$$$$ resort

Hurry to Ko Chang!!

ESSO   300 M   COURT

GEM SHOPS

5 HRS (6.00) 8.30 TO KO CHANG BY AC LEAVE BKK BY 120B AC 8.30 TO KO CHANG SAME DAY. 170 B VIP

→ BANGKOK (E) 2 HRS • 14 SHRS

Attractive ride (3hrs) to Sa Kaeo for Arayaprathet see P.107

ศรีราชา (TRAD)

TRAT
1½ HRS ½ HR

LONG ROUTE FROM TRAT DIRECT THRO' CH BURI

BUSES SPEED PAST JCTN. WATCH FOR SIGNS

จันทบุรี CHANTHABURI GEMS,

½ HR 2-3/HR P/U 25B

6.00, 12.00 MINIBUS 2½ HRS

BAN PAE (PHE)

ONLY 30B

FREQ ½ HR   GUE TO '05
FEW

KO SAMET BEST BUT DEVELOPED ☼ '0's

to KSR 11.00, 250B

เกาะช้าง KO CHANG

KHLONG SON TOWN

HOURLY ON THE HOUR (NOV.-AP) X HR LAST 17.00

to Hat Lek for CAMBODIA

SAI KHAO (WHITE SAND BEACH)- MOST DEVELOPED   30B   7 FALLS
KHLONG PHRAO PLENTY OF ☼
KAIBE NICE BUT NO LONGER 'LONELY' CHEAP☼
BAILAN. V. QUIET, 3x ☼ EG JUNGLE HUT ☀ 150B

BANG BAO FISHING VILLAGE. GREAT SEAFOOD AT PIER.

SAI YAO 'LONG BEACH' 2x ☀. ISOLATED. CONTINUES TO KO WAI

(MOSTLY) A/C BUSES TO BANGKOK (BOTH ROUTES) + CHANTHABURI

To Bangkok + Hatlek

VARIOUS CO's. TOGETHER = ①

Petchaburi (Tanon)

150m

WITHIN CAR PARK
TRAD HOTEL DISGRACEFUL 350B 'A/C' ROOMS. AVOID!

KFC + SHOPS

Sukhumvit 50i

NASTY 120B ROOMS
@ 1B/min

★
GARDEN HOME. BEST IN TOWN FOR 100B+ CLEAN. NEW IF BASIC ROOMS ⊞ CAFÉ, GREAT FOOD

Thon charoen

100B

WINDY GH. ⊞, TINY, CLASSIC CANALSIDE TERRACE, FRIENDLY, INFO. 70-100B

Sukhumvit Soi

FRIENDLY GH 60-100B
N.P. GH- DORM 70B+
FOREMOST GH①, 'JEAN'S CAFÉ
RESIDANG 150B+ RELATIVE COMFORT

to Laem Ngop

CANAL

TRAT (TRAD)
TRAVELLER FRIENDLY SMALL TRANSIT TOWN. GH's HAVE INFO FOR ISLANDS, AREA BY THE CANAL HAS SOME CHARM.

to Trat

LAEM NGOP
FERRIES + ISLE VIEWS
← 5mins walk →

$
CHUT KAEW GH. 80B+. RATHER RUN-DOWN, BASIC

DRIED FISH STORE
★REAN TALAY RESTAURANT, ⊞, VIEWS! SIGN IN THAI ONLY... LOOK FOR TEL. NO 597092 (MARKED)

BOAT TICKETS SOLD HERE TOO! 50B MAP OF ISLANDS WORTH THE MONEY

MARINE POLICE

PARK H.Q.   W.C.

NAVAL BATTLE MEMO-RIAL
MAIN JETTY

P/U to Trat
⊞ Trat BOAT TICKETS

500B
TRAVEL AGENTS. CMB VISAS, @2.5B/min

TOURIST POLICE

MORE VIEWS FROM OLD JETTY (UNDER RECONSTRUCTION)

ISLAND OPTIONS
•$ = PACKAGE TOUR ISLE/RESORT, 1500B+.

EXCEPT THOSE MARKED ✈ ++, THERE IS 1 BOAT/DAY TO EACH (NOV.-APRIL) FROM LAEM NGOP. MOST ✈13.00, RET 8.00

AO THAMMA-CHAT
CENTRE POINT
LAEM NGOP
← 10Km →
CAR FERRY
AO SAPPA ROD
DAN KAO
DAN MAI KHLONG NONSI
LAEM HIN
SAI KHAO ☼
KAI BAE ☼
BANG BAO
SALAK KHOK
KHLONG PO
LAEM SOK
SAI YAO ☼
KO PHRAO NOK $
KO NGAM $
KO LAOYA
KO WAI 2x ⛺ 150-400B 'CORAL'/'PARADISE' QUIET, ROCKY
KO KHAM 150B ⛺ $10 incl MEALS
KO MAK SEV ⛺+☼. 'LAZY DAY'/ 'FANTASIA', 'SUNSET', 'HOLIDAY BEACH'
KO RAYANG NOK ⛺ 500B
1/WEEK?
KO KUT (KUUD)
SUN

Rap 140	Exp 68	Ord 420	Ord 74	Rap 142	SP 22	Ord 422	Ord 230	Ord 426	Ord 432	Ord 234	Ord 232	Ord 228	Rap 136	Exp 72	Ord 234	**S. Isaan Trains** Type & number	Ord 431	Ord 425	Ord 421	SP21	Ord 419	RAP 135	Ord 231	Ord 227	Exp 71	Rap 139	Exp 73	Rap 141	Ord 229
19.40	18.15		18.35	16.15	15.45	12.45		8.40		6.55	6.35		4.55			**UBON** RATCH ATHANI	8.35	13.45	15.40	17.10	18.10		21.00			04.45	05.35	07.20	10.45
22.48	20.47	19.30	21.27	18.22	19.58	16.24	13.55	9.20	12.04	10.04	7.45		6.08	4.55		**SURIN**	5.23	10.48	13.17	13.42	17.45	15.13	21.25	21.59	01.30	03.04	04.52	06.00	07.44	9.22
23.53	22.07	20.27	20.56	19.05	20.56	17.21	15.03	11.02	13.00	11.02		8.02	8.35	6.08		**BURIRAM**	9.46	12.31	12.58	16.49	18.01	20.30	00.30	02.15	04.56	04.56	06.04	08.06
02.34	23.32	22.44	23.03	20.46	23.03	19.33	18.35	12.15	15.50	13.28	10.37	10.37	8.41		7.26	**KHORAT** (N. Ratchasima)	7.30	10.35	10.55	14.55	16.31	17.58	21.59	00.37	03.12	03.12	03.16	05.51
04.57	00.34	00.52	02.03	21.37	21.37		19.09		17.40	15.05	13.58	13.58	10.05	10.25	06.05	**PAK CHONG**	9.26	10.48	13.03	14.43	16.06	19.53	22.42	22.37	01.43	00.15	01.08
07.41	03.36	03.02	03.59	01.20		20.06		17.41	18.36	13.39	13.11	13.11	14.00			**AYUTTHAYA**	7.36	8.33	10.48	12.42	13.29	17.12	20.22	22.37	21.54	00.15	01.08
08.40	03.12	03.49		02.08	03.03	20.55	21.40	18.16	16.51	14.17	15.05					**BKK AIRPORT**	6.51	7.48	10.00	11.58	12.35	15.25	19.39	21.54	22.37	22.37	23.33	00.17
09.35	04.00	04.35		03.05		21.40	19.30	17.45		14.55						**BANGKOK** Hualamphong	6.05	6.50	9.10	11.05	11.45	15.05	18.45	21.00	21.50	22.45	23.25	00.17

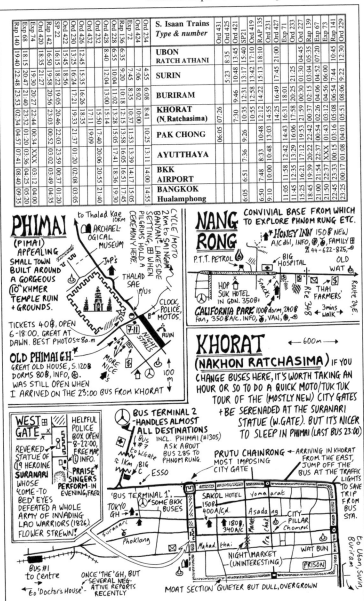

PHIMAI (PIMAI) APPEALING SMALL TOWN BUILT AROUND A GORGEOUS 10° KHMER TEMPLE RUIN + GROUNDS. TICKETS 40฿, OPEN 6-18:00. GREAT AT DAWN. BEST PHOTOS ≈ 8a.m

OLD PHIMAI G.H. GREAT OLD HOUSE, S.120฿ DORMS 80฿, INFO. WAS STILL OPEN WHEN I ARRIVED ON THE 23:00 BUS FROM KHORAT

to Thalad Kae 10KM — ARCHAEOLOGICAL MUSEUM
J+P's
CYCLE MOTO 2KM to SAI NGAM BANYAN LAKESIDE SETTING, WHEN PILGRIMS HOLD A CEREMONY HERE.
THALAD SAE p/us
CLOCK, POLICE, MOTOS
7-11 · RUIN · NIGHT STALLS · MORE NICE · 100 m

NANG RONG CONVIVIAL BASE FROM WHICH TO EXPLORE PHNOM RUNG ETC.
★ HONEY INN 150฿ NEW A/C dbl, INFO, FAMILY ☎ 44-622-825,
P.T.T. PETROL
BIG HOSPITAL · OLD WAT
HOP SUK HOTEL IN GDN. 350฿
CALIFORNIA PARK 100฿ dorm, 240฿ Fan, 350฿ A/C. INFO, VAN.
snacks · THAI FARMERS · Rte 24E · Route 24E. · 3mins walk

KHORAT (NAKHON RATCHASIMA) ←600m→ IF YOU CHANGE BUSES HERE, IT'S WORTH TAKING AN HOUR OR SO TO DO A QUICK MOTO/TUK TUK TOUR OF THE (MOSTLY NEW) CITY GATES + BE SERENADED AT THE SURANARI STATUE (W.GATE). BUT ITS NICER TO SLEEP IN PHIMAI (LAST BUS 23:00)

BUS TERMINAL 2 -HANDLES ALMOST ALL DESTINATIONS INCL. PHIMAI (#1305) ASK ABOUT BUS 285 TO PHNOM RUNG.
BUS #7 to wGate ≈ 1Km · BIG C · ESSO

PRUTU CHAINRONG ← ARRIVING IN KHORAT FROM THE EAST, JUMP OFF THE BUS AT THE TRAFFIC LIGHTS TO SAVE TRIP FROM BUS STA.
MOST IMPOSING CITY GATE

'BUS TERMINAL 1', SOME BKK BUSES
TOKYO GH · Suranari · Phoklang
SAKOL HOTEL 150฿ 400A/Cd. · Yomarat · Asadang · CITY PILLAR Chompol
180฿ 340 A/C · Market chak · Mahad thai
NIGHT MARKET (UNINTERESTING) · WAT BUN · PRISON
MOAT SECTION QUIETER BUT DULL, OVERGROWN
to Ubon, Surin, Buriram

WEST GATE — HELPFUL POLICE BOX OPEN 8-22:00, FREE MAP, INFO.
REVERED STATUE OF 19 HEROINE SURANARI WHOSE 'COME-TO BED' EYES DEFEATED A WHOLE ARMY OF INVADING LAO WARRIORS (1826). FLOWER STREWN!
PRAISE SINGERS PERFORM IN EVENING, FREQ.
BUS #1 to Centre
to 'Doctor's House' — ONCE 'THE' GH, BUT SEVERAL NEGATIVE REPORTS RECENTLY

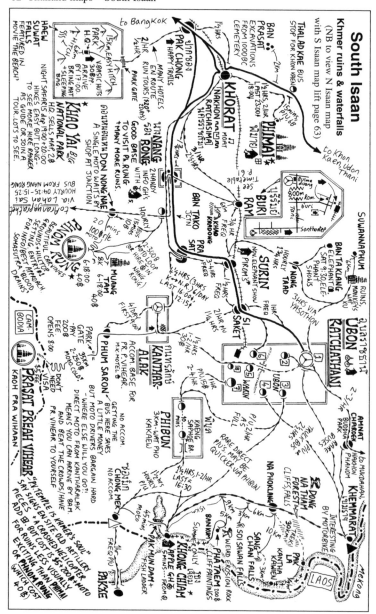

South Isaan

Khmer ruins & waterfalls

(NB to view N Isaan map
with S Isaan map lift page 63)

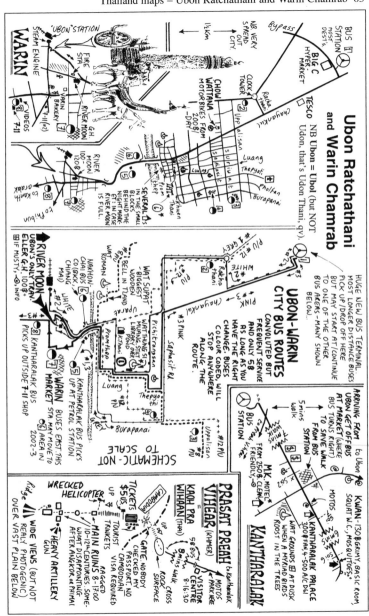

Ubon Ratchathani and Warin Chamrab

NB Ubon = Ubol (but NOT Udon, that's Udon Thani, qv).

UBON–WARIN CITY BUS ROUTES

CONVOLUTED BUT FREQUENT SERVICE AND ONLY 5฿ AS LONG AS YOU HAVE THE RIGHT CHANGE. BUSES COLOUR CODED WILL STOP ANYWHERE ALONG THE ROUTE.

SCHEMATIC - NOT TO SCALE

PRASAT PREAH VIHEAR (KHMER)
KAOH PRA WIHAAN (THAI)

WIDE VIEWS (BUT NOT REALLY PHOTOGENIC) OVER VAST PLAIN BELOW

WRECKED HELICOPTER

HEAVY ARTILLERY GUN

KANTHARALAK

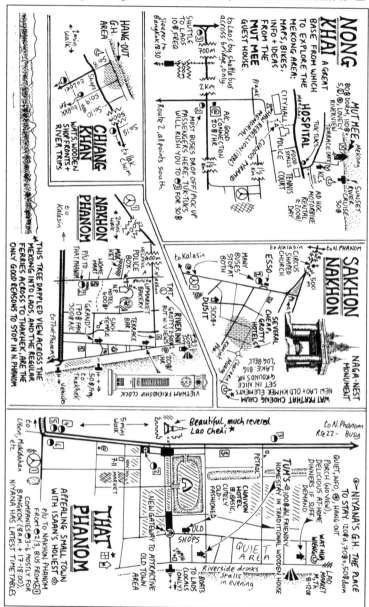

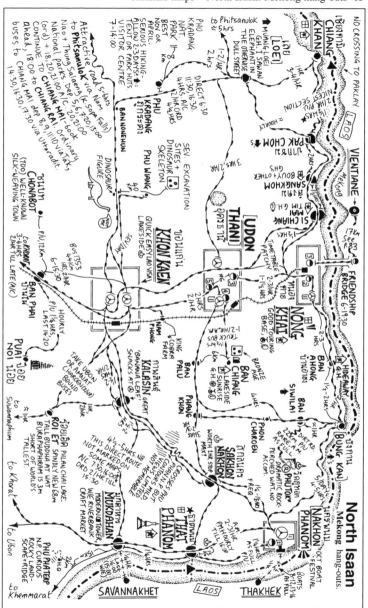

North Isaan
Mekong hang-outs.

North Isaan

Towns are friendly if dull & little English is spoken. Khon Kaen's handy for Lao visas, bypass Udon Thani if possible and use That Phanom or Nong Khai as starting points to relax along the Mekong. From Nong Khai to Chiang Khan you'll find some laid-back GH hang-outs, but elsewhere scenery can be disappointing.

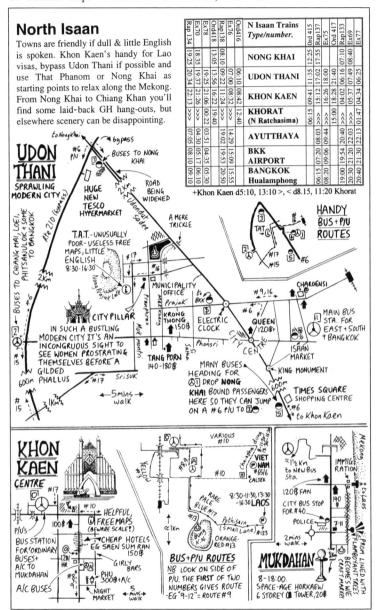

Rap 134	Ex70	Ex78	Rap 138	Ex76	Ord 416	Ord 418	N Isaan Trains Type/number.	Ord 415	Rap 137	Ex75	Ord 417	Rap 133	Ex77
19:25	18:35	13:05	08:10				**NONG KHAI**	12:25	17:55			07:10	08:40
20:34	19:37	13:56	09:22	07:00	08:32		**UDON THANI**	11:35	17:02	21:40		06:16	06:25
22:13	21:26	16:22	11:24	08:32	12:40		**KHON KAEN**	09:41	15:12	16:26	18:28	04:02	04:34
v	v	19:40	v	v			**KHORAT (N Ratchasima)**	06:15	>	15:00	>	>	01:47
07:05	04:30	03:51	19:02	14:29			**AYUTTHAYA**		08:03	09:44		20:40	22:13
08:10		04:35	19:53	15:09			**BKK AIRPORT**		07:20	09:06	19:54	21:20	21:30
09:10		06:10	20:50	15:55			**BANGKOK Hualamphong**	06:15	06:20	08:20	19:00	20:30	20:40

+Khon Kaen d5:10, 13:10 >, < d8.15, 11:20 Khorat

UDON THANI

SPRAWLING MODERN CITY

To Nong Khai — bypass
#6 P/U
BUSES TO NONG KHAI
HUGE NEW TESCO HYPERMARKET
ROAD BEING WIDENED
Udondit Sadee — 2km
A MERE TRICKLE
Rt 210 (bypass) — BUSES TO CHIANG MAI, LOEI, PHITSANULOK & SOME TO BANGKOK
BUSES TO CHIANG MAI, LOEI, PHITSANULOK — #6 2Km

T.A.T.- UNUSUALLY POOR- USELESS FREE MAPS, LITTLE ENGLISH 8:30-16:30
Nong Prajak Lake
#17 #16
MUNICIPALITY OFFICE Prajak
to BKK
KRONG THONG 150฿
ELECTRIC CLOCK
#9,16
#6
QUEEN 120฿+
CHAROENSI
MAIN BUS STA. FOR EAST + SOUTH + BANGKOK

CITY PILLAR
IN SUCH A BUSTLING MODERN CITY IT'S AN INCONGRUOUS SIGHT TO SEE WOMEN PROSTRATING THEMSELVES BEFORE A GILDED PHALLUS
600m — #15 #17 Srisuk Phonsri Sala — CITY CENTRE
TANG PORN 140-180฿
Mukkontri
ISAAN MARKET
KING MONUMENT
600m
TIMES SQUARE SHOPPING CENTRE #6 to Khon Kaen
MANY BUSES HEADING FOR ① DROP NONG KHAI BOUND PASSENGERS HERE SO THEY CAN JUMP ON A #6 P/U TO ②
5mins walk 1Km #15

HANDY BUS + P/U ROUTES
TAT #3 #17 #15 #6

KHON KAEN

CENTRE #17
#10
P/U's 100฿
BUS STATION FOR "ORDINARY" BUSES + A/C TO MUKDAHAN
A/C BUSES
@ HELPFUL, FREE MAPS (BEWARE SCALE!)
CHEAP HOTELS EG SAEN SUM RAN 150฿
GIRLY BARS
PHU 300฿+A/C
#8 NIGHT MARKET 5 mins walk
YELLOW #3
VARIOUS #10
Chaophaya dong
VIET NAM #65/6
#10 CALTEX
RARE PALE BLUE #17
8:30-11:30, 13:30 -16:30 LAOS
Pothisarn (small lane) #123
Bung K.N. ORANGE- RED #13
≈1km

BUS+P/U ROUTES
NB LOOK ON SIDE OF P/U. THE FIRST OF TWO NUMBERS GIVES ROUTE -EG "9-12"= ROUTE #9

MUKDAHAN

≈½ Km to New Bus Sta
Mekong — to Laos
IMMIGRATION
120฿ FAN
CITY BUS STOP FOR #40 140
POLICE 7-11
2mins walk
FROM LINED WITH FLAMBOYANT TREES BECOMES 1ML CRAFT MARKET
8-18:00. SPACE-AGE HORKAEW 6 STOREY ① TOWER, 20฿
1Km

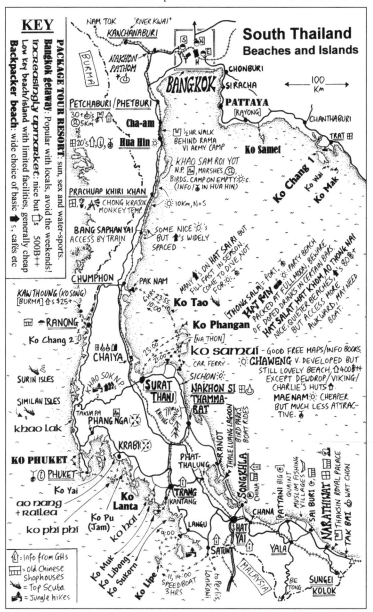

South Thailand
Beaches and Islands

KEY

PACKAGE TOUR RESORT: sun, sex and water-sports.

Bangkok getaway: Popular with locals, avoid the weekends! **increasingly upmarket:** nice but ⬆s 500B++

Low key beach/island: with limited facilities, generally cheap ⬆s, cafés etc

Backpacker beach: wide choice of basic

NAM TOK
'RIVER KWAI'
KANCHANABURI

BURMA

NAKHON PATHOM

CHONBURI
BANGKOK
SIRACHA
PATTAYA [RAYONG]
CHANTHABURI
TRAT

100 Km

PETCHABURI / PHETBURI
30+⬆s ⬆ 5km
Cha-am
20's Hua Hin
½ HR WALK BEHIND RAMA VI ARMY CAMP
Ko Samet
Ko Chang 1
Ko Wai
Ko Mak

KHAO SAM ROI YOT N.P. MARSHES, BIRDS. CAMP ON EMPTY ☼ S. (INFO in HUA HIN)

PRACHUAP KHIRI KHAN
CHONG KRAJOK MONKEY TEMP.
☼ 10KM, N+S

BANG SAPHAN YAI ACCESS BY TRAIN
SOME NICE ☼'s BUT ⬆'s WIDELY SPACED

CHUMPHON
PAK NAM
MANY ⬆s ON HAT SAI RI BUT FILL FAST IN SEASON. ☼ COME TO DIVE. NOT FOR ☼:

KAW THOUNG (KO SONG) [BURMA] ⬆s $25+
RANONG
Ko Chang 2
Ko Tao
⬆HRS ±3:55 10:00

SURIN ISLES
CHAIYA
Ko Phangan [NA THON]
23:00 2:00

SIMILAN ISLES
KHAO SOK N.P.
ko samui - GOOD FREE MAPS/INFO BOOKS
CAR FERRY
CHAWENG v. DEVELOPED BUT STILL LOVELY BEACH, ⬆400B++ EXCEPT DEWDROP/ VIKING/ CHARLIE'S HUTS ⬆.
MAE NAM: ☼ CHEAPER BUT MUCH LESS ATTRACTIVE.

khao lak
TAKUA PA
PHANG NGA
SURAT THANI
SICHON:☼
NAKHON SI THAMMA-BAT
KLONG CHINA

KO PHUKET
PHUKET
Ko Yai
KRABI
PHAT-THALUNG
THALE LUANG LAGOON
BIRD PARK, BOAT RIDES

ao nang + railea
Ko Lanta
TRANG
KANTANG
SONGKHLA
CHINA
PATTANI BIG QUAINT MUSLIM FISHING VILLAGE ☼s
SAI BURI
THAKSIN ROYAL PALACE
TAK BAI WAT CHON
NARATHIWAT

ko phi phi
Ko Pu (Jam)
ko hai
CHANA
BE TONG

Ko Muk
Ko Libong Ko Sukorn
Ko Lipe
LANGU
4:00
HAT YAI
SATUN
11, 14:00 SPEEDBOAT 3 HRS
to Perlis, Lankawi
MALAYSIA
YALA
SUNGEI KOLOK

[THONG SALA] = PORT. ☼ PARTY BEACH
HAT RIN ☼: BEWARE OF DOPED DRINKS IN CERTAIN BARS.
HAT SALAT HAT YHOM AO THONG NAI
HAT KHOM NICE QUIETER BEACHES ⬆s 90B+ BUT ACCESS MORE AWKWARD, MAY NEED BOAT.

⬆ = Info from GHs
= Old Chinese Shophouses
= Top Scuba
= Jungle hikes

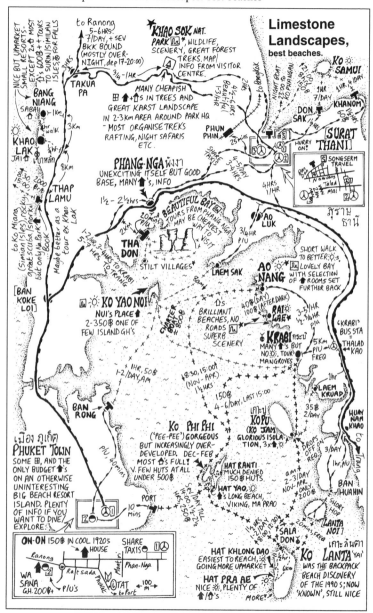

	BANGKOK H=H'phong/ T=Thonburi
	NAKHON PATHOM
	PETCHABURI
	HUA HIN
	P.K.K.
	BANG SAPHAN
	CHUMPHON
	CHAIYA
	SURAT* THANI
	PHATT-HALUNG
	HAT YAI
	SUNGEI KOLOK
	<Destin Origin>
	Trains South Type/no.

BANGKOK: H=Hualamphong main sta, T=Thonburi (across river from KSR). **PKK** = PRACHUAP KHIRI KHAN, **NST** = NAKHON SI THAMMARAT. **SURAT THANI** station is actually at Phunphin (13km). Additional trains Sungei Kolok to Yala d 15:30 (2hrs) and Yala to NST d 6:30 arr 13:35

PETCHABURI เพชรบุรี (PHETBURI)

HUA HIN หัวหิน — WATERFRONT/STILT GH'S — CHEAP G.H.'s — SOFITEL GRAND 1920s RAILWAY HOTEL

P.K.K. ประจวบ คีรีขันธ์ — CHONG KRAJOK MONKEY WAT — Khlong Kyat

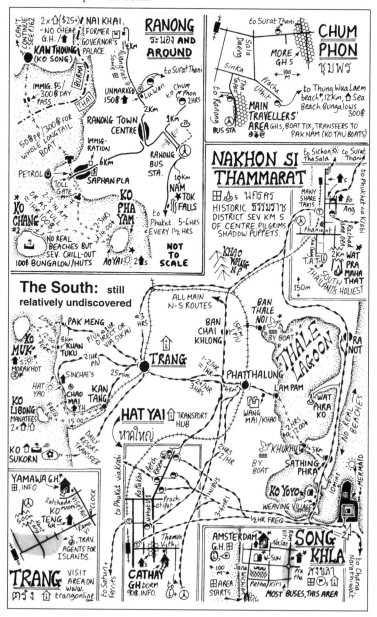

The South: still relatively undiscovered

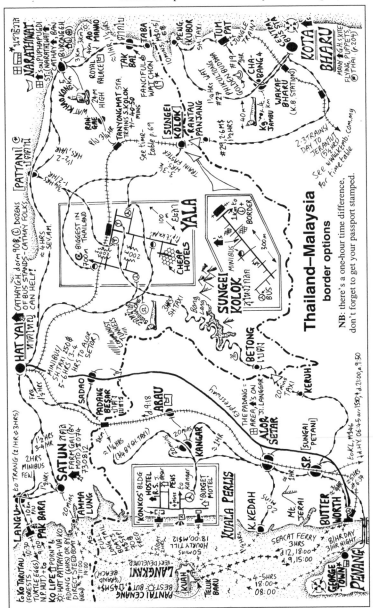

LAOS
LAO PEOPLES' DEMOCRATIC REPUBLIC (PDR)

Introduction

There aren't many countries in Asia that have so few tourist 'sights' and yet so much appeal. Laos has no 'Great Walls', no magnificent monuments, no picture-postcard beaches – even the temples which litter neighbouring Thailand are scarcer here.

The charm of Laos is that life appears to be in low gear. Sleepy villages snuggle amongst infinite folds of green mountains interspersed with hidden caves and lush river views. The locals seem to exude an infectious serenity. Every morning at dawn, while legions of spliffed-out backpackers snooze, the pious are on the street giving alms to silent, saffron-robed monks (even if imported chocolate bars are now included with the sticky rice and fruit offerings).

Laos, however, has a darker side – its eastern flank was carpet-bombed by the US in the 1970s and the country retains certain bureaucratic souvenirs from a communist era that hasn't formally ended. But Lenin is safely locked up in the Vientiane Revolutionary Museum, and most people seem happy to smile and chat when you approach them, or to leave you undisturbed if you choose to spend your day watching the Mekong flow by.

Laos is the least densely-populated country in Asia yet has some 68 ethnic groups. The national language itself is effectively the same as Isaan – the language of north-east Thailand which Bangkok folk consider a hillbilly form of Thai.

The government leading this mirage country came to power in a 1975 coup which ousted the royal family; it has since embarked on the formidable task of forging some national unity.

❏ **Country ratings – Laos**

● **Expense $$** Very cheap. Even Vientiane now has $2 dorm beds. In the northern villages it's often hard to pay more than $1 for a bed. Rather more in the south and in Louang Prabang where prices triple during the water-throwing 'new year' season.

● **Value for money ★★★☆☆** So cheap that you can't complain.

● **Getting around ★☆☆☆☆** There are few bus routes, though pick-ups and trucks serve wilder areas. Everything breaks down.

● **English spoken ★☆☆☆☆** Improving rapidly in areas that travellers frequent but still relatively limited overall. Phrase book very handy. French sometimes useful, if only to interpret the pronunciation of transliterated names.

● **Woman alone ★★★★☆** No problem.

● **For vegetarians ★★★☆☆** If you can explain you are a *satavapet* (vegetarian) most places can serve meatless local dishes.

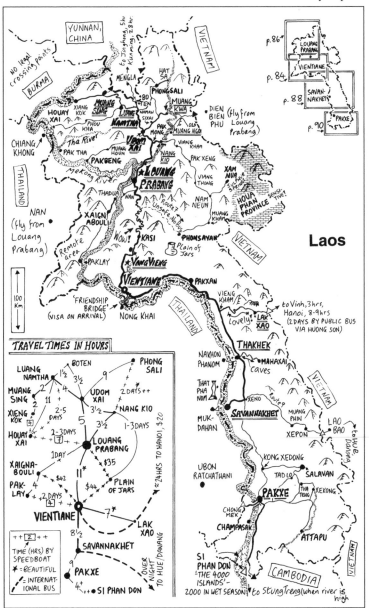

❑ **Essential information for travellers – Laos**

● **Visa** Required. Easy. two-week or one-month options. Extensions only possible in Vientiane.

● **Currency** Kip. US$1=K7950, the Thai Baht (B1=K180) doubles as a second currency in many areas: easier to exchange cash than travellers' cheques and a marginally better rate than for US$.

● **Time zone** 7 hours ahead of GMT (same as Thailand and Indochina; 1hr behind China).

● **Religious tone** A deep Buddhist undertone beneath a largely secular surface. Also animist and hill-tribe faiths.

● **Health factors** Cholera is prevalent. There's also a moderate, drug-resistant malaria risk outside Vientiane.

● **Special dangers** Temptations of opium and the evangelically-powerful weed. Unexploded bombs in the Plain of Jars and Ho Chi Minh trail areas. Forgetting to leave.

● **Social conventions** Laos are easy-going but basic Buddhist conventions should be observed (remove shoes, decent dress etc in temples). The traditional *nap* greeting is identical to the Thai *wei* (palms placed together prayer-like at chest level) and should be returned when given. Treat family guesthouses like private homes which means removing your shoes and behaving more like a guest than a paying customer.

● **Key tips** Rivers flow north–south – southbound river trips are consequently considerably faster than northbound ones.

Wrap your valuables in several layers of plastic, especially if you're visiting during Pi Mai (Lao New Year, mid-April). Otherwise everything will be soaked.

● **Traveller hubs** Vang Vieng (inner tubing, weed), Luang Namtha and Muang Sing (hill-tribe treks, opium), Si Phan Don, Louang Prabang, Muang Ngoi, Nang Kio.

According to some human rights' observers, those who boycott Burma should also boycott Laos. They argue that while the Burmese opposition has been quashed, in Laos it has never been allowed in the first place.

Laos is one of five countries which retains the nebulous classification 'communist' (along with Vietnam, Cuba, North Korea and China). But the Lao government has never been strongly driven by ideology. While there are plenty of hammers and sickles around Lao cities, the largest of them seem to be sponsored by Pepsi. The government doesn't appear to exercise much direct control yet one senses a subtle feeling of secrecy which pervades all Laos. The entire country, from politics to the transport network, runs on rumours.

HIGHLIGHTS

The scenery is fantastic along the Nam Ou river. The finest point – about 25 minutes north of tiny Muang Ngoi – is only accessible by boat.

Vang Vieng is also beautifully set though the town itself is beset with boisterous backpackers, supposedly being calm, but frequently forgetting. You can find similarly stunning karst landscapes without Westerners i) around Mahaxai, ii) in the area directly north of Kasi and iii) along the road to Lak Xao.

In the far south Si Phan Don is flat and accommodation is basic but the Mekong scene is mesmerizing with the ever-present hope of sighting the rare river dolphins.

The country's main tourist draw is temple-filled Louang Prabang where it's magical to watch processing monks collecting alms at dawn. The town's main attraction is its sleepy *olde worlde* quality. Ironically, so many tourists are coming that you'll need to hurry here before its very success undermines its appeal. Vientiane is quietly attractive and you could do much worse than simply renting a motorbike and heading out into the countryside an hour or two to the north.

In the search for the 'undiscovered', travellers are increasingly aiming for Phongsali but the town isn't really that inspiring – better to stop part way along the Udom Xai–Muang Kwa road where the scenery is nice and the costumed local tribes-people's only contact with Westerners is selling them snacks as they whizz by on a bus roof.

WHEN TO GO

The coolest, driest season is November to January. Days are comfortable in short sleeves. At lower elevations a light sweater is the most you'll need at night, though in the hills it can get surprisingly cold and foggy. March and April are the hottest months.

Lao New Year/water festival *(Pi Mai)* in April is a week of mayhem that is fun if you don't mind getting soaked to the skin. Day after day. Transport still runs but kids bombard anything that moves with water bombs, buckets and hose pipes. Room prices in Louang Prabang hostels and hotels triple or quadruple in this period and for the three main days of Pi Mai you will be lucky to find a room at all there (finding accommodation is not a problem in other towns, though).

The monsoon season is from May to October. The rain is sporadic and pleasant but its effect is to turn most of the country's unpaved roads into impassable quagmires. River levels rise dramatically making boat travel easier.

Practical information

VISAS AND FORMALITIES
Visa strategy
Visas usually do not state the period of stay when initially stamped into your passport so you might be tempted to believe you can stay forever. Sadly, this is not the case. A **tourist visa** allows a two-week stay and costs $25–60 depending upon nationality and the processing time (same day costs about 50% more than three working days). Visas are cheap for Swedes and Hong Kong citizens, but pricey for Canadians.

A **business/entry visa** requires no actual business motive – it is simply the name for a one-month visa and it offers the possibility of an extension. **Transit visas** give an unextendable five-day stay but in some consulates (eg Kunming) cost exactly the same as a tourist visa so aren't worth applying for.

For a flat $30, tourist (but not business) visas are available on arrival at the airports of Louang Prabang and Vientiane, or at the Friendship Bridge from Nong Khai (but no other land borders).

Visa services in the Thai border towns of Chiang Kong and Nong Khai cost considerably more as they have to courier your passport down to the consulate at Khon Kaen where you could get the visa yourself – it took me only 20 minutes!

❑ **Geo-political information – Laos**
Population: 5.6 million (2001), 4.9m (1993), 3.6m (1985).
Area: 236,800 sq km.
Capital: Vientiane (pop 190,000, 450,000 metro area).
Other major cities: Savannakhet (60,000); Pakxe (50,000); Xam Nua (40,000);
Thakhek, Louang Prabang (27,000), Pakxan (21,000).
GNP per capita: $1,600 (2000 est), $160 (1988).
Currency history: Kip/US$1 – April 2002: K7950, Oct 1999: K7100, Feb 1998:
K2444, Oct 1997: K1300, 1994: K720, 1990: K709.
Major exports/economy: Electrical power to Thailand, opium, coffee, tin, gypsum,
tourism, Beer Lao.
Ethnic mix: Extremely complex. Statistics divide Lao Loum (ie 'lowland' Lao, 67%),
Lao Soung ('highland' ie Hmong family hill tribes, 22%), Mien/Yao (9%), Chinese
1% and Vietnamese less than 1%.
Official languages: Lao (spoken by only 67% as a first language).
Religious mix: Buddhist (Therevada).
Landmarks of national history: **1353–71**: First Lao nation called Lane Xang (land
of a million elephants) developed under Fa Ngum with the capital at Louang Prabang
until the mid-16th century. **1571–4**: Burmese invasion caused collapse. **1713**: Country
split into Champusak (south) and Vietnamese-controlled mini-kingdoms of Louang
Prabang and Vientiane. **1778**: Thai invasion, kings ruled on within Thai empire.
1886–7: French forces bullied Thailand into withdrawing and declared a French protectorate in 1893. **March 1945**: Laos declared independent by the Japanese occupation force. **1946**: The French returned but recognized the autonomy of Laos under the
king of Louang Prabang. **1949**: Independence within the French Union. **Late 1950s**:
UK, France and the USSR backed different Lao factions from the USA and Thailand
in repeated power struggles. **1962**: Country divided into two north–south strips with
communist Pathet-Lao/Viet Minh forces controlling the east – an overspill of the
Vietnam war. **1965–73**: USAF massive bombing campaign against Pathet Lao made
Laos the 'most bombed nation in history'. **1973**: Vietnam ceasefire. **1975**: Laos fell to
Pathet Lao, People's Democratic Republic declared. Widespread exodus of former
elite and middle classes to Australia etc.
Leader: Khamtay Siphandone re-appointed president March 2001. Prime Minister
Boungnang Volachit.
Pressing political issues: Complete lack of political opposition, effects of sudden
tourist influx, unexploded ordinance, infrastructure problems.

Registration

Laos once required all travellers to sign in at
each province they visited. Louang Prabang,
the last bastion of this bureaucratic nonsense
gave up the game in 2000.

Extensions

Tourist and business visas are extendable,
but only in Vientiane through a travel agency
($2+/day) and only when your current visa is
within a few days of expiring. Thus, if you
want to spend a significant time in Laos but
aren't planning on being in Vientiane during

the second week of your stay (when a tourist
visa would expire) it's worth starting out
with a one-month business visa.

If you're only going to be a few days
late it's possible to pay a $5 fine at the bor-
der for each day you've overstayed.

MONEY

In towns along the Thai border, Thai baht can
be used as easily as kip. US dollars cash can
easily be exchanged – informally at some
market stalls, hotels or jewellery stores, and
officially at exchange booths. Other curren-

cies (euros, pounds, yen etc) can be exchanged only in Vientiane. Beware of Thai banks which might insist that you exchange to baht before exchanging to kip (this means double commission for them).

Travellers' cheques can also be exchanged in Louang Prabang and Vientiane. The commission structure varies: 2% is typical, there's a $2 minimum at Thai banks, or pay K500 per cheque at **Vientiane Commercial Bank** with better rates and only 0.125% commission. Exchange booths charge 2% with no minimum. Credit card advances are possible in Vientiane only; a flat charge of $5 is payable.

TRANSPORT
In vast contrast to China or Thailand, Lao public transport is slow, crowded and pretty sporadic. Vehicles may be slightly more comfortable than in Cambodia but departures are decidedly less frequent. Set off in the early morning and don't expect to get very far after lunch. Many roads have been sealed or upgraded in the last few years, but some are already pretty threadbare again. The awful Savannakhet–Pakxe road is nothing short of an ordeal – unbelievable for the country's main north–south road. Many roads still get washed out by rain and estimated journey times should be seen as only the broadest approximations. Slow your expectations – this is the Lao PDR – **P**lease **D**on't **R**ush.

Bus
The majority of routes, in the very limited network, radiate from the Vientiane area. Public buses and minibuses leave reasonably close to their pre-determined times (even when they aren't full) and are very cheap (roughly $0.30 per hour's ride). The few new private services are less predictable and slightly more expensive. When demand is high (almost always) plastic chairs in the bus aisles increase capacity on both government and private 'express' buses (a real misnomer). The last local services usually leave around 5.30pm. Minibuses have replaced trucks on some recently paved rural roads, but these get increasingly uncomfortable

month by month as faults in the tarmac mature into fully-grown pot-holes.

Pick-ups and big trucks
Rough roads and a sparse population make pick-up trucks a sensible alternative to rural buses, and only larger, high clearance lorries can cope with the worst mud tracks. Target schedules of a sort exist but vehicles tend to leave when full – mostly in the early mornings from near a town's market. Useful items to have on truck journeys include sunglasses, a mask or bandanna (to fight dust inhalation), a warm pullover (for misty mornings and the post sunset wind-chill), sturdy waterproof bags (to protect your luggage) and rainwear – a pick-up's makeshift canvas roof won't prevent you getting soaked if it rains (or if it's the water-throwing festival!)

To enjoy the scenery at your own pace you can often charter the same pick-ups for about ten times the standard one-way fare.

Boat
Where roads are simply too rough, river transport takes over. Often the choice of craft is between grindingly slow cargo barges, short-distance motor-boats and manic long-tailed speedboats. The latter are low slung, torpedo-canoes that squeal like chain-saw-bearing mosquitoes and bounce across the swell at such a terrifying pace that your crash helmet is more of a talisman than genuine protection. They surf the turbulent Mekong gravy with reckless abandon between Houay Xai and Pakbeng and Louang Prabang (LP) for those with more courage than time. The truly suicidal could rent such a craft for around $200 (holding up to six people) for

the journey all the way from LP to Vientiane. It would be cheaper and easier on your ear drums to get a slow boat halfway (to Paklay) and join a regular speedboat from there ($20/person, four hours).

Some slow boat routes are scheduled (eg the alternative Houay Xai–LP service) but most are ad hoc cargo services that leave as needed. If you are told there is no boat going to your destination this often means that there is **no scheduled boat**. Ask at the piers and, with patience, you should eventually find something going your way. If you can't, it may be due to low water, high water or special conditions in a particular section of the river. Rather than giving up and being squashed into a truck, try hitching or taking a pick-up to a riverside village beyond the obstruction and finding a boat from there.

Scheduled boats usually stop for the night at villages with guesthouses. Cargo boats dock wherever they happen to be when it gets dark; you might be stuck on the boat. A sleeping bag, insect repellent and/or warm clothes are thus recommended, especially in the cool season. It is wise to have enough water and food for your trip. On any boat bring water-proofs and sun screen.

Slower, uncovered motorboats operate on the glorious Nam Ou river and make short hops to the occasional village markets along the Tha river. As long as you're not in a rush you'll usually find a boat going the way you want within a day or two – just relax at the pier and ask around (but note that 'So-pah' is not a town – it means the boatman is going fishing!).

Rapidly increasing tourism means that it's often easiest to gather a group of fellow travellers and charter your own boat. Prices may be better and boats emptier if you **find a boatman from the village** you want to visit as he will be going back anyway. Failing that, get a group together and charter the whole boat – it's often worth the extra money for the flexibility of occasional stops. However, you'll still stop to pick up passengers and chickens.

Air

Lao Aviation, the only domestic carrier, also offers handy hopper flights from Louang Prabang to Dien Bien Phu (Vietnam) and to Nan (Thailand). These flights cost less than $60 and save very long overland loops where there are no roads/border crossings.

Flights to Hanoi cost $108, Bangkok $70, Chiang Mai $85, Kunming $120 and Phnom Penh $130. Internal flights are reasonable value, though prices have risen and their motto of 'perpetual welcome' still often glosses over a reality of 'perpetual delay' – it can be wise to turn up at the airport and check the plane is actually there before paying for your ticket.

International departure tax is $5, payable in kip.

Other

Other varieties of local transport options include *tuk-tuks*, *jumbos* (the front is like a motorbike and the back like a small

Flights to Lao regional airports
http://www.lao-aviation.com for updates

HOE	Houay Xai	
LPQ	Louang Prabang	
LXG	Luang Namtha	
NEU	Xam Nua	
ODY	Udom Xai	
PKZ	Pakxe	
VTE	Vientiane	
XKH	Xieng Khouang (Phonsavan/Plain of Jars)	
ZBY	Xaignabouli (Sayaboury on time table)	
ZVK	Savannakhet	

pick-up), *motos* (motorbike taxis) and *samalors* (three-wheeled bicycle taxis).

Renting a bicycle ($2/day) or motorbike ($6–10/day) is a great alternative.

ACCOMMODATION

In villages and northern towns, guesthouse accommodation rarely costs more than $1–2, or $2.50–5 for rooms with attached bathrooms (should such fripperies exist). Smaller villages without a guesthouse may have a 'café' which doubles as a sleeping area at night; K1000 is typical for a place on the floor. Ask for a *hangindu* (literally 'sleep, eat, drink place'). Villagers are exceedingly friendly.

Towns facing Thailand across the Mekong tend to be rather more expensive with no real budget options at all in Thakhek and few in Savannakhet, but a growing handful of basic dorms are now available for $2/pp in Vientiane (or $5 for a spartan room). In several towns, forking out $15–25 or so can get you a room in a delightful old colonial mansion and is worth the splurge. Louang Prabang is increasingly geared to fly-in upper market tourists but (except in mid-April) competition keeps prices down.

FOOD AND DRINK

Lao food is similar to Thai minus most of the seafood. The national dish is *fue* – a soup of vermicelli and meat which is often served with leaves which one tears up and adds as a condiment. Other dishes include *phakdak padek* (fish and sticky rice) and *khao poun* (cold rice vermicelli) which is a favourite at weddings.

Markets and street peddlers sell mysterious banana-leaf wrapped bundles – these gastronomic lucky dips are generally the best food deals available and usually you can get a ball of super sticky Laotian rice (*khao*) for a negligible extra charge.

Khao can also be fermented. The result is *lao lao*, a potent moonshine and the unofficial national drink (indeed, the name means 'Lao alcohol'). There is also *vin lao*, a wine made with black rice and lemon and *lao hai* – fermented rice to which water (use your own from a bottle!) is added to make an alcoholic drink. Locally-brewed Beer Lao is increasingly popular and even exported, though it's much cheaper on draft than in bottles (one litre of cold draft costs $0.80).

❏ So what did you expect for $3?

'When you are sleeping do not smoking' announces an inscrutable 'Law in Guest House' sign on the door. The room's the size of a milk carton and as sturdily built. As if to confirm the metaphor, part of the wall has been repaired by inserting a sheet of galvanized iron, stamped 'Siam Box Company'. Other walls are haphazardly hammered, rough wooden planks whose mosquito-tempting gaps, previous occupants have attempted to plug with assorted rags and grimy wads of toilet paper. In a different context this would be a contender for the Turner prize. But if you're crossing the room don't look up to admire. You'll need all your concentration to negotiate a safe path across the rough bare floorboards with the minimum of splinters – another, inappropriate house rule is 'no shoes'.

The bed seems clean enough: the under-sheet is discoloured but by years of hand-washing rather than by anything more sinister. Of course if you want a top sheet you bring your own. This being a relatively luxurious place there's an attached bathroom. Once you've stepped across the malarial pond at its centre there's a slip-seated Western WC and beside it a bucket into which soiled toilet paper should be thrown to prevent blocking the cantankerous sewerage system. The droopy showerhead has fallen from its dangling hook and nestles unappetizingly against the grimy bog-brush. The water pressure is far too low to make the jerry-built water-heater function, but who cares – the engrossing ant and gecko show is performed free, 24 hours a day.

THE DRUG SCENE

Smaller northern towns, famous for their wicked weed, are increasingly awash with off-duty Ko Phangan ravers, time-warp hippies and other assorted lost souls drawn to the cheap and casually-available opium. This has had the depressing effect of turning many local infant-school kids into drug-runners and has made yet another generation of South-East Asian villagers wonder what kind of youth the West is breeding! Some delighted travellers stay for months at a time in Muang Ngoi, Muang Sing or Vang Vieng forgetting all about visas and general hygiene. For others the 'scene' rather spoils those once idyllic hideaways. Beware that **police raids** do occur ($250+ fines are typical) especially in Vang Vieng opium dens.

Whether or not you intend to smoke, you might consider bringing cigarette papers with you – they are often in short supply and can prove a very sociable offering or a good bargaining tool amongst travellers.

STAYING IN TOUCH

Email is available from several cafés in Vientiane and Louang Prabang from 150K/min. Elsewhere facilities are rare but will surely develop as phone lines improve. Presently available in Savannakhet (400K/min) and Udom Xai (one unreliable shop).

Mail is cheaper than that sent from Thailand and packages sent from Vientiane arrive reliably.

International phone calls are easy to place in Vientiane, possible in Louang Prabang, and very difficult elsewhere, but nowhere offers the cheap internet phone deals available in Bangkok. Direct dial rates at the public phone office from Vientiane to the USA and Italy are: $3.30/min; Canada, UK, Germany: $2.80/min; France, Sweden: $1.50/min; Australia: $1.10/min. Dial 170 for an international operator. Or you can dial yourself using a phonecard. International country code: +856.

□ **Meeting the locals**

● The Patouxai Monument in Vientiane is a popular gathering place for students, especially on Sundays. Popular Lao singers include Phu Vieng and Bao Ghean.

● **Language** Lao has its own numbering system but Western-style numerals are more commonly used. However, toilets, destination boards etc (especially in rural areas) are often marked only in Lao characters. Fortunately, Lao is slightly easier to decipher than Thai. With both alphabets the main challenge is remembering that for many syllables, the vowel might be a squiggle written before, after and/or above the main consonant.

Another challenge is the conflict of transliteration systems. The pronunciation of 'S' and 'X' is indistinguishable yet each is written with its own symbol. Meanwhile there are some half-dozen vowel sounds transliterated with an 'A'. 'L' and 'R' are different renderings of the same letter, as are 'V and 'W', 'OW' and 'AO' etc. 'H' is silent before 'L'. French transcriptions often persist to confuse Anglophones further, notably Louang, a common alternative for Luang, and Vientiane which is how the capital's name sounded to the colonists. Phonetically it should be spelt Vieng Chan.

Some phrases in Lao:

Hello – *Sah-bai-dee*
Thank you (very much) – *Hawp-jai (le-lai)*
How much? (in kip) – *Tao-dai (keep)?*
Where are you going? – *Pai Sai?* (A greeting not an inquisition)
Do you have ___ ? – *Mee ___ bao?*
It tastes good – *Hong Ngam/See-bee-lai.*

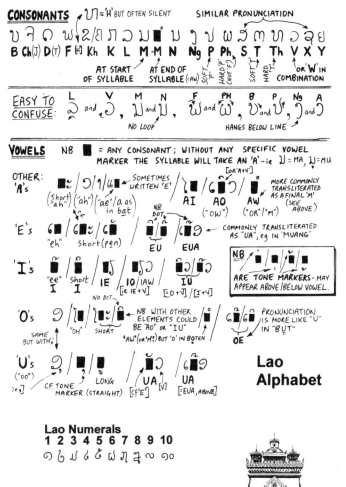

CONSONANTS

ປ = 'H' BUT OFTEN SILENT   SIMILAR PRONUNCIATION

B Ch(J) D(T) F (H) Kh K L M·M N Ng P Ph S T Th V X Y

AT START OF SYLLABLE
AT END OF SYLLABLE (-AN)
SOFT 'P'
HARD 'P' (NOT 'F')
SOFT 'T'
HARD 'T'
or 'W' IN COMBINATION

EASY TO CONFUSE:

L and ເ, M and N (NO LOOP), F and PH, B and P (HANGS BELOW LINE), Ng and A

VOWELS

NB ■ = ANY CONSONANT; WITHOUT ANY SPECIFIC VOWEL MARKER THE SYLLABLE WILL TAKE AN 'A' - ie ມ = MA, ມ = MU

OTHER 'A's
(short "ah") (ah) ("ae"/a as in bat) SOMETIMES WRITTEN 'E'
[or 'A+V']
AI AO AW ("OW") ("OR"/"M") MORE COMMONLY TRANSLITERATED AS A FINAL 'M' (SEE ABOVE)

'E's
"eh" short (pen) EU EUA COMMONLY TRANSLITERATED AS "UA", eg IN "MUANG"

NB ■ / ■ / ■ ARE TONE MARKERS - MAY APPEAR ABOVE/BELOW VOWEL.

'I's
"ee" I short I IE IO/IAW [ie IE+V] IU [EO+V] / [I+V]

'O's
"OH" short NO DOT NB WITH OTHER ELEMENTS COULD BE "AO" OR "IU" "AW" (OR "M") BUT 'O' IN BOTEN OE PRONUNCIATION IS MORE LIKE "U" IN "BUT"
SAME BUT WITH ↓

'U's
("oo") CF TONE MARKER (STRAIGHT) LONG UA [V] [CF 'E'] UA [=EUA, ABOVE]

Lao Alphabet

Lao Numerals
1 2 3 4 5 6 7 8 9 10

໑ ໒ ໓ ໔ ໕ ໖ ໗ ໘ ໙ ໑໐

Female	Male
ຍິງ	ຊາຍ
Laos WC signs	

PATOUXAI MONUMENT (VIENTIANE)

FURTHER INFORMATION
Books
Both Lonely Planet and Rough Guide produce pretty good Laos guide books. However, Laos is one of those places where information spread through the traveller grapevine is generally the most reliable. Vientiane has a limited selection of new and used books for onward destinations, but the bookstore near the Mut Mee Guesthouse in Nong Khai (across the border in Thailand) has a better selection than any in Laos.

Other books on Laos are difficult to find though Asia Books in Bangkok has a decent selection. *Laos and Its Culture* by Perala Ratwan, a former ambassador gives insights into the modern state. *Travels in Laos* by Lefevre (White Lotus Press) chronicles the travels of a Frenchman in the late 1800s.

Maps
Decent city maps of Vientiane and Louang Prabang can be found with a little searching in tourist shops and agencies in those respective cities.

Discover Laos, a vaguely useful magazine with a Vientiane city map pullout in the centre, used to be available free from Lao embassies, but seems to have disappeared of late. One of the most reliable sources of detailed Vientiane maps (in several pages) is the website 🖥 www.mekongexpress.com /laos/general/laos_map_index.htm.

Published maps of the entire country are frequently poor, thanks to the confusion of spellings and the rapidly changing state of the roads.

Useful websites
The best starting point to get a feel of the major routes is the wonderfully practical Passplanet, 🖥 www.passplanet.com/Laos/.

Great link sites include 🖥 www.laos-travel.net/links.htm.

Run by a Luang Namtha eco-tourism lodge, the website 🖥 www.theboatlanding .laopdr.com/touristinfo.html is great for north Laos travel information including great detail on the Tha river trip.

🖥 www.laosearch.net/ is a good links starting point and place to 'meet' others interested in anything to do with the country.

🖥 www.mekongexpress.com/laos/index.htm has some interesting, if old, maps and details, and a thorough listing of holidays and events.

🖥 www.haw-hamburg.de/pers/Kaspar-Sickermann/mgsing/emgs.html is a curiously over-detailed, if largely academic, study of Muang Sing town.

SPECIAL ICONS USED

🛕 **KAYSONE MONUMENT** HONOURING THE FIRST LAO P.D.R. PRIME MINISTER (DIED 1992)

💣 **SEVERELY DAMAGED** BY U.S. BOMBING 1964-73, LITTLE LEFT TO SEE.

 ATTRACTS TRAVELLERS WHO PREFER **SMOKING** SOMETHING STRONGER THAN TOBACCO:-LARGELY WITHOUT HASSLES

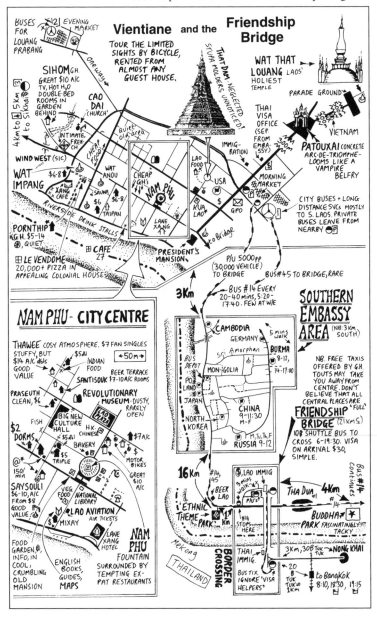

Vientiane and the Friendship Bridge

BUSES FOR LOUANG PRABANG

EVENING MARKET

TOUR THE LIMITED SIGHTS BY BICYCLE, RENTED FROM ALMOST ANY GUEST HOUSE.

THAT DAM, NEGLECTED STUPA MOLDERS UNNOTICED

WAT THAT LOUANG LAOS' HOLIEST TEMPLE

PARADE GROUND

SIHOM G.H. GREAT $10 A/C TV, HOT H₂O DOUBLE-BED ROOMS IN GARDEN BEHIND

CAO DAI (CHURCH)

INTIMATE FRENCH FOOD

one way

THAI VISA OFFICE (SEP. FROM EMBASSY)

IMMIGRATION

VIETNAM

PATOUXAI CONCRETE ARC-DE-TRIOMPHE-LOOMS LIKE A VAMPIRE BELFRY

WIND WEST (SIC)

4km to 5km to Sikhai

CHEAP FOOD

WAT IMPANG

$6-8

XANG CAFÉ

SAUNA $6

WAT ANOU

$4-8

TAIPAN

CHEAP G.H.'s

NAM PHU

LAO FOOD

USA

KUA LAO

$

GPO

MORNING MARKET

CITY BUSES + LONG DISTANCE SVCs MOSTLY TO S. LAOS. PRIVATE BUSES LEAVE FROM NEARBY

RIVERSIDE DRINK STALLS

LANE XANG

to Bridge

PORNTHIP G.H. $5-14 QUIET

LE VENDOME 20,000+ PIZZA IN APPEALING COLONIAL HOUSE

CAFÉ 27

PRESIDENT'S MANSION

P/u 5000pp (30,000 VEHICLE) TO BRIDGE

BUS#45 TO BRIDGE, RARE

3 Km

BUS #14 EVERY 20-40 mins, 5:20-17:40. FEW AT W/E

SOUTHERN EMBASSY AREA (NB: 3 KM SOUTH)

NAM PHU - CITY CENTRE

THAWEE COSY ATMOSPHERE. $7 FAN SINGLES STUFFY, BUT $14 A/C dbls GOOD VALUE

$5 A/C

INDIAN FOOD

←50m→

SANTISOUK $7-10 A/C ROOMS

BEER TERRACE

PRASEUTH CLEAN, $6

REVOLUTIONARY MUSEUM - DUSTY, RARELY OPEN

$2 DORMS

FISH

BIG NEW CULTURE HALL

LAO PLAZA

H.K. CHINESE

$5 A/C

$7 A/C

BAKERY

$5 TRIPLE

MOTOR BIKES

GREAT $10 A/C

@ 150/min

SAYSOULI $6-10, A/C FROM $8 GOOD VALUE

VEG FOOD

NATIONAL LIBRARY

LAO AVIATION AIR TICKETS

MIXAY

LANE XANG HOTEL

NAM PHU FOUNTAIN SURROUNDED BY TEMPTING EX-PAT RESTAURANTS

FOOD GARDEN, INFO, IN COOL, CRUMBLING OLD MANSION

ENGLISH BOOKS, GUIDES, MAPS

CAMBODIA

GERMANY

5 mins walk

Sri Amorphan

BURMA 8-12, 14-17:00

BUS DEPOT

MON-GOLIA

PO-LAND

JAPAN

CHINA 9-11:30 M-F

NORTH KOREA

RUSSIA 9-12

M, Tu, Th, F

NB. FREE TAXIS OFFERED BY G.H. TOUTS MAY TAKE YOU AWAY FROM CENTRE. DON'T BELIEVE THAT ALL CENTRAL PLACES ARE 'FULL'

FRIENDSHIP BRIDGE (21KmS)

10₿ SHUTTLE BUS TO CROSS 6-19:30. VISA ON ARRIVAL $30, SIMPLE.

16 Km

#14, 45

BEER LAO

ETHNIC THEME PARK 1 Km

#14 STOPS HERE

LAO IMMIG

3 mins walk

P/u's

THA DUA #1

4 Km

BUDDHA PARK FASCINATINGLY TACKY

Bus #14 continues

MEKONG

THAILAND

BORDER CROSSING

THAI IMMIG.

BUS TIX, IGNORE 'VISA HELPERS'

3 Km, 30₿ TUK TUK

NONG KHAI

20

TUK TUK 1 Km

to BANGKOK 8:10, 19:30, 11:15

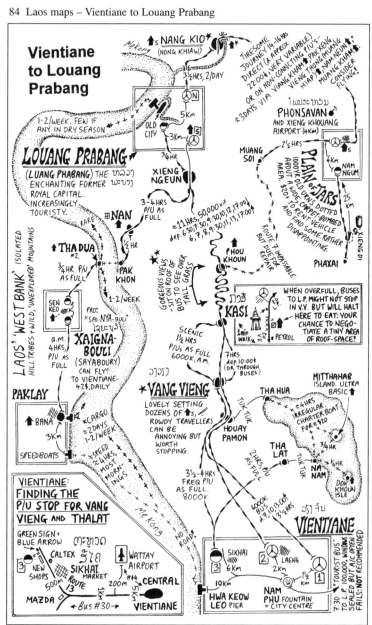

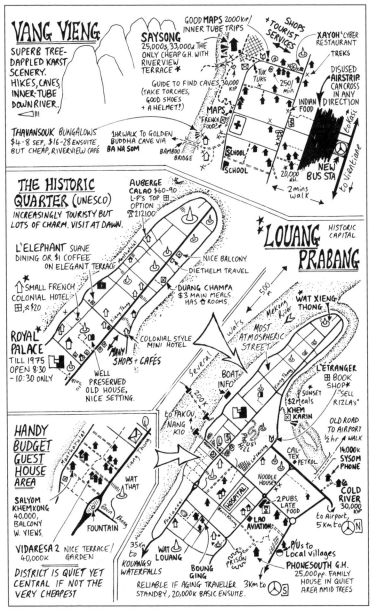

VANG VIENG

SUPERB TREE-DAPPLED KARST SCENERY. HIKES, CAVES, INNER-TUBE DOWN RIVER.

GOOD **MAPS** 2000kip/ INNER TUBE TRIPS

SHOPS + TOURIST SERVICES

XAYOH 'CYBER' RESTAURANT TREKS

SAYSONG 25,000s, 33,000d THE ONLY CHEAP G.H. WITH RIVERVIEW TERRACE *

GUIDE TO FIND CAVES, 30,000 (TAKE TORCHES, GOOD SHOES + A HELMET!)

TUK TUKS

250/ min

INDIAN FOOD

DISUSED AIRSTRIP CAN CROSS IN ANY DIRECTION

MAPS

FRENCH FOOD?

THAVANSOUK BUNGALOWS $4-8 Sep, $16-28 ENSUITE BUT CHEAP, RIVERVIEW CAFÉ

1HR WALK TO GOLDEN BUDDHA CAVE VIA **BA NA SOM**

BAMBOO BRIDGE

SCHOOL

SCHOOL

20,000 g.h.

NEW BUS STA

2mins walk

to Vientiane

to Kasi

THE HISTORIC QUARTER (UNESCO)

INCREASINGLY TOURISTY BUT LOTS OF CHARM. VISIT AT DAWN.

AUBERGE CALAO $60-90 L-P's TOP OPTION ☎ 212100

LOUANG PRABANG

HISTORIC CAPITAL

L'ELEPHANT SUAVE DINING OR $1 COFFEE ON ELEGANT TERRACE

NICE BALCONY

DIETHELM TRAVEL

SMALL FRENCH COLONIAL HOTEL ≈$20

DUANG CHAMPA $3 MAIN MEALS. HAS ⌂ ROOMS.

WAT XIENG THONG

Mekong River

500 m

ROYAL PALACE

TILL 1975 OPEN 8:30 - 10:30 ONLY

MANY SHOPS + CAFÉS

COLONIAL STYLE MINI HOTEL

WELL PRESERVED OLD HOUSE, NICE SETTING.

MOST ATMOSPHERIC STREET

Xieng Thong

several

BOAT INFO

L'ETRANGER BOOK SHOP "SELL RIZLA'S"

SUNSET

$2 MEALS

KHEM KARIN

200 k

to PAKOU, NANG KIO

OLD ROAD TO AIRPORT ½hr WALK

HANDY BUDGET GUEST HOUSE AREA

SALYOM KHEMKONG 40,000, BALCONY W. VIEWS.

WAT THAT

CAL-TEX PETROL

NOODLE HOUSE

14,000k **SYSOM** PHONE

COLD RIVER 30,000 kip

2 PUBS, LATE FOOD

to Airport, 5 km to ✈ N

VIDARESA 2 40,000k

NICE TERRACE/ GARDEN

FOUNTAIN

Boun Kheng

HOSPITAL

LAO AVIATION

P/Us to Local villages

PHONESOUTH G.H. 25,000pp. FAMILY HOUSE IN QUIET AREA AMID TREES

DISTRICT IS QUIET YET CENTRAL IF NOT THE VERY CHEAPEST

35km to KOUANGSI WATERFALLS

WAT LOUANG

BOUNG GING RELIABLE IF AGING TRAVELLER STANDBY, 20,000k BASIC ENSUITE.

PRISON

3km to ✈ S

North Laos

Northern Laos has seen an explosion of traveller interest in the last 5 years, notably in the hill-tribe areas around Muang Sing and Louang Namtha. You can expect to find backpackers on almost any rural bus or boat service (lucky as many boats only leave when there are sufficient passengers), and more pop up at even the smallest village backwater. While that's great for getting tips on accommodation & eating options, escaping the circuit requires you to be very self sufficient and to head for anywhere NOT mentioned on this map!

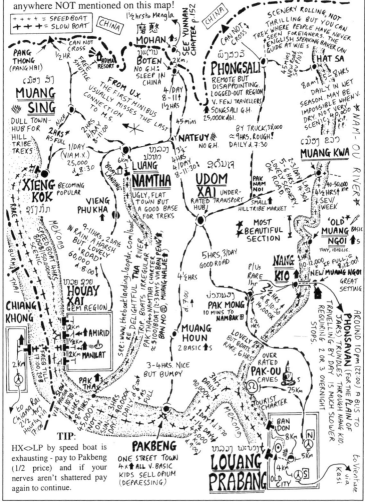

TIP:
HX<>LP by speed boat is exhausting – pay to Pakbeng (1/2 price) and if your nerves aren't shattered pay again to continue.

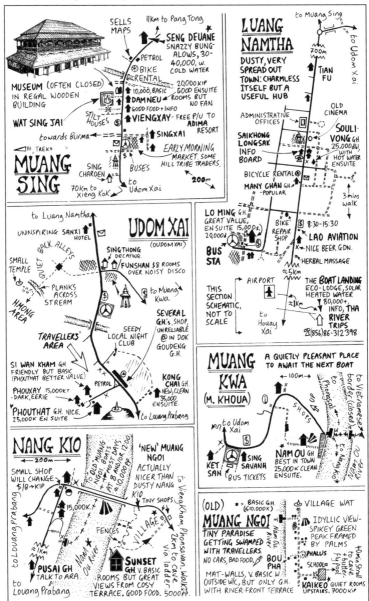

South Central Laos

Main roads are flat, dull & recently improved and most travellers are rapidly in transit to somewhere else, missing the intriguing scenery further inland which is totally devoid of tourist infrastructure. The easiest way to glimpse its wonders is on the northern of the two routes to Vietnam, via Lak Xao. Once 'discovered', parts of that green and dramatically scenic road are likely to become destinations in themselves. But for now the route's all yours! You'll see the best bits from the window of Hanoi TO Vientiane backpacker charabancs BUT NOT if you head the opposite direction (passes through at night). The rough and less interesting Lao Bao route suffered more from 1970s' American bombing.

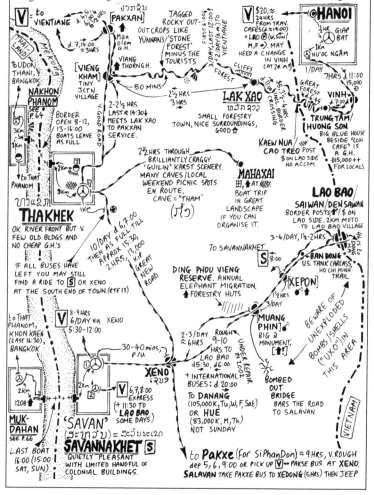

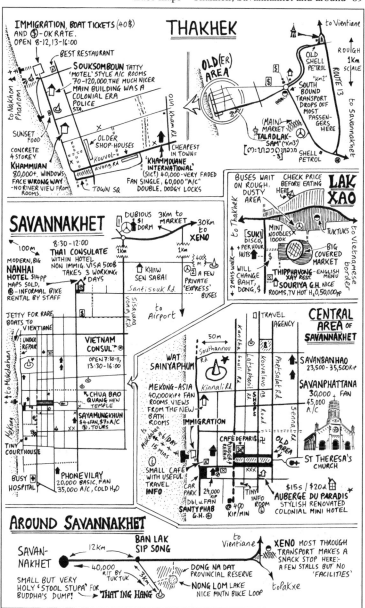

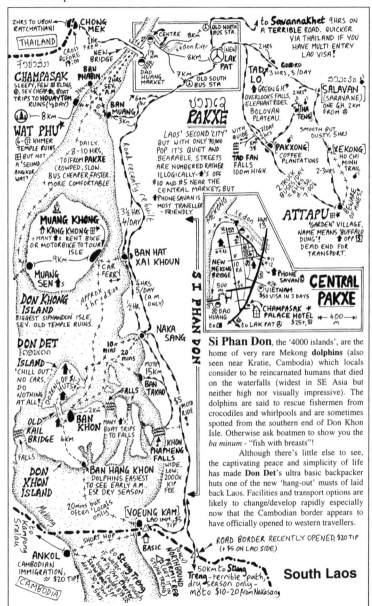

Si Phan Don, the '4000 islands', are the home of very rare Mekong **dolphins** (also seen near Kratie, Cambodia) which locals consider to be reincarnated humans that died on the waterfalls (widest in SE Asia but neither high nor visually impressive). The dolphins are said to rescue fishermen from crocodiles and whirlpools and are sometimes spotted from the southern end of Don Khon Isle. Otherwise ask boatmen to show you the *ba minum* - "fish with breasts"!

Although there's little else to see, the captivating peace and simplicity of life has made **Don Det**'s ultra basic backpacker huts one of the new 'hang-out' musts of laid back Laos. Facilities and transport options are likely to change/develop rapidly especially now that the Cambodian border appears to have officially opened to western travellers.

South Laos

CAMBODIA

Introduction

It's a thrilling time to visit Cambodia. Everything is in flux as the country's infamous roads are being rebuilt (not always where maps predict!) opening up areas that haven't seen visitors in a generation. Don't be blasé – there are still millions of landmines! – but for the first time in decades you can ride a motorbike into the wildest corners of the country without expecting to be shot by Khmer Rouge terrorists or have your savings extorted by renegade soldiers.

Collectively one of the most impressive sites on the planet, Angkor encompasses the Bayon's inscrutable stone faces, Angkor Wat's massive corn-cob towers, and a myriad of other ancient temples, a couple of which are still half-suffocated by contorted trees. Angkor is overwhelmingly Cambodia's main visitor magnet, and with tourist numbers doubling every year you'll have to hurry to see it before there's total package-tour gridlock.

The ancient Khmer culture that created and preceded Angkor left plenty of other much smaller but nonetheless interesting historical sites. Though most have been damaged by fighting or plundered by looters in the long civil war, pagoda searching is a great excuse to climb the knolls that poke abruptly out of the generally flat agricultural countryside.

Mondulkiri and Ratanakiri are higher, rolling provinces that retain some tracts of forest in a topography that makes the climate somewhat cooler than the plains. The area is very sparsely inhabited, mainly by shy ethnic minority villages, though you'd need to be a linguist or an anthropologist to notice the human differences (there are no 'hill-tribe costumes' here).

❏ **Country ratings – Cambodia**
- **Expense $$$** Budget for high miscellaneous costs (eg the $20–60 entry charge for Angkor, $25–50 'tips' and fees to cross the border to/from Laos).
- **Value for money** ★★★☆☆ Great for market food and mid-range guesthouses, poor for rock-bottom budget accommodation and restaurant meals. Good for moto rentals but pricey for long-distance transport.
- **Getting around** ★★☆☆☆ Abysmal, but undergoing rapid improvements.
- **English spoken** ★★★★☆ In Siem Reap/Angkor, ★★★☆☆ in Phnom Penh/Sihanoukville, ★★☆☆☆ in rural Cambodia.
- **Woman alone** ★★★★☆ Some lone women travellers have been hassled by lecherous rural moto drivers, but such annoyances are not widespread.
- **For vegetarians** ★★★☆☆ Some superb treats from market vendors. Fish is relatively rarely served.

❏ **Essential information for travellers – Cambodia**

● **Visa** Easy, $20. Available on arrival but only at Phnom Penh and Siem Reap international airports and on the Poipet and Hat Lek border crossings coming from Thailand.

● **Currency** Riel. US$1 = 3900–4000RIs. Bring US$ cash – notes of various denominations are helpful. West of Siem Reap, Thai Baht are the de facto currency.

● **Time zone** 7 hours ahead of GMT (the same as the rest of Indochina).

● **Religious tone** Buddhist but less visibly devout than Laos.

● **Special dangers** Land mines everywhere, guns in Phnom Penh, bandits on Highway 7 (recent reports suggest the problem has waned).

● **Health factors** Malaria is a problem in many rural areas, especially in Ratanakiri/Mondulkiri. Take precautions.

● **Social conventions** Buddhist mores but unlike Burma you don't need to remove your shoes in temple ruins – only in religious buildings that are still used. Increasingly it is considered rude to bring a machine gun into a hotel room or bank.

● **Traveller hubs** Narin and lake-area guesthouses (Phnom Penh), Weather Station Hill (Sihanoukville), Royal Hotel (Battambang). Siem Reap is full of tourists but many are on package tours.

Except for the low-key beach resort of Sihanoukville, Cambodia's coastline is almost utterly unexploited. Some gorgeous, pristine isles and beaches which will doubtless be resorts in the future are, as yet, empty for you to enjoy pretty much on your own, assuming that you're suitably self sufficient. And the new road from Koh Kong to Sre Ambel may, if only briefly (till the loggers rush in) open up glimpses of the rainforest treasures of the as yet totally-isolated Cardamon mountains.

Underlying any trip to Cambodia are the physical and emotional scars of the 'killing fields'. Almost everyone you meet will have suffered directly or indirectly as a result of the Khmer Rouge era. Shortly after seizing power in 1975, Pol Pot's regime emptied the cities and abolished money for the self-contradictory goal of creating a 'modernized, totally agrarian society'. Indoctrinated or bullied child soldiers were to murder anyone who had had contact with the West, those 'polluted' by business or wealth, those with an education, and even those who wore glasses and thus **might** be educated. In less than four years one-fifth of the population had died or fled. Those who were not killed were sent as slave labour to communal farms, as depicted in the powerful movie *The Killing Fields*. Brutal torture and extermination sites have been turned into ghoulish historical reminders (Sampeau, south of Battambang, and Tuol Sleng prison in Phnom Penh are more affecting

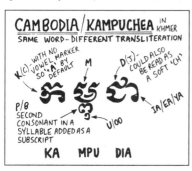

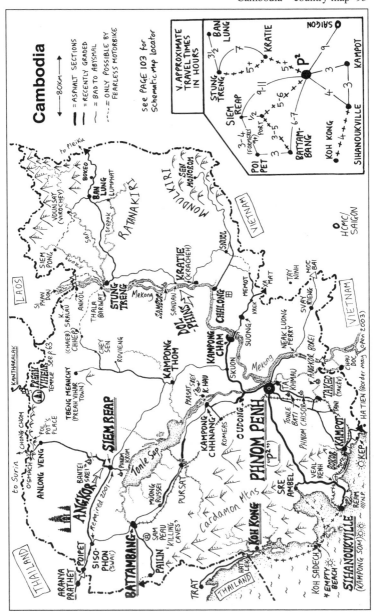

than the famous 'Killing Fields' memorial near Choeng Ek [15km south of central Phnom Penh]).

Cambodia was rescued from the Khmer Rouge by Vietnam's 1978/9 invasion. However, that didn't end the country's problems. Cambodia–Vietnam relations have never been cordial. And Vietnam was at that time enemy number one to the USA which protested more against the Vietnamese occupation than it ever had against the Pol Pot atrocities. The Khmer Rouge retreated into the hills as a terrorist-cum-smuggling organization but remained recognized by the UN as the official government! Despite the withdrawal of the Vietnamese in 1989, the reintroduction of the monarchy, and a UN monitored transitional period, the Khmer Rouge fought on till 1997 when Pol Pot was finally betrayed and captured, dying shortly thereafter of malaria. His death had been reported several times before, so like an anti-Jim Morrison, some people still don't believe he's really dead. Recently his cremation site above Anlong Veng has been starting to draw a few darkly-curious tourists, to very mixed reactions from the suspicious guards. Meanwhile Cambodia's political problems and issues of rampant corruption are by no means resolved, but the country seems to have survived the 2002 elections without the feared upheavals. As Cambodia edges towards a new era, it's a fascinating time for a visit if you keep yourself well informed.

HIGHLIGHTS

Angkor is *the* site. It may seem expensive ($20+) but it's unmissable. In comparison, all other attractions seem relatively modest, but just being able to get out into relatively uncharted areas (by moto/motorbike) makes exploring great fun – if you don't forget all the landmines!

The **south-coast boat ride** is delightful if the sea is calm, Phnom Penh's smart **terrace cafés** make for great lounging and it's great fun to find **your 'own' beach** on islands off Sihanoukville.

WHEN TO GO

The temperature in most of Cambodia remains a constant 34°C to 39°C year-round, though at slightly higher elevations it is significantly cooler eg in Mondulkiri and at Bokor (often lost in clouds at a mere 1079m). October to April is the driest time.

The wet season (May to September) transforms the country's slightly monotonous dry-flat landscapes into stunning emerald green vistas, though flooding makes boggy laterite roads even more difficult than usual.

PLANNING TACTICS

● Entry from Thailand means there's no need to get the visa in advance.
● If you're coming from/going to Laos, allow plenty of time and money – the border has its idiosyncrasies!
● If you're expecting to continue to Vietnam get a Vietnamese visa while you're still in Battambang or Sihanoukville rather than waiting for Phnom Penh.

❑ **Key tips**
● As soon as you arrive in Phnom Penh, Siem Reap or Sihanoukville the first thing to do is find a copy of the free 'Visitors Guide' (see p101). These have **maps**, reviews and pretty much all the practical information you need.
● Use the suggested **internet** sites to follow the constant changes, checking the posting date carefully for any travel information.
● If your first experience of Cambodia is **Poipet**, don't be put off! The touts here are uniquely annoying: people elsewhere are much nicer.
● **Commission** is paid on everything! Hotels, souvenir shops and ticket agents can give you a better price if you walk there rather than arriving by moto as they don't have to pay off the driver. Ask the moto for a café near where you really want to go, then sit a while till he's gone!
● **Beggars** There are so many thousands of 'deserving' mine victims and amputees that it's hard to refuse. But you'll soon be bankrupted if you don't have lots of very small riel change to give away – and if you give to one you're likely to be swamped by other hopefuls. It can get very upsetting.
● Looking for an old temple, ask for the '**prasat**'.
● Don't get blasé about safety. **Land-mine** dangers are real – see box below.

SAFETY

The safety situation in Cambodia has vastly improved since 1998. Visiting the Thai–Cambodian border was once suicidal. Now you can get a visa on arrival and even the awesomely appalling Poipet–Siem Reap road has been mostly rebuilt.

The main security worries these days are the ubiquitous **land mines**. They really could be almost anywhere. The Angkor site has been pretty thoroughly cleared of mines but you should still stick to trodden paths. Elsewhere, if children refuse to join you on a walk in a rural area, it probably means there are land mines. Even along Highway 6, the main highway, I saw that a group of de-miners had found something suspicious – only 40cm from the asphalt. So if you need a toilet stop don't just nip behind a bush. As new roads are built over the next few years, so more and more tourists are likely to 'forget' and step off the tarmac: for example, along the new Angkor–Anlong Veng road which goes through some very heavily-mined stretches.

Other dangers include the prevalence of **fire arms**. Certain areas of Phnom Penh are the most risky and it is generally wise to be back in your hotel by 9:30pm

❑ **Land mines**
Some mind-blowing statistics from CMAC (Cambodia Mine Action Committee):
● Total number of mine-related accidents: approximately 60,000, though the annual injury rate is dropping – 4789 incidents in 1997, 2046 in 1998, 808 in 2001.
● Average cost to clear land: $1.2 million per sq km.
● Total area cleared so far: 90 sq km.
● Total area left to clear: 3000 sq km!!!!
● Estimated total number of mines laid: 4–6,000,000.
● Number of villages believed still 'contaminated': 4025 (ie 46% of the nation).

❏ **Geo-political information – Cambodia**

Population: 12.9 million (2002 est), 11m (1997), 10.3m (1993), 5.7m (1962).

Area: 181,000 sq km.

Capital: Phnom Penh (P^2; 1.1 million).

Other major cities: Battambang (195,000); Siem Reap (140,000); Sihanoukville (95,000); Ta Khmau (50,000); Pursat, Takeo (40,000), Kampong Chhnang, Kampong Speu, Sisophon, Kratie, Kampot (over 20,000).

GNP per capita: $1300 (in 2000), average monthly income less than US$30.

Currency history: Riel/US$1 – April 2002: 4030RIs, Jan 2001: 3800RIs, Feb 1998: 3585RIs, Oct 1997: 3200RIs, Dec 1995: 2300RIs, Jan 1988: 159RIs. Between 1978 and 1979, under Pol Pot, money was abolished altogether.

Major exports/economy: tourism, garments, wood, fish, gemstones.

Ethnic mix: Khmer (92% figure includes the Muslim Cham), Vietnamese (5%), and Chinese (1%), various hill tribes including Tampuan, Brao, Jarai, Prou, Kachak, Raong and Krul in Ratanakiri, Phnong in Mondulkiri, Stieng around Snuol.

Official language: Khmer.

Religious mix: Buddhist (95%, pre-1976 Therevada Buddhism was the state religion), Muslim 4%. Christianity was legalized in 1990 but estimates put the number of believers at only 20,000.

Landmarks of national history: **6th century** AD: Kambuja (Khmer ancestors) conquered the Hindu Mekong kingdom of Funan. **802–836** Jayavarman II became the first 'god-king', conquest of neighbouring regions. In approx **890** Yasovarman I founded Angkor. **1113–1150** Hindu Khmer empire reached its zenith under Suryavarman II, Angkor Wat built. **1177** Sacking of Angkor by the Cham (linguistically Malay kingdom of southern Vietnam) shook royal faith in the Hindu deities. **1181–1219** Jayavarman VII rebuilt Angkor Thom (including the Bayon) as a Buddhist city. **1353 and 1431**: Angkor sacked by Thai armies, capital moved to Phnom Penh. **1863**: French colonial protectorate declared. **1949**: Independence within the French Union. **1955**: Monarchy established. **1975**: Khmer Rouge's disastrous communist-agrarian experiment, over a million died/fled. **1978/9**: Vietnamese invasion. **1992**: UNTAC oversaw the restoration of the constitutional monarchy.

Leaders: King Sihanouk is the figurehead but power is in the hands of Hun Sen, sole prime minister since the 'coup' in September 1997 when he deposed the co-PM, Prince Ranariddh, the king's son!

Pressing political issues: Land-mine clearance, shattered economy, corruption, smuggling of resources and illegal forestry, racism towards the Vietnamese minority.

'THSAY' THESE GREEN LOTUS PODS ARE CULTIVATED IN PONDS AROUND OUDONG - BREAK OPEN TO REVEAL THE PEA-FLAVOURED SEEDS: EDIBLE RAW.

or earlier until you have sized up the current situation. In Phnom Penh there have been several cases of tourists being robbed of their rented motorbikes at gunpoint. Reports of bandits on Highway 7 between Kratie and Stung Treng were once common, but most are now rather dated and travellers have started using the route more frequently of late. Check carefully though!

Practical information

VISAS AND FORMALITIES

One-month **tourist visas** are easy to arrange (usually $20, 24 hours). They are available on arrival at the airports in Phnom Penh and Siem Reap (two photos, $20), and at the two main border crossings with Thailand (1000B, ie around $25 but payable in Thai currency).

At the land borders, officers often demand to see a **cholera vaccination certificate**, or else you pay a 50B/$1 fee: despite the official appearance, this is a scam according to long-term residents – a blatant way to intimidate money out of first-time visitors. You'll get through if you confidently stride past saying 'no thank you!' – don't listen to their dire warnings (no, the paper they give you won't be checked on exiting Cambodia). If that sounds too confrontational, show them almost anything official-looking – eg a European medical information form or kidney donor card and say that that covers it!

If you're coming **by land from Laos or Vietnam** you should apply for the visa in advance but as late as possible before hitting the road. That's because the one-month validity and period of stay are the same for most Cambodian visas – ie from the moment your visa is issued the month starts to tick away.

Going **to Laos overland**, you need a border permit that you can get in Stung Treng immigration office (check with other travellers if this is still the case). The cost varies from $2 to $25 according to who helps you get it! Going the other way you don't need a permit, but either way there are 'tips' to pay to the border guards. Ironically these were cheaper when the border was officially closed but they can now total $25–30 per person, mostly on the Cambodian side – clean bills are required!

There are several **border crossings with Vietnam** but until very recently only the Moc Bai crossing was open. Following the completion of the Kampong Cham bridge at the time of writing, the Xa Mat border will hopefully open allowing Phnom Penh–Saigon traffic to take the easier route via Tay Ninh. The boat service between Chau Doc and Neak Luong allows you to head straight into Phnom Penh from the Mekong delta. For several years, false alarms have claimed that the Kep–Ha Tien border had opened – when I checked it certainly hadn't, but fresh reports in late 2002 claim it really has. If true this would be excellent news as you could link Kampot in Cambodia to Vietnam's Phu Quoc Island without back tracking. The border between Pleiku and Banlung in Ratanakiri remains closed as of 2002, though the road has been upgraded – a good omen?! As we went to press the border between Anlong Veng and Chong Chom (for Surin, Thailand) had reportedly just opened.

Visa extensions are possible through several travel agencies and guesthouses in Phnom Penh, and generally cost $50 for one extra month, $90 for three.

Onward visas

Sihanoukville and Battambang (but not Phnom Penh) are the best places anywhere to get your **Vietnamese visas** – they are issued within minutes, you can get long stays, and the consulates are open seven days a week! If you insist on getting Vietnamese visas in Phnom Penh (P^2) ironically it's sometimes cheaper to use visa services than to go to the embassy (426 Monivong; P^2 ☎ 720022, 362531, open 8–11am, 2–4:30pm, a visa takes three to five working days). That's not the case, however, for **Chinese visas** (256 Mao Tse Tung, P^2 ☎ 720022, 720920) or **Lao** (15-17 Mao Tse Tung, P^2 ☎ 720022, ☎ 426441/982632) visas.

MONEY

Cambodia's official monetary unit is the *riel*. However, the de facto currency for most transactions is the US dollar (but see over). Prices are often quoted in dollars and greenbacks are accepted (and preferred) virtually everywhere, except in markets and small villages. Only small change is given in riels.

There is no black market so, generally if you pay for a 1000RIs item with a $1 bill, you will get 3000RIs change. No discussion is needed. Nonetheless one feels less like a tourist if not well stocked with riels and having the right money makes for more convincing bargaining. Thai Baht are easily exchangeable for riel throughout Cambodia, and is the currency of choice in Poipet, Sisophon, Koh Kong and, to some extent, Battambang.

Travellers' cheques (preferably in US$) are awkward but can be changed for 2% commission at a few banks in Phnom Penh, Sihanoukville, Battambang and Siem Reap. In the same towns you can get **credit card cash advances** (2%) at the Cambodia Commercial Bank and Mekong Bank. As yet there are no ATMs, though things will change rapidly as tourists start flooding in.

TRANSPORT
Buses and pick-ups
Many 'roads' have potholes that will kill a car at 20 paces. So the bus system is limited to the few paved sections of highway (notably Phnom Penh–Sihanoukville). This is likely to change very quickly as a major road-building programme is underway. But for now public transport on most routes is by **pick-up truck**. Unlike the covered vehicles in Laos, these are simply open-backed flat-beds into which bodies and luggage squeeze themselves as best they can. If it rains, a plastic tarp is thrown over everything/everyone as a makeshift shelter. If you stump up the extra cash you can ride inside the cab. Generally there will be six passengers squeezed into that claustrophobic cab (two beside the driver, four in the seat behind). If you can afford it, it's worth having two people pay for three of the latter spaces (or three for four). Even if you don't want the luxury, consider that Westerners usually do take up an unfair amount of space and fidget into the bargain. So it is only fair on your fellow passengers. NB Negotiate the price (and write it down to confirm) but don't pay till you arrive! Tourists are often asked for money up-front – don't be pressured!

Most departures are in the mornings when there's a chaos of competing trucks and their touts trying to bundle you aboard. But whenever there's sufficient demand more trucks will run, some leaving Phnom Penh for Battambang as late as 4pm.

Where **bus services** do run, eg Phnom Penh to Takeo, Kampong Cham, Oudong and Sihanoukville there is a choice of companies: Genting generally offers the best range of departures and nicest vehicles, albeit at a slightly higher price. Capitol Guest House runs several tours and its own Sihanoukville bus service, which is useful if you're staying nearby.

Bangkok–Siem Reap tourist offers
Now that the Sisophon–Siem Reap road has been repaired (meaning a two-hour journey in 2002 instead of seven hours in 2001!) the Bangkok–Siem Reap route is easier than ever. Several tourist services are available to/from Kao San Road. Such services used to involve changing vehicle at the border with many people disappointed by the rough Cambodian truck they're thrown on to!

With the road rebuilt, everything changed and the cost ($15–30) of the trip plummeted – some eastbound fares fell as low as 100B ($2.50)!!! There is, of course, a catch. The cheapest journey may be dragged out for many extra hours to give you the appetite for meal stops at commission-paying restaurants. And on arriving in Siem Reap late in the evening you may be a virtual captive of the guesthouse where you arrive, the owner of which will have subsidized the fare and will be very reluctant to let you 'escape'. If you accept these hassles, it's a bargain. But do-it-yourself is easy, despite the very annoying touts in Poipet.

Taxi and share taxi
Where buses are infrequent but the roads are good enough not to need pick-ups (eg Phnom Penh to Kampot), share taxis are the most sensible form of transport. For six times the one-way fare you can rent the whole car, as long as you leave early enough for the driver to get passengers for the return leg. This can make a lot of sense if you have a small group

but make sure the driver knows both the route and the stops you want before departing as this will affect the price: eg Phnom Penh–Kampot direct would cost about $15 for a car, via Takeo with two long stops en route would be about $30.

Train

Until recently trains were a regular target for the Khmer Rouge who enjoyed blowing up the tracks for a bit of sport, or test-firing bazookas at passing locos. Until 2000 the front carriage was thus used as a 'sacrifice', clearing any mines on the line by simply running over them. Anyone brave/foolhardy enough to ride in it could travel for free. Things have settled down these days: trains remain slow but generally arrive intact. And you even have to pay (though only 45Rls/km).

There are two lines: Phnom Penh–Battambang and Phnom Penh–Sihanoukville via Kampot. Both run three times a week leaving Monday, Wednesday and Friday from Phnom Penh at 6:30am returning 6:30am Tuesday, Thursday and Saturday, around 12,000RIs. The most popular section for tourists is the Kampot–Sihanoukville run (4365RIs) which is beautiful and saves the dreadful stretch of mud 'road' east of Veal Renh. Despite many maps which suggest the contrary, there is no cross border service between Sisophon and Poipet/Aranyaprathet, Thailand.

Air

Royal Air Cambodge, once the country's national airline, went bankrupt in October 2001. However, three mainly domestic services remain: **RPP** (Royal Phnom Penh Airlines, P² ☎ 217419, 🖳 www.royalpnhair.com), **SRA** (Siem Reap Airways, P² ☎ 720022, 🖳 www.siemreapairways.com/) and **PrA** (President Airlines, P² ☎ 720022, 212887). Each operates one or more flights daily between Phnom Penh and Siem Reap – it is whispered that well-placed shareholders in the various airlines are behind the long delays in resurfacing of the nation's roads ... in a small country like Cambodia, good roads would destroy the airline business.

RPP also links Phnom Penh to Battambang (daily), Koh Kong (Monday, Wednesday, Saturday), Mondulkiri/Sen Monorom (Monday, $55), Ratanakiri/Banlung (Sunday, $55), and Stung Treng ($45, Monday, Wednesday, Saturday).

PrA flies Siem Reap–Koh Kong (twice a week) and has been known to run very handy flights between Sen Monorom and Banlung.

There has been an exponential growth in international flights to Siem Reap notably from Bangkok, but also from Saigon, Phuket (inbound only returning to Sukothai on Bangkok Airlines), Vientiane via Pakxe (Tue, Fri on Lao Aviation) and Singapore (Silk Air). Departure tax is $4/8 (local/int'l) from Siem Reap, $10/20 from Phnom Penh.

> ### ❏ Cambodian airport codes
> BBM = Battambang
> KKZ = Koh Kong
> MWV = Mondulkiri (Sen Monorom)
> PNH = Phnom Penh
> RBE = Ratanakiri (Banlung)
> REP = Siem Reap
> TNX = Stung Treng

Boat

Despite some foreigner markups, speedboats are cheaper than flying (though not a giveaway), more comfortable (despite the bumps) than the awful roads and usually much faster too.

The main routes go up the Mekong from Phnom Penh to Kratie (and beyond to the Lao border when water is high), Phnom Penh to Siem Reap (a very popular backpacker route to Angkor), Siem Reap to Battambang (mini boats at a scary lick and the gorgeous coastal run from Sihanoukville to Koh Kong (dangerous if there's much surf). There are also a plethora of other boat services hopping between smaller river towns.

Slow boats generally cost about half the price and take two to three times longer. This would be painfully slow on the rather dull Phnom Penh–Siem Reap run, but is worth considering between Kratie and Kampong

Cham where there's somewhat more river life to enjoy. Downstream is obviously faster than upstream. In the dry season many rivers can become too low to navigate (including certain sections of the Mekong north of Kratie).

For a real desert island experience get dropped on one of the desert islands off Sihanoukville or Kep – be sure to arrange pick up details carefully and don't forget to take enough food and water!!

Motorbike and moto (motodop)
It is increasingly easy to rent mopeds from as little as $4–5/day and trail bikes for $6–10, not just in Phnom Penh but also Kampot, and Sihanoukville. Beware that you are responsible if the bike is stolen – a real danger particularly in Phnom Penh. Also, in the countryside, be very aware that there may be land mines mere inches off the tarmac even on brand-new roads! Renting in Battambang is more difficult and in Siem Reap pressure from moto drivers means that rentals are generally not allowed. This rule changes with the wind, but even if you can rent, for visiting the Angkor temples, a moto is a cheaper and safer option.

Drivers of the ubiquitous motos (chauffeured motorbike taxis) charge $4–10/day (usually $6) depending on the distance travelled and how much the driver reckons himself to be a guide as well as a ride. In Siem Reap competition is so fierce for customers that, on arrival, a moto driver will often be prepared to drive you around town for free looking for a hotel. This is not a scam – the idea is that, in return, you'll use his services to tour Angkor next day. If you don't like him and don't plan to employ him, it's only fair to give at least a tip for the hotel ride. Motos at the airport work on a similar basis: note that the $1 fee you pay to the Tourist Transport Association is not given to your driver.

Motos are the normal means of **city transport** too with drivers generally recognizable by their trademark base-ball hats – short hops are usually 500–1000Rls (5-10 Thai Baht in Koh Kong, Poipet, Sisophon). If you're arriving in a town and already know where you want to stay, either walk or get the moto to take you to a nearby café or landmark, not to the guesthouse itself. That way you can save up to $1/night that the guesthouse would have to pay in commission to the driver!

Bicycle
A few bicycles are finally becoming available for rent in Siem Reap, but although cycling around Angkor Thom is a brilliant experience, the first 7km from Siem Reap to the archaeological park entrance is sweaty and the whole site of Angkor is so spread out that a moto is generally more convenient.

ACCOMMODATION
The majority of guesthouses are brand new and built to a pretty decent standard with en suite facilities and, often, air-conditioning. These are a good deal at around $10–15/double B&B but for ultra-budget travellers the cheapest $2–5 options are pretty miserable. Nonetheless, with backpackers flooding in, it's likely that more dorm accommodation will spring up in the next year or two. Couples can often save money by sharing a 'single' room – the term implies that there's one bed but that's often a double bed in mid-range places.

FOOD AND DRINK
Both the riverfront in Phnom Penh and the old quarter of Siem Reap have some delightfully-atmospheric restaurants with dollar prices aimed at expats and wealthier tourists: these are worth the splurge and good value in global if not South-East Asian terms. Elsewhere, eating is a rather hit and miss affair – with the best deals almost always coming from roadside food stalls and markets where women ladle out unidentifiable but generally excellent concoctions from unmarked saucepans: 500Rls a scoop, plus 500Rls for some rice and you're set. Junction towns and river ports bring out more snack sellers, including the infamous fried spiders of Skuon and roast beetles in Neak Luong.

Bars range from the delightfully cool, neo-colonial atmosphere of Phnom Penh's FCC or Siem Reap's Red Piano to a range of disgraceful whorehouses where armed brawls are not uncommon as the clientele get drunker. These ubiquitous 'karaoke' places were officially closed by presidential decree in early 2002 but it is unlikely that they'll remain shut for long.

SEX AND DRUGS

Cambodia is trying to clean up its 'new Thailand' sex image and in April 2002 was reported to have considered expelling Gary Glitter who has spent several months there since his release from British jail (he'd been charged with downloading child sex material from the web). While 'happy' pizzas are liable to get you very giggly, there is not such an obvious opium scene as you'll find in Laos.

STAYING IN TOUCH

The **postal system** does function but post-cards sent from the Phnom Penh GPO certainly didn't catch the plane prominently advertised, taking over a month to arrive in Europe. The poste restante doesn't have a fail safe record for holding mail, either.

Domestic **telephone** calls are easiest from the ubiquitous little roadside stands which advertise the codes to which they can connect you (typically from 500RIs). MPTC and Camintel phone offices will place international calls for you (but this is more expensive). International country code: +855, dial out code is 007. City codes: Battambang: 053, Kampong Cham: 042, Kampong Chhnang: 026, Kampong Thom: 062, Kampot: 033, Koh Kong: 035, Siem Reap: 063, Sihanoukville: 034, Phnom Penh: 023, Takeo: 032.

MPTC's Caminet generally has the best deal on **internet access** but at around $3 per hour this is still pricey and slow compared to Thailand. At present, access is limited to Phnom Penh, Siem Reap and Sihanoukville plus a few places in Battambang (expensive and slow) but by the time you read this there will surely be many more.

ACTIVITIES
Hiking

The combination of land mines in the west, unexploded ordnance (UXO) and insecurity in the north-east and intensive agriculture in the central plains makes Cambodia a particularly poor choice for hikers. Ratanakiri and Mondulkiri provinces would be your best bet but you'll need a good guide and plenty of time to get there.

Work

With foreigners arriving in droves there is no longer the desperate shortage of English teachers that once pushed casual teaching wages to around $20/hour, but vacancies still occur.

Unlike Thailand one can own land in Cambodia and there is not (yet) an off-puttingly huge minimum investment for a foreigner to start a small business. Thus there is a rush of small-time European business-types moving across from Pattaya, Phuket etc and setting up small hotels and cafés, particularly in Phnom Penh and Sihanoukville.

FURTHER INFORMATION
Maps and books

Cambodia is very well served by a series of free, regularly updated, map-brochure-listings pamphlets. The best is the 'Visitors Guide' series with separate issues for Phnom Penh, Siem Reap and Sihanoukville (🖳 www.canbypublications.com). If you can't find any of them, the fortnightly *Phnom Penh Post* (3500RIs) has a passable city map and some listings.

Website 🖳 www.canbypublications .com/miscpages/books.htm is also useful for listing many of the most relevant books written about Cambodia.

There is little incentive to buy a guide book given all the free information and the rapid pace of change. If you do need one, $3 bootleg Lonely Planet guides (relatively poor) and various architectural guides to Angkor ($1–2) are available in Siem Reap and at the gates of Angkor itself (plus more expensively in Phnom Penh's central market).

Obviously original (ie non-bootlegged) books are much more expensive. But especially in Phnom Penh there is a very good selection available, notably in the Mekong Libris bookshop (opposite the post office), and Monument Books (at 46 Norodom Blvd). There you'll find *Adventure Cambodia*, an inspiring new guide book by Jacobson & Visakay which gives practical details of their journeys into the wildest corners of the country (though sadly their town plans are dangerous fiction with a wildly varying scale and random omissions). Look out for books by Jeff Zepp, including his

Field Guide to Cambodian Pagodas. Robert Philpott's *Coast of Cambodia* is the best source available for the south. London Books at 77, 240th St, has second-hand books.

The International Travel Map company produces a Cambodia map but will have trouble keeping pace with the new road building.

❏ **Meeting the locals**

● **The people** Cambodians are generally much more anti-Vietnam than anti-Khmer Rouge. Running around Phnom Penh yelling 'Up with Pol Pot!' might not bring you more than a few dirty looks; walking around silently with a Ho Chi Minh t-shirt could bring you some threats.

● **Language** The beautiful Khmer alphabet has more letters than any other. They congregate in craggy calligraphic clusters, eyeing potential readers with a cocky disdain. And to add to the tease, the cursive form looks, at first glance, like an altogether different script. Below I have given the main letters in both their forms, but make no attempt to explain the full intricacies of the writing system, and leave to you the unbridled delights of the vowel system! A good starting point (failing reincarnation as a Khmer) is 🖳 www.learnkhmer.com which sounds out each (cursive) letter just for you as well as showing you the handwriting.

Transliterating Cambodian words can be a bigger minefield than the country itself. Kampuchea and Cambodia are actually one and the same – different renderings of the same consonant clusters Ka+mpu+dia (see graphic p92).

Fortunately for the traveller, many signs have at least some Latin component.

Some phrases in Khmer/Cambodian:
Hello – *chum-reep su-or*
How's it going? – *sok sabay ta?*
Thank you – *or koun*
This food is good – *mohope nis ch-gang*
Is the road to _____ safe? – *tei plov tov _____ sroul ta?*
Cheap hotel – *hotel thork* (the word 'hotel' is commonly used)

Khmer/Cambodian alphabet

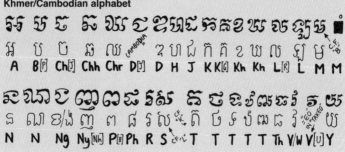

Useful websites

More than for any other country in South-East Asia, websites on Cambodia are extremely helpful and genuinely informative. Given the incredible pace of change, any traveller is well advised to consult the internet and to check carefully the dates of any information posted.

💻 www.btinternet.com/~andy.brouwer/contents.htm is a personal site that goes into immense detail and keeps up to date. Check out the very detailed Ray Zepp reports too, find the 'Map' page for border-crossing updates, ask questions at 💻 http://pub90.ezboard.com/bandybrouwerscambodiacommunity.

💻 http://talesofasia.com/Cambodia/Overland/index.htm for exhaustive detail on the Bangkok–Angkor Wat route and its pitfalls. Gordon Sharpless, the author, lives in Siem Reap so has the very latest information on travel in western Cambodia.

💻 www.kohkong.com/kohkong/overland.html has similar step by step detail for the coastal route from Trat to Koh Kong.

Very helpful travel situation summaries plus useful links can be accessed on George Moore's well-maintained 💻 http://rectravel.com/khlavn/.

💻 www.canbypublications.com/ is the handy site of the free booklet company.

Cambodia Information Centre's homepage, 💻 www.cambodia.org/ is good for downloading Khmer fonts, but other links are poorly maintained.

Go to 💻 www.nexus.net/~911gfx/cambodia.html for a very detailed if out of date and very slow to download series of Cambodia maps.

💻 www.angkor-ruins.com/ has an encyclopaedic photographic coverage of the temples in the Angkor complex. Though much of the text is in Japanese there's basic English titling and the photos of the lesser temples are worth looking at before you bother to go a long way to see a small pile of stones.

Special icons

☠ Killing Fields Site
⌂ Recommended moto driver
▣ Sections of road very bad
▦ Much of road appalling
⛨ Prasat (ancient Khmer temple ruin)
🏛 More extensive temple ruins
▨ Area of town retains a hint of colonial charm
⛊ Independence monument (see Takeo map for typical design)
P² Phnom Penh

Cambodia – locator map

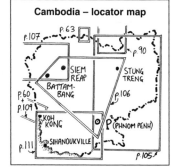

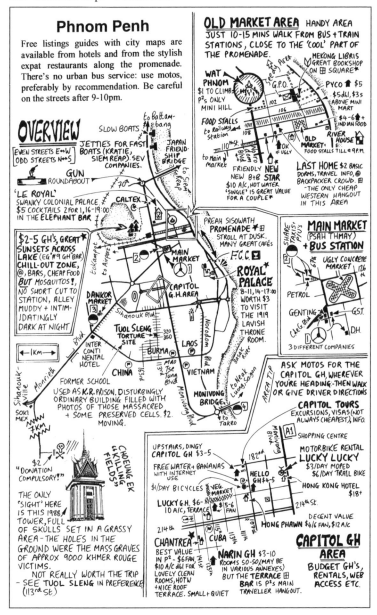

Phnom Penh

Free listings guides with city maps are available from hotels and from the stylish expat restaurants along the promenade. There's no urban bus service: use motos, preferably by recommendation. Be careful on the streets after 9-10pm.

OVERVIEW

EVEN STREETS E↔W
ODD STREETS N↔S

SLOW BOATS
to Battambang

JETTIES FOR FAST BOATS (KRATIE, SIEM REAP). SEV COMPANIES.

JAPAN FRIENDSHIP BRIDGE

GUN ROUNDABOUT

'LE ROYAL'
SWANKY COLONIAL PALACE. $5 COCKTAILS 2 FOR 1, 16-19:00 IN THE ELEPHANT BAR

70°

to Siem Reap

CALTEX

$2-5 GH's, GREAT SUNSETS ACROSS LAKE (EG "#9 GH BAR) CHILL-OUT ZONE, @, BARS, CHEAP FOOD BUT MOSQUITOS!, NO SHORT CUT TO STATION, ALLEY MUDDY + INTIMIDATINGLY DARK AT NIGHT

Tokkampot

to Airport

MAIN MARKET

2

CAPITOL G.H. AREA

DANKOR MARKET
3

Sihanouk Blvd.

TUOL SLENG TORTURE SITE
320 350

BURMA

LAOS

Noradom Blvd.

PREAH SISOWATH PROMENADE ★ STROLL AT DUSK. MANY GREAT CAFÉS

F.C.C.

ROYAL PALACE
8-11, 14-17:00 WORTH $3 TO VISIT THE 1919 LAVISH THRONE ROOM.

←|1 Km|→

INTER CONTINENTAL HOTEL

FORMER SCHOOL USED AS K.R. PRISON. DISTURBINGLY ORDINARY BUILDING FILLED WITH PHOTOS OF THOSE MASSACRED + SOME PRESERVED CELLS. $2. MOVING.

CHINA

Sihanouk-ville

Monirath Blvd.

SOKI MEX
7KM

MAO Tse Tung Blvd.

VIETNAM

Monivong Blvd.

MONIVONG BRIDGE

to Neak Lung/Saigon

to Takeo

$2 "DONATION COMPULSORY!"

CHOEUNG EK "KILLING FIELDS"

THE ONLY 'SIGHT' HERE IS THIS 1988 TOWER, FULL OF SKULLS SET IN A GRASSY AREA - THE HOLES IN THE GROUND WERE THE MASS GRAVES OF APPROX 9000 KHMER ROUGE VICTIMS.
    NOT REALLY WORTH THE TRIP - SEE TUOL SLENG IN PREFERENCE (113rd St.)

OLD MARKET AREA

HANDY AREA JUST 10-15 MINS WALK FROM BUS + TRAIN STATIONS, CLOSE TO THE 'COOL' PART OF THE PROMENADE.

WAT PHNOM
$1 TO CLIMB- P's ONLY MINI HILL

MEKONG LIBRIS GREAT BOOKSHOP ON ⊞ SQUARE ★

G.P.O.

102

106

PYCO 🏠 $5
$5 dbl, $3 s ABOVE MINI MART

$4-6 🏠 + INDIAN FOOD

FOOD STALLS
to Railway Station

108

110

to Main Market

OK IF UGLY

OLD MARKET
FOOD STALLS TILL ≈ 9 P.M.

RIVER HOUSE

FRIENDLY NEW NEW 8+8 STAR $10 A/C, HOT WATER 'SINGLE' IS GREAT VALUE FOR A COUPLE ★

LAST HOME $2 BASIC DORMS, TRAVEL INFO, BACKPACKER CROWD. ⊞ - THE ONLY CHEAP WESTERN HANGOUT IN THIS AREA

MAIN MARKET
(PSAH THMAY)
+ BUS STATION

SHARE TAXIS/ P'U's

UGLY CONCRETE MARKET

126

PETROL

GENTING

G.S.T.

ClG GH

D.H.

3 DIFFERENT COMPANIES

AREA TIP

ASK MOTOS FOR THE CAPITOL GH, WHEREVER YOU'RE HEADING - THEN WALK OR GIVE DRIVER DIRECTIONS

CAPITOL TOURS
EXCURSIONS, VISAS (NOT ALWAYS CHEAPEST), INFO.

A1 SHOPPING CENTRE

182nd

MOTORBIKE RENTAL
LUCKY LUCKY
$3/DAY MOPED $6/DAY TRAIL BIKE

UPSTAIRS, DINGY CAPITOL GH $3-5

FREE WATER + BANANAS WITH INTERNET USE

$1/DAY BICYCLES

VEG. MARKET

HELLO GH $4-5

HONG KONG HOTEL $18+

LUCKY G.H. $6- 10 A/C, TERRACE

$5-6 FAN

214th St.

DECENT VALUE
HONG PHAWN $4/6 FAN, $12 A/C

214th

CHANTREA
BEST VALUE IN P's - $6 FAN, $10 A/C dbl FOR LOVELY CLEAN ROOMS, HOT W + NICE ROOF TERRACE. SMALL + QUIET

CUBA

NARIN GH $3-10
ROOMS SO-SO (MAY BE IN VARIOUS ANNEXES) BUT THE TERRACE ⊞ BAR IS P's MAIN TRAVELLER HANGOUT.

CAPITOL GH AREA

BUDGET GH's, RENTALS, WEB ACCESS ETC.

[@@] = **see** http://www.btinternet.com/~andy.brouwer/miscz.htm

East Cambodia

Travel conditions are in constant flux with roads rebuilt one year, washed out the next.

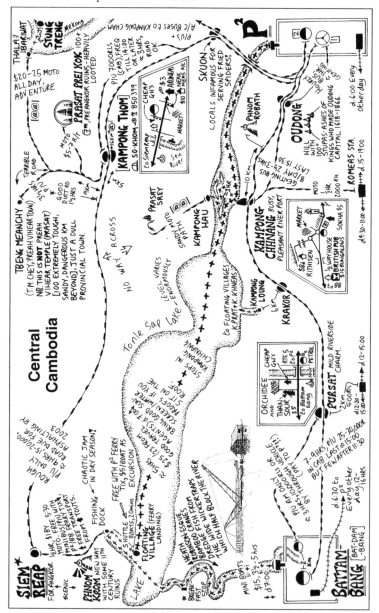

Bangkok - Angkor
Details of the options regularly
updated on http://talesofasia.com/Cambodia/Overland/index.htm

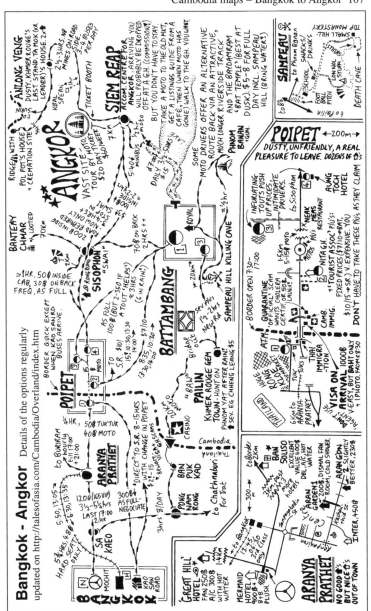

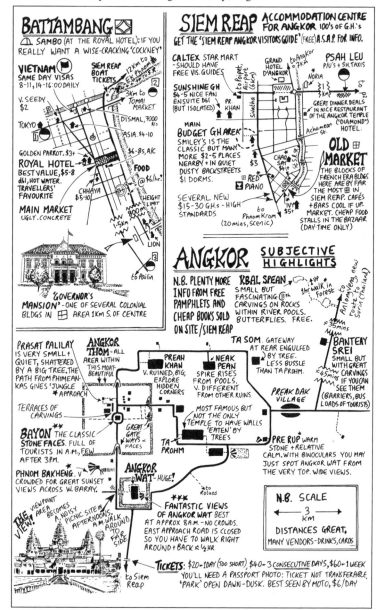

BATTAMBANG

SAMBO (AT THE ROYAL HOTEL): IF YOU REALLY WANT A WISE-CRACKING 'COCKNEY'

VIETNAM SAME DAY VISAS 8-11, 14-16:00 DAILY
V. SEEDY $2

SIEM REAP BOAT TICKETS

12km to PHNOM

3km to TOMAI MARKET

TOKYO

DISMAL, 7000 Ris

ASIA. $4-10

GOLDEN PARROT, $3+

$6-8s, A/C

ROYAL HOTEL BEST VALUE, $5-8 dbl, HOT WATER. TRAVELLERS' FAVOURITE

FOOD

CHHAYA $5-10

a $6/hr.

HEIGHT LIMIT 800m

MAIN MARKET UGLY, CONCRETE

1-5km

LION

to Pailin

'GOVERNOR'S MANSION' - ONE OF SEVERAL COLONIAL BLDGS IN ⊞ AREA 1KM S. OF CENTRE

SIEM REAP
ACCOMMODATION CENTRE FOR ANGKOR 100's of G.H.'s
GET THE 'SIEM REAP ANGKOR VISITORS GUIDE' (FREE) A.S.A.P. FOR INFO.

CALTEX STAR MART - SHOULD HAVE FREE VIS. GUIDES

to Poipet, Airport (6km)

GRAND HOTEL D'ANGKOR

to Angkor ~7km

PSAH LEU P/U's + SH. TAXIS

NORIA

SUNSHINE GH $4-5 NICE FAN ENSUITE Dbl (BUT ISOLATED)

PR. KHAN

Swatha

GREAT DINNER DEALS IN NICE RESTAURANT ON THE ANGKOR TEMPLE ('DIAMOND') HOTEL.

Achemean St.

MAIN BUDGET GH AREA SMILEY'S IS THE CLASSIC BUT MANY MORE $2-5 PLACES NEARBY + IN QUIET DUSTY BACKSTREETS $1 DORMS.

CHAO SAY $3

RED PIANO

OLD MARKET ⊞

THE BLOCKS OF FRENCH ERA BLDGS HERE ARE BY FAR THE MOST ⊞ IN SIEM REAP. CAFÉS + BARS COOL IF UP-MARKET. CHEAP FOOD STALLS IN THE BAZAAR (DAY-TIME ONLY)

SEVERAL NEW $15-30 GH's - HIGH STANDARDS

IVY $5+

to Phnom Krom (20 mins, Scenic)

ANGKOR SUBJECTIVE HIGHLIGHTS

N.B. PLENTY MORE INFO FROM FREE PAMPHLETS AND CHEAP BOOKS SOLD ON SITE / SIEM REAP

KBAL SPEAN SMALL BUT FASCINATING 11th CARVINGS ON ROCKS WITHIN RIVER POOLS. BUTTERFLIES. FREE.

1hr up in Forest

An Long Veng, new route to Surin (Thailand)

~35 mins

TA SOM. GATEWAY AT REAR ENGULFED BY TREE. LESS BUSSLE THAN TA PROHM.

BANTERY SREI SMALL BUT WITH GREAT CARVINGS IF YOU CAN SEE THEM (BARRIERS, BUS LOADS OF TOURISTS)

~45 mins

PRASAT PALILAY IS VERY SMALL + QUIET, SHATTERED BY A BIG TREE. THE PATH FROM PHIMEANKAS GIVES 'JUNGLE' APPROACH

ANGKOR THOM = ALL AREA WITHIN THIS MOAT. BEAUTIFUL

PREAH KHAN V. RUINED, BIG; EXPLORE HIDDEN CORNERS

NEAK PEAN SPIRE RISES FROM POOLS. V. DIFFERENT FROM OTHER RUINS

PREAK DAK VILLAGE

TERRACES OF CARVINGS

MOST FAMOUS BUT NOT THE ONLY TEMPLE TO HAVE WALLS 'EATEN' BY TREES

BAYON ⭐⭐ THE CLASSIC STONE FACES. FULL OF TOURISTS IN A.M., FEW AFTER 3PM.

GREAT GATE WAYS WITH FACES

TA PROHM

PRE RUP WARM STONE + RELATIVE CALM. WITH BINOCULARS YOU MAY JUST SPOT ANGKOR WAT FROM THE VERY TOP. WIDE VIEWS.

PHNOM BAKHENG V. CROWDED FOR GREAT SUNSET VIEWS ACROSS W. BARAY.

ANGKOR WAT - HUGE!

to Roluos

THE VIEW. VIEWPOINT AREA BECOMES A NOISY PICNIC SITE IN AFTERNOONS. A.M. WALK AROUND TO FAR SIDE

⭐⭐⭐ **FANTASTIC VIEWS OF ANGKOR WAT BEST AT APPROX 8 A.M. - NO CROWDS. EAST APPROACH ROAD IS CLOSED SO YOU HAVE TO WALK RIGHT AROUND + BACK ≈ ½ HR**

N.B. SCALE
3 km
DISTANCES GREAT, MANY VENDORS - DRINKS, CARDS

to Siem Reap

TICKETS: $20=1 DAY (TOO SHORT), $40=3 CONSECUTIVE DAYS, $60=1 WEEK
YOU'LL NEED A PASSPORT PHOTO: TICKET NOT TRANSFERABLE. 'PARK' OPEN DAWN-DUSK. BEST SEEN BY MOTO, $6/DAY

KOH KONG

7km to Airport
picnic spot,
mangrove
views
enroute

1km to Osresronoh

HUGE NEW BRIDGE UNDER CONSTRUCTION

←200→ m

600m
800m
600m
600m

KOH PICH
$5-8 GOOD ENSUITE ROOMS BUT INCONVENIENT LOCATION

to Sihanoukville Sre Ambel

SMALL INFO ROOM

150฿ BASIC,

OTTO's ฿50฿,
⊞ DINNER VENUE, EXCURSION IDEAS

BOAT TICKETS

KOH KONG HOTEL 100฿

PENH CHELH 150-200฿

POYSEAN 100฿

AIR TICKETS

to many more G.H.'s

TAXI BOATS
20฿ ACROSS RIVER (PP),
4-500฿ FOR 2-3 HOUR UPRIVER TRIPS THROUGH LUSH JUNGLE TO ROCKY RAPIDS (2-3 PEOPLE)

HTTP://KohKong.com/KohKong - useful site but no @ yet in Koh Kong to view it!

TRAT
MANY ⬆'s,
$/ATMs
@'s

BORDER CONNEC-TIONS

25฿ plu 1-1½ HRS

100฿ 1¼ HRS MINIBUS

THAILAND

KHLONG YAI ⬆'s

≈20mins 1-2/hr 12฿

BORDER (V. SHORT WALK)
OPEN 7-17:00

HAT LEK (TINY, SHOPS BUT NO G.H, NO $ - GET BAHT IN SIHANOUKVILLE IF HEADING TO THAILAND

CASINOS 10฿/CHIP MINIMUM

to Rapids

≈20mins, 50฿pp + through mangroves: FOR THOSE RUSHING TO THE BOAT OR BORDER

10mins, 20฿ moto! 50฿ taxi

20฿pp (MIN 2/hr)

BA KLONG
5-10mins

2+3

BRIEF STOP

KOH KONG

to Sihanouk- ville d 8:00, $25
+ Sre Ambel d 6:40, 7:10, $15

CAMBODIA

Koh Kong boat notes

> Don't buy **tickets** from touts/moto drivers - they may not be valid.

> Check the **weather**. In rough seas the boats don't run, and if they do they're dangerous. The tiny Sre Ambel boats are particularly vulnerable. The site http://www.cnn.com/WEATHER/html/KampongSomCambodia.html may help.

> Sitting on the **roof** is great for views, but be prepared for deafening engine noise, minimal grip (scary when rough!), sunburn, spray & possible sudden rain showers.

> Boats stop for 2 mins on the tiny island of **Koh Sadech**. Facing the port/village is a tempting, totally undeveloped 8km long sandy beach. Bring tent, food and water!

> **P² to Bangkok in 24hrs?**: if the 7:30am bus arrives on time in Sihanoukville there's JUST enough time to grab a moto to the port for the noon boat to Koh Kong. Hurry off the boat at Ba Klong and onto the first connecting skiff to be early in the queue at the border and get through before the Thai side closes at 5pm. There's a Trat-Bangkok bus at 11pm.

Heading east, chances are slimmer: you'll need to be first in the queue at the border when it opens at 7am, but the earliest (6am) mini-bus from Trat to Hat Lek probably won't get you there quite in time. Anyway, why rush? Koh Kong may be a little dull but river trips to nearby waterfalls & beaches are really appealing. Note that the huge **bridge** at Koh Kong should be complete by the time you read this and will make connections much easier. Once the KK-Sre Ambel **road** is finished, the boat services may be suspended altogether.

> Regularly **updated info** from http://www.kohkong.com/kohkong/overland.html

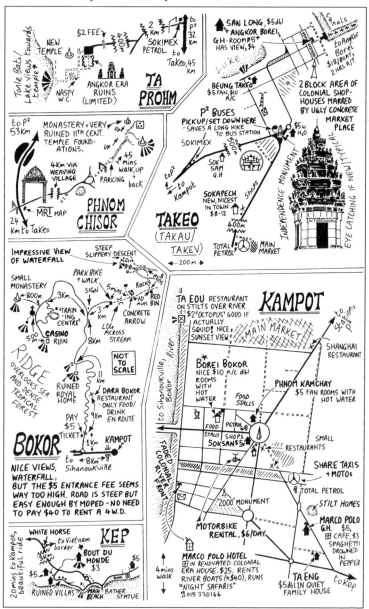

South Cambodia

NB Rent a motorbike to tour Sihanoukville & area; also in Kampot to visit Bokor, Kep et al. You can charter a P²-Kampot share taxi to take you via Ta Prohm, Phnom Chisor and Takao: $20-25 if you start early and arrive by around 1-2pm.

KOH KONG

~4HRS ~600₵ DAILY IF SEA IS CALM

SRE AMBEL 18 Km

d.v. variable

4½HRS 12-14:00 ALTERNATE DAYS

BOAT & 40 10:30, 300₵ 3 HRS

3 HRS SHARE TAXI, 30₵

P²

5½-8 HRS ALL DAYS

SHARE TAXI, 3 HRS

SHARE TAXI

HOURLY GENTING BUS, 2 HRS

PHNOM CHISOR ~4Km

★ WATERFALL

BOKOR
GHOST CASINO

⚑ MOTO
40 Km STEEPLY UP

[ANGK TASOM]

TA PROHM 3 Km

14Km MOTO

1Km SCENIC

BOAT $18, 2HRS r/t

TAKEO

ANGKOR BOREI ⚑ PHNOM DA

VEAL RENH

45 mins as FULL-SHARE TAXI

12 BUSES/DAY RUN BY 4 COMPANIES d. 8-14:00₵ 7:30-13:30₵ (EXTRA AT WEEKENDS)

SHARE TAXI 2-2½HRS AS FULL

XDAAK PHOTOGENIC FISHING HAMLET

KAMPOT GENTLY CHARMING RIVERTOWN

½hr MOTO

KEP LUSH BUT DESOLATE EX-RESORT, POOR BEACH, $10 ISLAND TRIP

MOTO 100R

SIHAN-OUKVILLE

Sihanoukville

ATTRACTIVE, LOW-KEY BEACHES OR A LAUNCH POINT FOR ISLAND ADVENTURE.

On arrival get a **free Sihanoukville Visitors Guide**, eg from Star Mart. Includes maps, sights, food, GHs etc.

to P² GOOD MOPED $4/DAY SHARE TAXIS

STAR MART + PETROL STATION MAP/GUIDE

to Ochheu-teal ☼

BACKPACKERS' AREA

MEALY CHENDA ⬆
DADA ⬆
VICTORY ⬆

SHORT STREET OF TRAVELLER CAFÉS incl. MASH, MELTING POT (BOAT TRIPS)

SEA STAR ⬆
NIRVANA ⬆

'BEACH CLUB' G.H. ⊞ - NOT ON THE BEACH, BUT HIP (IF ULTRA BASIC) AND RUN BY A WELL INFORMED 'FRENCH' PHYSIOTHERAPIST. MAT BEDS $2, FREE PICKUP IF YOU CALL (012) 808813. KICKBOXING CLASSES.

← 1km →

to Koh Kong

to Port

to station

GOLDEN BUDDHA

to Down Town area

VICTORY BEACH

HAWAII BEACH

BIG UGLY PORT

WEATHER STATION HILL

BACKPACKERS' HILL

BOAT TICKETS 1000₵

to brewery

to Phnom Penh (route 4)

DOWNTOWN AREA

BUS STATIONS

VIETNAM CONSULATE 7:30-11, 13:30-16 DAILY!

SUNSET VIEW RESTO.

INDEPENDENCE BEACH

SOKHA BEACH

LIONS

MIDRANGE BEACH HOTELS

OCHHEUTEAL BEACH

Nicest Beaches

BUS COMPANIES
Ⓐ ☯ GENTING
Ⓑ ☯ G.S.T.
Ⓒ ☯ CAPITOL
Ⓓ ☯ D.H.
EACH HAS 2-5 SERVICES/DAY TO PHNOM PENH.

EAT, RENT A BIKE AND GET OUT A.S.A.P!

SEVERAL GOOD VALUE FAMILY GH's $10-20 ENSUITE ON ROADS SET FURTHER BACK. NOT ALL WILL HAVE ENGLISH SIGNS EG. ⚑A = APSARA GREAT $12 A/C, E, Dbl, SITTING AREA ★

SPOOKY SHELL OF A 1970's HOTEL "NO PAY FEE, NO POLICE GUARD" THREATENS A SIGN DEMANDING 1000Rls TO CLIMB FOR THE SEA-VIEWS + 'SHINING' ATMOSPHERE.

VIETNAM

Introduction

Vietnam was always a most unlikely candidate for communism. The Vietnamese people ooze business zest and entrepreneurial enthusiasm, making what is still on paper a 'socialist people's republic' one of the most vibrantly capitalist countries anywhere. Having withstood two decades of bloody-minded post-war international boycotts and resultant economic stagnation, the country transformed itself through the 1990s.

The locals, always quick to spot ways to make a buck, sometimes seem to care about nothing else. One can't blame them. Vietnam is one of the poorest countries in Asia. A college professor makes only $40/month and to survive he must extort bribes from students. Similarly, patients bribe doctors for operations. And everyone bribes the police for everything ... and for nothing. 'We give money so they be our friends,' said one shopkeeper noting that 'bad fortune' falls on those who do not pay.

Tourists sometimes feel themselves to be a constant target for beggars, persistent shoe-shine boys, postcard sellers, and overcharging virtually anywhere. It's enough to make you jump on the next plane, bus, or cyclo out of Vietnam. But give it time. With a smile and a little patience you can usually break through the 'money barrier' and find the delightful people on the other side. Returning frequently to the same business can win you respect. Every day during a week in Hanoi, I rented bicycles from the same lady. The first day I haggled. By the third her price was trustworthy. On the fifth day she decided not to charge at all.

❑ **Country ratings – Vietnam**
- **Expense $$$** Less than $12/day is possible if you bargain heavily and fight against foreigner pricing. But often accommodation is likely to set you back $10+.
- **Value for money** ★★☆☆☆ Standards vary greatly within the price ranges.
- **Getting around** ★★★★☆ Trains are comfortable but incur foreigner pricing. The 'open ticket' and tour minibuses are convenient. Public buses can be hellish and not necessarily cheaper for non-Vietnamese.
- **English spoken** ★★★★☆ In tourist areas, business folk are increasingly proficient while sales-kids can even imitate various regional British accents. ★★☆☆☆ In the more remote provinces things are tougher, a knowledge of French just might be handy with the very oldest people.
- **Woman alone** ★★★★☆ Shouldn't be a problem.
- **For vegetarians** ★★★☆☆ Traces of meat seem to sneak into most local dishes (especially in the north) but vegetarian options are common in travellers' cafés.

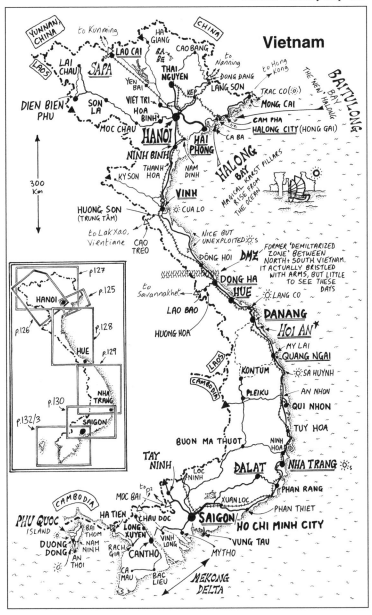

❏ **Essential information for travellers – Vietnam**
● **Visa** Required. $30–70, the best places to apply are Battambang or Sihanoukville, Cambodia.
● **Currency** Dong. US$1= Đ14,500. Now pretty stable. Cash gets a better rate and is easier to exchange than travellers' cheques.
● **Time zone** 7 hours ahead of GMT (same as Thailand, Laos, Cambodia; 1hr behind China).
● **Health factors** Drinking tap water is not recommended; mineral water is readily available. There's a malaria risk in the Mekong Delta.
● **Special dangers** Beware of unexploded mines and bombs along the Laos border.
● **Social conventions** Crossing your index and middle fingers (a sign of good luck in the West) is a rude gesture in Vietnam. The Vietnamese often cross their arms when listening intently.
    Age is respected in Vietnam – direct eye contact with older people (ie grandparental age) is considered rude.
    The person who invites another to a meal pays the bill.
● **Key tips** Don't underestimate how annoyingly slow and overpriced the public bus system can be! The open-ticket café buses are great for long hauls but don't forget to slow down between legs, venture out of the traveller hubs and actually get to know the real people! It's the same anywhere, but is easily forgotten in Vietnam.
● **Traveller hubs** Sapa, Cat Ba, old Hanoi, Hoi An, Hue, Nha Trang, Dalat, Saigon and anywhere else that the café buses stop.
● **Festivals** Unless you have close friends in Vietnam, there's little incentive to visit during *Tet* (Vietnamese New Year, four days in February or March according to the lunar calendar). It's mostly a family affair with the majority of shops and money-changers closed and few buses running. Tourist hotels aren't likely to be full so you shouldn't have a problem finding a place to stay, but that won't stop some guesthouse owners trying to charge you double!

Elsewhere, guesthouse staff who started out appearing cold and money grabbing, grew to be friends, started inviting me to family dinners and finally waved me off with Vietnamese candies and shots of brandy as a farewell. With persistence you can really find a Vietnam to savour.

HIGHLIGHTS

Sapa and the highlands beyond for craggy mountain views, rice terraces and a colourful array of tribal people, magical Halong and its neighbouring bays full of surreal karst pillars and caves, charming old Hoi An, and watching conical-hatted merchants dangle a mass of goods from their *gwang ganh* poles even in old Hanoi.

TRAVEL TACTICS

Tourist Vietnam tends to be one long north–south route with well-worn stops en route and a few excursions at either end (Halong Bay being the country's crown jewel). Since trains are artificially pricey and local buses packed to the gunnels for a gouged foreigner price, backpackers in Vietnam are drawn inexorably to the frequent, generally reliable, competitively-priced tour minibuses. These are very handy and you get to know plenty of other foreigners. However, it is all too easy to get locked into a travel-bubble and to have little interaction with the Vietnam beyond the guesthouses and the long, long road.

CÔNG NGHIỆP HÓA, HIỆN ĐẠI HÓA, ĐẤT VỮNG BƯỚC TIẾN VÀO THẾ KỶ 21

With the exception of charming Hoi An, pretty much all of the most visually interesting places are north of Vinh, from which you can now loop into Laos on a scenic cross-border route. If you want to make more of a month in Vietnam, consider renouncing the south altogether and taking more time to get out and about on a motorbike around Sapa or the little visited area north-east of Halong Bay. And take longer in old Hanoi.

I am not convinced that all those kilometres from Vinh to Saigon are really worth the effort – Lang Co is rather idyllic but a few minutes is enough, Nha Trang's beaches are OK but prices are high (and with a disproportionate number of thieves to worry about), Dalat is humorously ordinary, Hue is historic but very much more ruined than one might hope and paying $4–5 for each of the so-so royal tombs seems steep if you've been to Phnom Rung (Thailand) or Prambanan (Indonesia).

The DMZ sites are at best lumpy undulations that are of very much specialist interest to veterans of the 1970s' American war. More interesting war sites are the Cu Chi tunnels which, along with semi-interesting Saigon and the bucolic, steaming Mekong Delta, you might consider visiting as a separate side trip from Cambodia – if so consider getting away from it all on Phu Quoc Island, before it becomes Vietnam's Ko Samui.

WHEN TO GO

The climate differs between the regions. Saigon and the south has the most predictable climate. It is always hot and rain usually falls in heavy afternoon spurts, particularly from July to January. The Mekong Delta receives even more rain – flooding is possible during September and October. December is the best month to visit the south.

The north-central area is usually best in February and March but varies greatly from year to year. It is wet from May to January with the worst rains in October and November – flooding commonly makes minor roads impassable. Yet a little further south, the beaches of Nha Trang have their best season from June to October, and the rain in October/November is generally pretty limited.

Hanoi and Halong Bay, in the north, have the most pleasant temperatures in October and November – clear skies, short sleeve days, long-sleeve nights. December to February is cooler (some days will require a sweater) and, more importantly, cloudy. Halong Bay, which is so magnificent in the sunshine, looks rather ordinary on an overcast day. In March the heat sets in and then, in May, the monsoons. The mountainous areas receive less rain and more moderate temperatures.

Dalat offers a year-round respite from the heat of Saigon. In December, in fact, Dalat can be chilly, and the northern mountains can be downright freezing.

❏ **Geo-political information – Vietnam**

Population: Estimates vary between 80 and 86 million, 74.5m (1995), 52.7m (1979).
Area: 325,360 sq km.
Capital: Hanoi (1.3 million/2.5m for the whole metropolitan area).
Other major cities: Ho Chi Minh City (incl Saigon) (3.3m/5.7m); Haiphong (570,000/1.7m); Danang (450,000); Nha Trang, Hue, Cantho, (250,000); Nam Dinh, Rach Gia, Vung Tau, Qui Nhon (190,000); Long Xuyen (150,000); Hong Gai, Phan Thiet, Cam Pha (140,000); Thai Nguyen, Buon Ma Thuot, Dalat (130,000), My Tho (120,000).
GNP per capita: $1950 (2000), $190 (1994).
Currency history: Dong/US$1 – April 2002: Đ14,500, Mar 2001: Đ13,900, Feb 1998: Đ12,280, Sep 1997: Đ11,600, Dec 1994: Đ11,079, Dec 1993: Đ10,820.
Major exports/economy: Oil, rice (reforms in the 1990s took Vietnam from being a net importer to the world's third biggest exporter!), coffee, tea, seafood, rubber, clothing, shoes.
Ethnic mix: 90+% Vietnamese, 3% Chinese (though many fled after the 1979 war – the census details are old!), Khmer, Cham, Hmong, various hill tribes.
Official language: Vietnamese.
Religious mix: Various forms of Buddhism, Cao Dai (3%), Christian (7%).
Landmarks of national history: 111BC: Conquered by Chinese emperor Wu Ti. AD939: Ngo Quyen defeated the Chinese. **1044**: Capital moved to Hanoi. **1371**: Hanoi stormed by Champa army. **1471**: Champa conquered and absorbed. **1802**: Vietnam united after period of north–south division. **1847**: Missionaries expelled. **1858**: French invasion began at Danang. **1867**: French colony declared in the Mekong Delta (called Cochin China) **1883**: The French took Hue, the imperial capital, and declared the northern protectorate of Annam and Tonkin. **July 1954**: Division into north and south following Dien Bien Phu battle where the French were defeated. **1965**: US intervention began. **Jan 1973**: Ceasefire. **1975**: Saigon fell, 200,000 people fled. **1979**: Border war with China and invasion of Cambodia to oust Pol Pot. **3 Feb 1994**: US embargo lifted.
Leaders: President: Tran Duc Luong, Prime Minister Phan Van Khai, General Secretary of the Communist Party (powerful position) Le Kha Phieu.
Pressing political issues: Fight against 'Social Evils' (public morals campaign), anti-corruption drive and 'self criticism campaign' in the Communist party as it seeks to renew its legitimacy while opening the capitalist market, Spratley Islands dispute with China et al.

KEY REMINDER
Emphasising the positive:

THIS FONT = somewhere interesting

⊞ = atmospheric, quaint, charming…

★ = recommended

✸★ = a must (a rare accolade indeed!)

Practical information

VISAS AND FORMALITIES
Visa strategy
Citizens of ASEAN countries can visit visa free, but all other nationalities require a visa.

One-month tourist visas for Vietnam typically cost around $50 and take between three and ten days (usually a week) to issue and paying extra will not speed that along (but see below for exceptions).

Until 2000 you had to state the entry and exit point if arriving/leaving by land which was a considerable headache. Thankfully that rule has been abolished and where the visa has a line marked 'entry point', the consul should now write *Ta ca cac cua khau* or *Qua cua khau* (ie any legal border crossing).

Many consuls (especially those in South-East Asian capitals including Bangkok) still issue 'set date' visas. This means the stay you're allowed begins and ends on exact stated dates rather than being a month from the date of arrival – annoying if, as with many travellers, you fall in love with Laos or Yunnan en route and want to slow down your progress. However, if you apply in the consulate at either Sihanoukville or Battambang (both in Cambodia) you pay less ($35/30 respectively), wait only a matter of hours or even minutes and get a visa that starts from the date of entry, within three months of issue.

Some Kao San Rd (Bangkok) agencies can get you a three-month, multi-entry business visa, though these may cost as much as $150.

Given two working days many travel agencies/guesthouses in Hanoi and HCMC can arrange one-month visa extensions ($27–50) and re-entry permits ($15–25). If you're visiting Laos or Yunnan and then coming back to Vietnam, the latter saves a lot of trouble as double-entry visas are hard to come by, and re-applying in Laos or China is painfully slow (no consulate in Yunnan at all). If you're going to Cambodia just pick up a new visa in Battambang or Sihanoukville.

MONEY
As though named for 'fnnnrrs' (Finbar Saunders) by Viz Comic, the Vietnamese currency is known as the Đong and you'll soon have your hands on an impressive wad. US$ cash can be changed virtually anywhere: banks, guesthouses, jewellery shops are the safest bets. Rates are generally better in the bigger cities than in rural areas. Travellers' cheques can be exchanged in major banks (8–11:30am Mon to Fri plus some afternoons) but also now at certain tourist guesthouses, even in Sapa, if you're not worried about a poor exchange rate.

At Vietcombank cash advances are free on MasterCard and JCB but there's a 4% commission on Visa. ANZ Bank has Cirrus ATMs in Hanoi (14 Le Thai To Street) and Ho Chi Minh City (11 Me Linh Street).

Keep at least some handy small bills in US$ currency for border towns and weekend emergencies.

TRANSPORT
Public bus and minibus
Vietnam has an extensive bus network but services are generally uncomfortable, slow and can require several changes to reach rural destinations. Express buses stop only at designated bus stations and have priority over local buses at ferry crossings. Long-distance buses often depart between 4 and 6am, with the better-quality ones leaving first. Minibuses depart when (over)full on popular shorter hop routes.

The standard fare for Vietnamese on a local bus is about Đ15,000 for every 100km. However, especially in the south, bus drivers/bus stations tend to charge foreigners up to 400% more. Vigorous bargaining can somewhat reduce the quoted price, but don't count on it. More than a few travellers have also felt cheated to find that public buses don't go exactly where they'd expected. Whether by deliberate ploy or through linguistic misunderstanding (eg buses 'to' the Laos border that actually go 'toward' the Laos border), this adds to the unpopularity of public buses amongst backpackers.

Café minibus
The gap has been filled by a network of 'café' tours and minibus services. Operating from backpacker cafés and hostels these serve destinations specifically of interest to independent travellers and are faster, more comfortable and not necessarily any more expensive than foreigner-priced public buses. They may even stop at key view points en route for brief photo opportunities.

Very popular are the hop-on hop-off 'open ticket' services between Saigon and Hanoi. These typically take about five days stopping the night at Dalat, Nha Trang, Hoi An, and Hue with drop offs in Ninh Binh, Vinh and at some beaches. At each stop you can decide to stay longer and simply re-book for the next leg the day before you're ready to leave. Prices ($20–35) vary both according to the organizers and according to who sells you the ticket. Perhaps the best known and most reliable is operated daily by Sinh Café.

Note, however, that in 2002 even ticket agents were advising people to take the train instead of the road between Vinh and Hue as the latter had degraded so severely. Hopefully repairs will be complete by the time you read this.

On a café bus you'll be dropped and picked up from a specific guesthouse. This is very convenient if you choose to stay there, but don't be bullied into accepting accommodation you don't like. Similarly, it's worth bringing food for the journey in case the bus stops for lunch at an overpriced restaurant with suspiciously unpriced menus.

Train
'Reunification Express' (S1/S2) trains now cover the 1726km of single-track railway between Saigon and Hanoi in 32 hours. Other daily services take either 39 or 41 hours, stopping at most intermediate stations. Train fares would be similar to the cost of café minibuses if it weren't for the roughly 300% foreigner surcharge. Smaller stations used to be unaware of the foreigner prices, but these days the mark-up is pretty rigorously applied even in the remotest country station.

Classes are similar to those in neighbouring China: hard and soft seat, hard and soft berth, and deluxe. Soft seat is comfortable – generally more so than the bus – but tickets sell quickly as they are very popular with Vietnamese. Hard sleeper is the best deal for overnight runs and fares should include a blanket and pillow, to be provided by your compartment attendant. Upper berths are marginally cheaper than middle and lower ones, but they are cramped and get terribly hot in summer.

While it is usually possible to get tickets for departure the same day, booking ahead is wise for weekends and essential well in advance of national holidays. And since most foreigner booking desks only open from around 7am, you have to **buy ahead for early morning departures**.

Air
Internal flights are reasonably frequent but not a particular bargain, eg Hanoi–Danang $70, Saigon–Hanoi $132 (three a day).

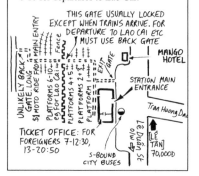

Hanoi Ga (train station)
Getting to the platform is not always as easy as you'd expect. You may need to take a motorbike taxi to reach platforms 6-10 for departures to Lao Cai.

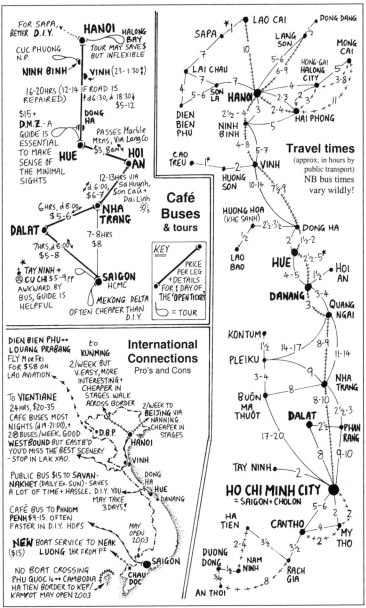

FOR SAPA, BETTER D.I.Y.

HANOI

HALONG BAY
TOUR MAY SAVE $ BUT INFLEXIBLE

CUC PHUONG N.P.

NINH BINH

VINH (23-1:30‡)

16-20HRS (12-14 IF ROAD IS REPAIRED)
↓d6:30, d.18:30↑
$5-12

$15+
D.M.Z. - A GUIDE IS ESSENTIAL TO MAKE SENSE OF THE MINIMAL SIGHTS

DONG HA

PASSES Marble Mtns. Via Lang Co
$3, 8am*

HUE

HOI AN

12-13HRS VIA Sa Huynh, Son Cau + Dai Linh
↓d.6:00,
$6-7

6HRS, d8:00
$5-6

NHA TRANG

DALAT

7THRS, d 8:00
$5-8

7-8HRS
$8

TAY NINH + @ CU CHI $5-9 PP AWKWARD BY BUS, GUIDE IS HELPFUL

SAIGON HCMC

MEKONG DELTA OFTEN CHEAPER THAN D.I.Y.

Café Buses & tours

KEY

PRICE PER LEG + DETAILS FOR 1 DAY OF THE 'OPEN TICKET'

↺ = TOUR

Travel times
(approx. in hours by public transport)
NB bus times vary wildly!

LAO CAI
DONG DANG
SAPA   1
LANG SON   2
LAI CHAU   7
MONG CAI
7   10   5-6
6-9   HONG-GAI HALONG CITY   5
4   3-8
SON LA   7
4   5-6   **HANOI**   2-3   2
DIEN BIEN PHU   2½-4   3   2-4   HAI PHONG   11
NINH BINH   5
CAO TREU   1*   4-8   5-7
2   **VINH**
HUONG SON   10-14   7½-9
HUONG HOA (KHE SANH)   2½-3½   **DONG HA**
½   2   1½-2
LAO BAO   **HUE**   ×2½-5*
4-5   1½   **HOI AN**
DANANG   3-4
3   **QUANG NGAI**
KONTUM   1½   14-17   8-9
PLEIKU   11-14
3-4   9   **NHA TRANG**
BUÔN MA THUÔT   8   8-10
17-20   **DALAT**   2½-3
2½   **PHAN RANG**
TAY NINH   8   9-10
2
HO CHI MINH CITY
= SAIGON + CHOLON
5-6   2   2
HA TIEN   **CANTHO**   4   **MY THO**
2-4   3½   3½   2
DUONG DONG   NAM NINH   RACH GIA
½   8
¾   **AN THOI**

International Connections
Pro's and Cons

DIEN BIEN PHU ↔ LOUANG PRABANG FLY M or FRI FOR $58 ON LAO AVIATION

To **VIENTIANE** 24HRS, $20-35. CAFE BUSES MOST NIGHTS (d19-21:00), + 2@ BUSES/WEEK. GOOD WESTBOUND BUT EAST B'D YOU'D MISS THE BEST SCENERY - STOP IN LAK XAO.

PUBLIC BUS $15 TO **SAVAN-NAKHET** (DAILY Ex. SUN) - SAVES A LOT OF TIME + HASSLE. D.I.Y. YOU MAY TAKE 3 DAYS!

CAFÉ BUS TO PHNOM PENH $9-15. OFTEN FASTER IN D.I.Y. HOPS

NEW BOAT SERVICE TO NEAK LUONG 1HR FROM P² ($15)

NO BOAT CROSSING PHU QUOC Is ↔ CAMBODIA HA TIEN BORDER TO KEP/ KAMPOT MAY OPEN 2003

to KUNMING 2/WEEK BUT V.EASY, MORE INTERESTING + CHEAPER IN STAGES. WALK ACROSS BORDER

2/WEEK TO BEIJING VIA NANNING. CHEAPER IN STAGES

•D.B.P.

•HANOI

•VINH

DONG HA

HUE

DANANG

MAY OPEN 2003

•SAIGON

CHAU DOC

You can fly Hanoi–Vientiane for $100, Hanoi–Bangkok for $175.

International departure tax is $10, domestic Đ20,000.

Motorcycle

Motorbikes can be rented in most tourist centres and are particularly recommended for visiting the Mekong Delta and northern hill-tribe villages. A 100cc Honda Dream typically costs $6–9 per day with lower rates negotiable for rentals of more than two days. As one motorcycle rental contract said you should 'be able to be driver to avoid being accident.' However, you're unlikely to be asked to show any kind of driver's licence. Note that fuel is more expensive in country areas than in cities and is usually sold at street-side stalls in cans and plastic bottles.

If you buy a motorbike for your time in Vietnam you'll generally do better buying in Hanoi and selling in Saigon where prices are 10–15% higher. Check notice-boards in traveller cafés for second-hand deals. Be sure to check that the registration card has the motorcycle licence plate and engine number marked correctly on it – whoever has this card owns the motorcycle. An old Soviet-made Minsk (around $200 for a 125cc) may not be noted for reliability but has more street credibility than a Honda. Bikes over 150cc incur a special import duty and are thus significantly more expensive.

Bicycles, Cyclos and Xe Oms

For around $1/day it's easy to rent a **bicycle** in almost any tourist area.

The ubiquitous three-wheeled **cyclo** is a back-to-front rickshaw. Driving a cyclo is more profitable than teaching, especially for English speakers who can make money from affluent tourists. Rates start at around Đ10–15,000.

Motos (xe om – literally 'hugging vehicle') are generally faster and slightly cheaper (less effort required!) if less atmospheric.

Hitchhiking

Rather than sticking out a thumb, wave your entire arm up and down with the palm of your hand facing down. Hitchhikers report great success but ascertain carefully whether your driver expects to be paid; an amount comparable to the bus fare is reasonable.

Boat

A boat trip is the only way to fully appreciate the glory of Halong Bay – conveniently the boat from Haiphong to Hong Gai takes you through some of the best scenery. The Mekong Delta region has an extensive network of river-crossing ferries and longer-distance services that, especially in the wet season, are often more convenient going by road. Cargo ships ply the length of the Vietnamese coast and are worth considering if you have the patience and the sea legs.

❏ **Vietnam war sites**

Everywhere in Vietnam is deeply connected to the sad decades of war, which resulted in the virtual obliteration of most of the country's historic cities (notably Hue) and citadels (Vinh etc). The following is a list of places where aspects of the war remain the overriding reason for a visit:

● **Dien Bien Phu** Last stand of the French forces. Now a dusty admin town.
● **Quang Ngai** For visits to My Lai, site of the infamous massacre which further increased anti-war sentiments in the US.
● **Khe Sanh** Former French combat base; salesmen hawk rusty 'dog tags'.
● **Between Saigon and Cantho** The flag of South Vietnam is still faintly visible under the paint on one of the bridges you'll pass.
● **Demilitarized Zone (DMZ)** Ludicrous misnomer for what was one of the world's most lethally armed no-man's lands until the north and south were reunited in 1975. Tours will show you a few ditches.

❏ Man bites dog

The Vietnamese do, indeed, eat dog meat *(thit chay)*. Dark-haired dogs are supposed to taste better than light. Both are considered a delicacy and eaten mostly by men, because, as one male Vietnamese explained mysteriously to me 'Dog meat you must eat slowly with wine, so women don't like. Women like to eat quickly.' A Vietnamese woman had a more plausible explanation: 'It tastes bad'.

From the 15th to the end of the lunar month is the most fortuitous time to delight in canine cuisine. At the start of the month eating dog meat is bad luck and many *thit chay* places are closed. In Hanoi there is a gaggle of *thit chay* places on the lake north of the old centre. A selection of cuts with noodles can be had for Ð40,000. And, if you don't finish, you can always ask the waiter to put the rest in a....!

ACCOMMODATION

Mid-range tourist accommodation is a relative bargain in much of Vietnam if you're prepared to pay around $7–10/double. However, there is relatively little choice in the $2–5 range with the exception of a few backpacker dorms in the big cities. Grimy 'local' hotels that might ask Ð20,000 from a Vietnamese guest often charge foreigners $5 so there is little incentive to slum it.

Many 'café tours' include passable accommodation in the deal for much less than you'd pay if you showed up alone. In smaller villages if there's no *khach san* (hotel) or *nha khach* (guesthouse) villagers might be able to arrange floor space in a house or local school.

FOOD AND DRINK

Common ingredients to look out for include rice *(com)*, fish *(ca)*, squid *(muc)*, chillies *(ot)*, vegetables *(rau)*, crab *(cua)*, pork *(heo)*, beef *(bo)*, chicken *(ga)*, and potatoes *(khoai [tay])*. These are usually easy to spot within a menu name – eg *pho* is a noodle soup, (often served for breakfast): thus *pho ga* is noodle soup with chicken.

A typical Vietnamese meal gives you various salad/meat dishes which should be rolled in special leaves or rice-paper circles and dunked in sauce like a cold spring roll. Dishes vary greatly between the regions but most use *nuoc mam* (fermented fish sauce), or a pungent shrimp equivalent called *mam tom*.

Especially in the south, try stuffed crêpes *(bang xeo)*. French bread is ubiquitous and street trolleys will delight in whipping you up a paté-filled baguette.

Tea is of great social importance: it is thought to cement relationships and to calm interpersonal tensions. Refusing a cup of tea when you visit someone's house could be misunderstood as being insensitively rude. Many hotels provide a flask of tea in the room for their guests.

Traditionally, ordering coffee got you a tall glass with a little condensed milk at the bottom and a slow-dripping metal filter pot on top. However, an increasing proportion of the celebrated Vietnamese coffee crop now goes for export these days. Thus, local cafés are likely to serve instant coffee from Thailand unless you specifically ask for *feen café*.

Beer is very popular amongst Vietnamese men, with draft *(bia hoi)* much cheaper than bottled equivalents.

STAYING IN TOUCH

Mail is expensive (Ð12,000 to North America) but fairly reliable if you watch the stamp being franked.

International telephone calls are outrageously expensive, up to $11/min – wait till you reach Thailand to call home. The international phone code is +84, Hanoi is 04, and HCMC 08.

Email is getting cheaper (from Ð150/min in Hanoi, Ð2000/min in Sapa!), with connection possible in most traveller areas, though very slow in more remote spots.

ACTIVITIES
Scuba diving

The easiest place to dive is off the isles around Nha Trang, though dynamite fishing has spoilt most of the coral. Equipment hire and double boat dive cost from $50. Phu Quoc Island (off the Cambodian coast) is much better and is just starting to develop, with a few hotels renting equipment.

Shopping

Trademark conical hats make great, cheap souvenirs. Tailoring is very reasonable as are decent silks and other fabrics, though you'll need to bargain and examine the quality carefully. Vietnam is a bootleg bargain basement selling what may be the world's cheapest music CDs at around Đ10–12,000.

FURTHER INFORMATION
Advice and guide books

Basic travel information and travel advice can be found through traveller cafés. Although most really want to sell you a tour, many such cafés have noticeboards, and the backpacker sitting beside you has probably just been where you want to go. However, it can often be difficult to get past the 'it's in the book' attitude: an underlying assumption being that you're carrying the Lonely Planet *Vietnam* guide. Actually there is a fair choice of other guides too, including a reliable Rough Guide and several options in French. Trailblazer's *Vietnam by Rail* is aimed at those sticking to the tracks.

There is a fair chance of swapping guide books in Hanoi, Sapa or Saigon guesthouses or cafés – Lonely Planet *China* guides have been sighted in the Green Bamboo book swap in Hanoi. The capital also has a 'Lonely Planet Bookshop': it's nothing whatever to do with the travel publisher, but is helpful and reasonably well stocked.

City street peddlers all seem to have the same selection of cheap photocopied books: Lonely Planet's *Vietnamese Phrasebook* ($1), Graham Greene's *The Quiet American* ($3) and *The Sorrow of War*. Bookstores and street stalls also sell coffee-table picture books and various background works. Try looking near the GPO in any town.

Maps

Decent city maps of Hanoi, Saigon and Hue, are sold by roaming map-salesmen who will probably leap on you before you have a chance to look for them. A rare selection of detailed, French-era topographical maps is sold from an unassuming stall at 61 Trang Tien St, Hanoi, in an alley beside the Bodega Café. These maps are not on show so ask specifically. While clearly out of date, they remain the most useful maps available for motorbike explorations in the north.

CAO DAI CATHEDRAL NEAR TAY NINH

> ❏ **Cao Dai – the religion**
> Uniquely Vietnamese, some two million followers of Cao Dai-ism revere a selection of great prophets from Buddha, Lao-Tsu and Jesus to Victor Hugo.
>
> Synthesized as a religion by 1920s' mystic Ngo Minh Chieu it became a major force in South Vietnam especially before the 1975 communist takeover. The religion uses an all-seeing eye/triangle symbol, eg on a great, jade sphere in the brilliantly-gaudy main cathedral, Tay Ninh. The design is uncannily similar to the equivalent on a US$1 bill.

❑ Meeting the locals

● **The people** Almost every Vietnamese adult can, and often will, share stories of bravery and fortitude from the decades of strife their country endured in the years of anti-colonial war. The suffering, destruction and death that America and France caused in this sliver of South-East Asia is unfathomable. And yet there seems to be no discrimination against visitors from those countries. The forgiving attitude of the local people is, in itself, a reason to make the trip. One traveller whose father had bombed Vietnam as a US Air Force pilot shared his amazement as he sat in a Hanoi café: 'a smiling old woman who lost every single member of her family brought me free cups of tea waving away the bad memories. "That was then. We take care of each other now" she said!'.

Don't overlook the discreet pressure on local people that remains in what is still (despite the veneer of 'new thinking') a communist country. Discussion of political topics should be broached sensitively.

● **Language** Although written in a Latin script, spoken Vietnamese has many regional dialects and six accent tones which makes it a difficult language to pick up. In the north, 'r', 'gi', the uncrossed 'd' and 'z' are all pronounced like an English 'z'. These sounds become more like the English transliteration as you head south. The crossed 'Đ' is a hard, English-style 'd'.

Some phrases in Vietnamese (transliterated as they sounded to me; official Vietnamese in parentheses):

Hello – *Sin chao [xin chao]*
How are you? – *(An) ko kwé kong? [(Anh) có khoûe khoâng]*
Fine – *Ko kwe [Cou khoûe]*
And you? – *Kon ban? [Con baïn]*
Thank you <u>very much</u> – *Kam-ern <u>zat new</u> [cam on <u>rat nhieu</u>]*
No worries – *Kong ko zee [Khoâng cou gi]*
Delicious – *Ngon lam [Ngoân Laém]*
How much is it? – *Zar bao new? [Gia bao nhieu?]*
Too expensive – *Dut kwa [Naet qua]*

Useful websites

⌨ www.sinhcafe.com/english_info/info_opentour.htm has up-to-date details of the famous hop-on hop-off bus ticket, but there's lots more to the site – eg rail timetables and prices (click 'Transports').

⌨ www.queencafe.com.vn/index1.htm is the site of one of Sinh's main competitors, with details of numerous tours if you can wait for the slow download!

⌨ http://icarus.shu.edu/gallery/V_Portfolio/ is a site of great photos with a mechanism for viewers to comment or ask questions inspired by what they see.

⌨ http://vietnamtourism.hypermart.net/visa.htm gives you a printable visa application form if you plan to apply in the US.

⌨ http://grunt.space.swri.edu/visit.htm is an excellent resource with loads of Vietnam pictures, great maps and aerial photos, travel reports, language resources etc and is of particular relevance to those interested in the American war angle.

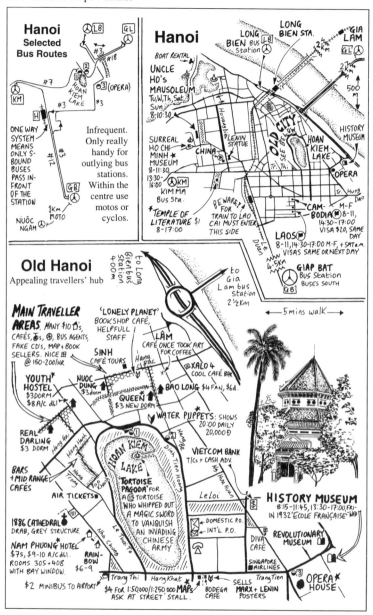

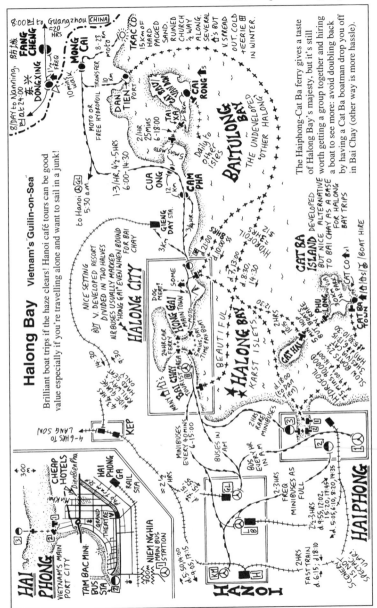

Halong Bay Vietnam's "Guilin-on-Sea"

Brilliant boat trips if the haze clears! Hanoi café tours can be good value especially if you're travelling alone and want to sail in a junk!

The Haiphong-Cat Ba ferry gives a taste of Halong Bay's majesty, but it's still worth getting a group together and hiring a boat to see more: avoid doubling back by having a Cat Ba boatman drop you off in Bai Chay (other way is more hassle).

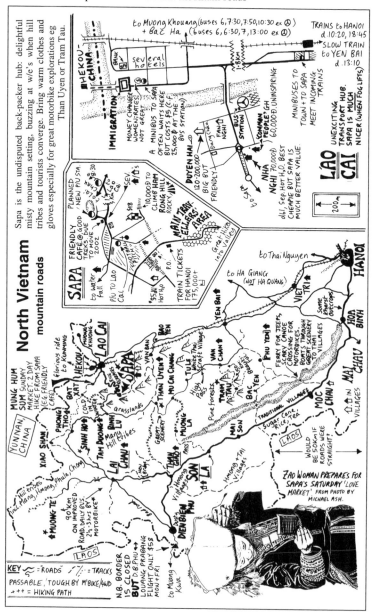

North Vietnam
mountain roads

Sapa is the undisputed back-packer hub: delightful misty mountain setting, buzzing at w/e's when hill tribes and tourists converge. Bring warm clothes and gloves especially for great motorbike explorations eg Than Uyen or Tram Tau.

to Muong Khouang (buses 6, 7:30, 7:50, 10:30 ex Ⓧ)
+ Bac Ha (buses 6, 6:30, 7, 13:00 ex ①)

HEKOU CHINA

several hotels

IMMIGRATION

Money changers women x rates! Not great

A MINIBUS TO SAPA OR TEN WAITS HERE BUT COSTS ₱5 (c.f. 25,000₫ AT THE BUS STATION)

DUYEN HAI 120-200,000₫ BIG BUT FRIENDLY

NHA NGHI (70,000₫)

TRAINS to HANOI d. 10:20, 18:45

SLOW TRAIN to YEN BAI d. 13:10

BUS STATION

CONG PEOPLE'S CH 60,000₫ UNINSPIRING

FAN NGHI

MINIBUSES TO TOWN + TO SAPA MEET INCOMING TRAINS

LAO CAI
UNEXCITING TRANSPORT HUB. SAPA IS MUCH NICER (WHEN FOG LIFTS)

d. Ul, Sep hot H.O. BEST CHEAPE BUT SAPA IS MUCH BETTER VALUE

⟷ 200m ⟷

SAPA
FRIENDLY TREKS @ GOOD E. FRIENDLY CAFE

PLANNED NEW RLY STA.

GOOD CAFE, bve 2002

10,000₫ TO CLIMB HAM RONG HILL (ROCKY)

MAIN TRAVELLERS' AREA

Great hikes into valley

to water fall

Plu Tu Lao Cai

TRAIN TICKETS FOR HANOI 175,000₫

to Thai Nguyen

to Ha Giang (NOT HA QUANG)

YEN BAI

VIET TRI

HANOI

Some khurst outcrops

MUONG HUM SUM SUNDAY MARKET. 2 DAY HIKE FROM SAPA (E.G. FRIENDLY CAFE)

glorious ride to Kunming

YUNNAN, CHINA

XIAO SHAN

PHONG THO

BAT XAT

SINH HO*

TAM DUONG

BINH LU

LAO CAI

HEKOU

SAPA

grasslands

COLD

THAN UYEN

BAO YEN

MU CANG CHAI

TULE White Thai Tribe Village

VAN CHAN

PHU YEN

Ferry for Jeeps, scary canoe crossing for motorbikes. BOATS THROUGH GREAT SCENERY TO TRAM VILLAGES

HOA BINH

High Pass

TRAM TAU

BAC YEN

TRADITIONAL VILLAGES

MOC CHAU

Ⓓ IN VILLAGES

MAI CHAU

Pine forests

LAI CHAU

Hill tribes Tai, Mang, Hmong, Phula Chong

MUONG TE

90km ON IMPROVED ROAD DAILY BUS 2½-3 hrs BY MOTORBIKE

MUONG LA

GREAT SCENERY

THAN UYEN

MAI SON

SON LA

Sugar Cane, Rice, tea

Hmong + Tai villages

LAOS

WOULD BE 50km IF ROADS WERE STRAIGHT!

Hmong Village

DIEN BIEN PHU

N.B. BORDER IS CLOSED BUT D.B.PHU → LOUANG PRABANG FLIGHT ONLY $58 MON→FRI

to Muong Kwa

KEY ∿ = ROADS ⁄⁄ = TRACKS
PASSABLE, TOUGH BY M'BIKE/4WD
×++ = HIKING PATH

ZAO WOMAN PREPARES FOR SAPA'S SATURDAY 'LOVE MARKET' FROM PHOTO BY MICHAEL ASH.

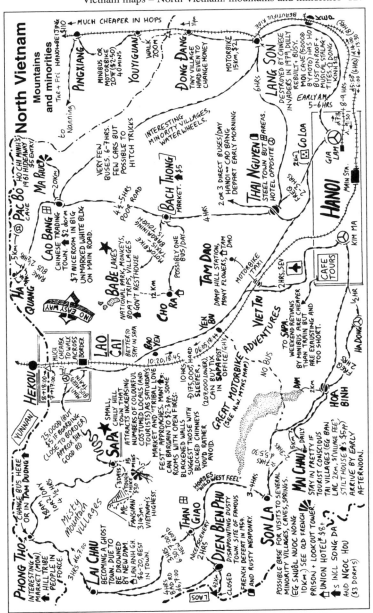

North Vietnam
Mountains and minorities

← MUCH CHEAPER IN HOPS

Tue + Fri HANOI→BEIJING $110

BEAUTIFUL RIDE

PINGXIANG — MINIBUS OR MOTORBIKE 20₫ ($2-50) 40 MINS

YOUYIGUAN WALK 200m

DONG DANG — TINY VILLAGE. HARD EVEN TO CHANGE MONEY. MOTORBIKE 15km, $2

11pm ↓

to Nanning

LANG SON DESTROYED BY CHINESE INVADERS IN 1979, DULLY REBUILT, BUSY. MOI CAVE (5000₫) BY MOTO) HAS HO BUST ON ROOF TYRES & MUSICAL STALAC TITES 1 DONG KINH 3₫

6HRS

EARLY AM 5-6 HRS

INTERESTING MINORITY VILLAGES, WATERWHEELS.

@PAC BO CAVE HO CHI MINH'S 1961 HIDEAWAY ($5 ENTRY)

MA PHUC 20km

VERY FEW BUSES 6-7HRS. FEW CARS BUT POSSIBLE TO HITCH TRUCKS

BACH THONG MARKET. $5

2 OR 3 DIRECT BUSES/DAY HANOI↔CAO BANG DEPART EARLY MORNING

THAI NGUYEN STEEL TOWN BUT BARES. HOTEL OPPOSITE @

4½-5HRS POOR ROAD

CAO BANG CHINESE TRADING TOWN. $2 DORM $7 NICE ROOM IN BIG UNMARKED WHITE BLDG ON MAIN ROAD.

MOTORBIKE TAXI BARGAINING TOUGH

BABE LAKES ★ NATIONAL PARK, MONKEYS, BOAT TRIPS, GOVT RESTHOUSE

CHO RA 12 Km

POSSIBLY ONE BUS/DAY

TAM DAO 1 TAM DAO DAMP HILL STATION, MANY FLOWERS,

CO LOA 2km

HANOI GIA LAM Main Sta. KIM MA

8-9 HRS 45:50 (SHG) 414-15:30 6:00 (SHG) KINH 31₫

MOTORBIKE TAXI 2HRS, 5EV

HA QUANG 5km RARE BUS HOUR

NO EASY WAY

LAO CAI BETTER TO STAY IN SAPA

HEKOU MUCH NEARER TO WALK ACROSS BORDER

25,000₫ BUS HERE $5 IF BOARDING CLOSE TO BORDER APPROX 1HR GOOD RD

8-11:00 ← 12:30→ MUCH NEARER TO

YEN BAI 10:20, 18:45 06:05, 18:44

10 HRS ←₫175,000) HARD SLEEPER,

₫207,000 LOWER (207,000₫) BEST. CAN BUY TIX IN SAPA OFFICE (24HR)

VIET TRI

GREAT MOTORBIKE ADVENTURES (SEE N.W. MTNS MAP)

TO SAPA. WEEKEND RETURNS BY MINIBUS ARE CHEAPER THAN TRAIN BUT ARE EXHAUSTING AND TOO SHORT.

HADONG ½ HR

CAFE TOURS

NO BUS

HOA BINH 2km

YUNNAN!

SAPA ★ SMALL, CHILLY HILL TOWN THAT ATTRACTS INCREASING NUMBERS OF COLOURFUL COSTUMED LOCALS (AND TOURISTS). AS SATURDAY MARKET AND SUN LOVE FEST APPROACHES, MANY ₫'s CAN BARGAIN TO 2-3pm. SOME ROOMS WITH OPEN FIRES: SUGGEST THOSE WITH BLACKENED WALLS BLOCKED CHIMNEYS YOU'D RATHER AVOID.

HORSES WILD WEST FEEL

MAI CHAU STAY IN PRETTY IF TOURIST CONSCIOUS TAI VILLAGES (EG BAN LAC 2km, $1 VILLAGE FEE) STILT HOUSE $'s $5pp) ARRIVE BY EARLY AFTERNOON.

2½ HRS 09:55, 13:30 5km

3-4 HRS

PHONG THO INTERESTING MARKET (MON). HILL TRIBE PEOPLE IN FORCE.

CHANGE BUS HERE OR IN TAM DUONG

8AM A DAY 10-12 HRS 4 1½ HRS

3HRS 06,7:00

Misty Mountain Villages

3 DAYS HIKE

ME- $30 FANSIPAN 3143m VIETNAM'S HIGHEST.

1½ TOWER 15 MINS

LAI CHAU BECOMING A GHOST TOWN. DUE TO BE DROWNED BY NEW DAM. 1 LAN ANH GH. $6-20, BEST IN TOWN.

3HR, 07:00 BAD RD

THAN GIAO NICE SCENERY

DIEN BIEN PHU DISAPPEARING DUSTY TOWN. SITE OF FAMOUS FRENCH DEFEAT IN 1954. CLOSED 1 AND RUSTY WEAPONRY.

42km

4 HRS BAD RD 06,7:00

SON LA POSSIBLE BASE FOR VISITS TO SEVERAL MINORITY VILLAGES, CAVES, SPRINGS. (EG SNOOL NUOC NONG 10km) SEE OLD FRENCH PRISON + LOOKOUT TOWER 1 UNION HOTEL $8+ S INCL SONG DA AND NGOC HOU (33 DORMS)

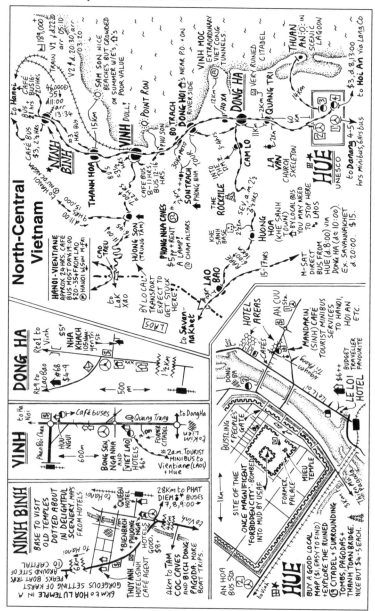

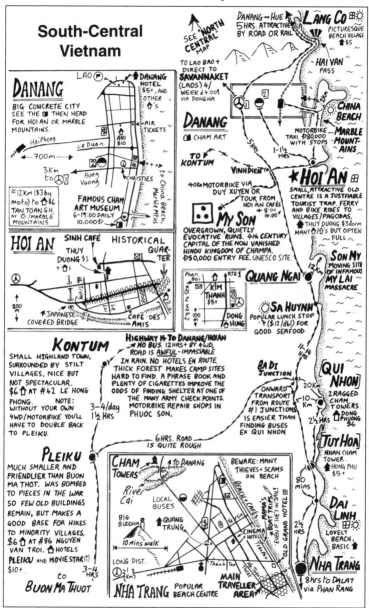

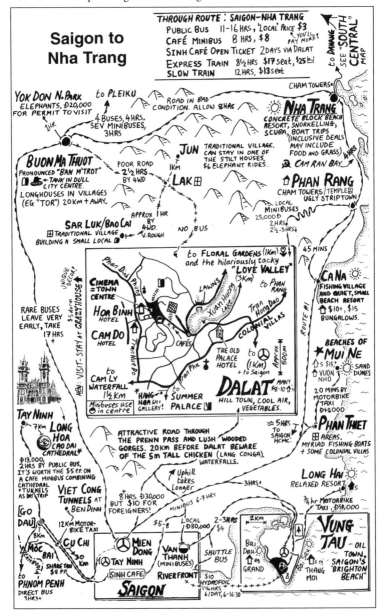

Saigon to Nha Trang

THROUGH ROUTE : SAIGON–NHA TRANG
PUBLIC BUS   11–16 HRS, 'LOCAL' PRICE $3
CAFÉ MINIBUS   8 HRS, $8   YOU'LL PAY MORE!
SINH CAFÉ OPEN TICKET 2 DAYS VIA DALAT
EXPRESS TRAIN   8½ HRS $17 seat, $25
SLOW TRAIN   12 HRS, $13 seat

to DANANG
SEE "SOUTH CENTRAL" MAP

CHAM TOWERS

YOK DON N. PARK
ELEPHANTS, Đ20,000
FOR PERMIT TO VISIT
1 HR

to PLEIKU

ROAD IN BAD
CONDITION. ALLOW 8 HRS

Nha Trang
CONCRETE BLOCK BEACH
RESORT, SNORKELLING,
SCUBA, BOAT TRIPS
(INCLUSIVE DEALS
MAY INCLUDE
FOOD AND GRASS)

4 BUSES, 4 HRS.
SEV MINIBUSES,
3 HRS

JUN   TRADITIONAL VILLAGE.
CAN STAY IN ONE OF
THE STILT HOUSES.
$6 ELEPHANT RIDES.
1 KM

CAM RAN BAY   4 HRS

BUON MA THUOT
PRONOUNCED "BAN M'TROT"
+ TANK IN DULL
CITY CENTRE
LONGHOUSES IN VILLAGES
(EG "TOR") 20 KM + AWAY.

POOR ROAD
2½ HRS
BY 4WD

LAK

PHAN RANG
CHAM TOWERS / TEMPLE
UGLY STRIPTOWN

LOCAL
MINIBUSES
25,000Đ
2 HRS
2½–3 HRS+

SAR LUK / BAO CAI
TRADITIONAL VILLAGE
BUILDING A SMALL LOCAL

APPROX 1 HR
BY
4WD
V. ROUGH

NO BUS

45 MINS

to FLORAL GARDENS (1KM)
and the hilariously tacky
"LOVE VALLEY"
(3KM)

Ca Na
FISHING VILLAGE
AND QUIET, SMALL
BEACH RESORT
$10+, $15
BUNGALOWS

RARE BUSES
LEAVE VERY
EARLY, TAKE
17 +

to PHAN
RANG

Phan Dinh Phung

CINEMA
= TOWN
CENTRE

LAWNS

XUAN HUONG LAKE

COLONIAL VILLAS

Tran Hung Dao

ROUTE #1

UNIQUE DECOR!

NB: VISIT - STAY AT CRAZYHOUSE

$5 dorm $15room

HOA BINH
HOTEL

CAM DO
HOTEL

Tran Hung Dao

to PHAN
RANG

Approx
500m

BEACHES OF
MUI NE
$15, $5+
VUON
NHO
SAND
DUNES

CAFÉS

Tran Hieu Do

THE OLD
PALACE
HOTEL

to
(1KM)
+ to SAIGON

20 MINS BY
MOTORBIKE
TAXI
Đ40000

to
CAM LY
WATERFALL
1½ KM

Tran Phu

DALAT MANY
$8–10 +
HILL TOWN, COOL AIR,
VEGETABLES.

MINIBUSES USE
in centre

HANG
NGA
GALLERY!

**SUMMER
PALACE**

PHAN THIET
AREAS.
MYRIAD FISHING BOATS
+ SOME COLONIAL VILLAS

TAY NINH
7 KM **LONG
HOA**
CAO DAI
CATHEDRAL
Đ13,000,
2 HRS BY PUBLIC BUS.
IT'S WORTH THE $5 P.P. ON
A CAFÉ MINIBUS COMBINING
CATHEDRAL
+ TUNNELS
AS DAY TRIP

ATTRACTIVE ROAD THROUGH
THE PRENN PASS AND LUSH WOODED
GORGES. 20 KM BEFORE DALAT BEWARE
OF THE 5m TALL CHICKEN (LANG CONGA).
WATERFALLS.

5 HRS
TO
SAIGON/
HCMC

LONG HAI
RELAXED RESORT

[GO
DAU]
8 KM

**VIET CONG
TUNNELS** AT
BEN DINH

Uphill
takes
longer

3 HRS+

¾ hr MOTORBIKE
TAXI, Đ58,000

12 KM MOTOR-
BIKE TAXI

8 HRS Đ30,000
BUT $10 FOR
FOREIGNERS!

MINIBUS 6–7 HRS

2 KM

**VUNG
TAU** – OIL
TOWN,
SAIGON'S
'BRIGHTON
BEACH"

**MOC
BAI**
SHARE TAXI
$8 P.P.

CU CHI
30
KM

$5–8

LOCAL
Đ80,000

2–3 HRS
$4

Bai
Dau

GRAND

1 S
THANG
MOI

to
PHNOM PENH
DIRECT BUS
9 HRS+

**MIEN
DONG**

**VAN
THANH**
(MINIBUSES)

SHUTTLE
BUS

$10
HYDROFOIL
1¼–4 HRS
6/DAY, 6–16:30

TAY NINH

[SINH CAFÉ]

RIVERFRONT

SAIGON

Saigon
(Ho Chi Minh City)

Saigon (shown above) combined with Cholon (appealing old Chinese quarter) forms Ho Chi Minh City. This bustling metropolis is Vietnam's economic engine and is at the cutting edge of the country's 'new thinking'. If Hanoi is like a grandfather's house, dusty but full of interesting bits and pieces, then Saigon is like a college student's flat – open, active, and full of life. There are limited tourist sites but the city is well set up for budget travellers and is a place that grows on those who stay for more than a few days.

Transport

Buses heading north use the Mien Dong bus station. Towards the Cambodian border use the Tay Ninh bus station. For the Mekong Delta use Cholon Tay (especially for Mytho) or Mien Tay bus stations. Local regional buses eg from Vung Tau, operate out of Van Thanh stn. All of these departure points are connected by city bus to Ben Than Market, or you can hop on a motorcycle taxi for $1 or so from the Pham Ngu Lao 'traveller ghetto'. Taxis from the airport cost $5+ but if you walk five minutes to the main road you can hop on a $1-2 moto.

Mekong Delta transportation

'Café' tours rush from town to riverside town for a very reasonable price. However, as there's nothing that really rates as a sight, you may feel happier retiring to a random town that takes your fancy and getting to know it. Any larger town will have its riverside cameos and cafés and getting around is fairly easy.

Public buses seem to go from everywhere to everywhere else except from where you happen to be. If so, head onto the main highway (usually 2-3km from town centres) and flag one down. Beware that roads tend to flood in summer. More relaxing/frustrating depending on your schedule are the inter-town ferries. Waterways outnumber roads and very slow boats go almost anywhere – if there appears to be no service you're probably at the wrong pier. Some docks are well out of town. Take food for the journey and be prepared to arrive whenever.

Chartering a boat is worthwhile as a way to cruise the backwaters at your own pace, and can be very cheaply done if you find an unofficial boatman. Police want all foreigners to use official (pricey) tourist craft claiming (often justifiably) that local boats are unsafe. So don't be overly alarmed if the 'boat' you've hired initially turns out to be a motorbike whisking you off to a secluded jetty beyond official view. My Tho is most accustomed to tourists and there are (too) many boat touts ready to help you. In Ben Tre things are more relaxed and the waterways are more scenic. Bargain carefully.

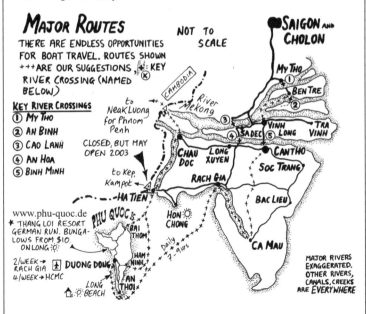

Where does the boat to .... leave from? = *O dau don tau be di ....?*

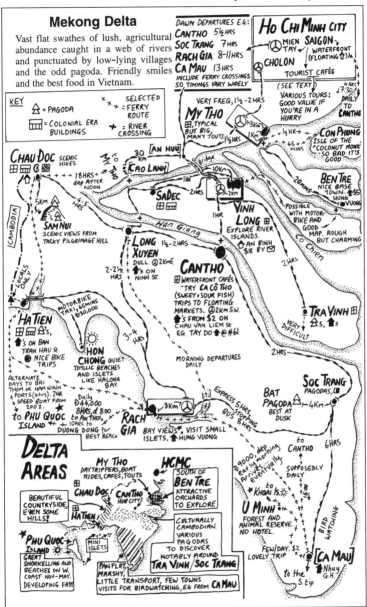

Mekong Delta

Vast flat swathes of lush, agricultural abundance caught in a web of rivers and punctuated by low-lying villages and the odd pagoda. Friendly smiles and the best food in Vietnam.

DAWN DEPARTURES E.G.:
CANTHO 5½HRS
SOC TRANG 7HRS
RACH GIA 8-11HRS
CA MAU 13HRS
INCLUDE FERRY CROSSINGS SO TIMINGS VARY WIDELY

HO CHI MINH CITY
MIEN SAIGON
TAY WATERFRONT (FLOATING ⌂)
CHOLON TOURIST CAFÉS (SEE TEXT)
4 HRS 17:30 DAILY TO CANTHO

VARIOUS TOURS: GOOD VALUE IF YOU'RE IN A HURRY

KEY
⌂ = PAGODA
▥ = COLONIAL ERA BUILDINGS
× × ⁺ ⁺ = SELECTED FERRY ROUTE
✚ = RIVER CROSSING

VERY FREQ, 1½-2HRS
MY THO
▥, TYPICAL BUT BIG, MANY TOUTS 1½HRS
1 KM ½HR
CON PHUNG ISLE OF THE "COCONUT MONK" "SO BAD IT'S GOOD"
45 MINS

[AN HUU]
30 KM
[CAO LANH]
BRIDGE
10KM
20MINS
BEN TRE NICE BASE TOWN. 45 HUNG VUONG

CHAU DOC SCENIC HIKES
▥ ⌂ ⌂
18HRS+ dep AFTER NOON
4-5
5KM
1HR
SADEC ▥▥
1HR
2HRS ~2km
VINH LONG ▥ Explore River Islands.
⌂ AN BINH $8 BY ⌂

POSSIBLE WITH MOTORBIKE AND GOOD MAP. ROUGH BUT CHARMING
Co Chien
2HRS

CAMBODIA
SAM NUI SCENIC VIEWS FROM TACKY PILGRIMAGE HILL
LOCALS ONLY
Han Giang
LONG 1½-2HRS XUYEN DULL. ⌂2kmE. ⌂'S ON NINH ST.
2-2½ HRS
CANTHO ▥ WATERFRONT CAFÉS -TRY CA CÔ THO (SWEET+SOUR FISH) TRIPS TO FLOATING MARKETS. ⌂2km S.W. ⌂'S FROM $2 ON CHAU VAN LIEM St EG. TAY DO ⌂ @ #61
TRA VINH ▥ ⌂s, ⌂s
VERY DIFFICULT

HA TIEN ▥ ▥ ⌂'s
⌂'s ON BAN TRAN HAU St. ● NICE BIKE TRIPS
MOTORBIKE TAXI, 65MINS ₫30,000
3-4 HRS
HON CHONG QUIET IDYLLIC BEACHES AND ISLETS LIKE HALONG BAY.
2HRS
SOC TRANG PAGODAS, ⌂
⌂ -4KM
BAT PAGODA ⌂ BEST AT DUSK

ALTERNATE DAYS TO BAI THOM or HAM NINH PORTS (4HRS). 2HR SPEED BOAT FROM 2002. ★
to PHU QUOC ISLAND
Daily ₫44,000 8HRS, d 8:00 to AN THOI, 10HRS to DUONG DONG for BEST BEACH
3KM
RACH GIA BAY VIEWS, VISIT SMALL ISLETS. ⌂ HUNG VUONG
MORNING DEPARTURES DAILY
EXPRESS 5HRS STOPPING BUS 8HRS
to CANTHO
₫9000 dep EARLY MORNING. ARRIVE EVENTUALLY.
SUPPOSEDLY DAILY
6HRS
BIRD WATCHING

DELTA AREAS
MY THO DAYTRIPPERS, BOAT RIDES, CAFÉS, TOUTS
HCMC
SOUTH OF BEN TRE ATTRACTIVE ORCHARDS TO EXPLORE
to KHOAI Is.

BEAUTIFUL COUNTRYSIDE EVEN SOME HILLS!
CHAU DOC ▥ CANTHO HUB CITY!
HA TIEN !
CULTURALLY CAMBODIAN. VARIOUS PAGODAS TO DISCOVER NOTABLY AROUND TRA VINH / SOC TRANG
U MINH FOREST AND ANIMAL RESERVE. NO HOTEL.
FEW/DAY. $2 LOVELY TRIP
to the S. tip
[CA MAU] NHUY G.H.

★ PHU QUOC ISLAND
GREAT SNORKELLING AND BEACHES ON W. COAST NOV-MAY. DEVELOPING FAST
MINI ISLETS
PAN FLAT, MARSHY, LITTLE TRANSPORT, FEW TOWNS VISITS FOR BIRDWATCHING, EG FROM CA MAU

YUNNAN
(SOUTH-WEST CHINA)

Introduction

By Chinese standards it's a quaint, country backwater. But coming from Vietnam or particularly from Laos, entering Yunnan is like walking into the future.

Towns glisten with new glass towers, many roads are newly paved, transport is frequent and efficient and across the spectrum, the population is looking increasingly prosperous: from traditional-minded Dai villagers, to meditative Naxi song-bird rearers to the trendy, dyed-red-headed Han youths in the nightclubs of Kunming.

For once-sleepy market towns such as Jing Hong, the transformation in the last decade has been nothing short of astonishing. While language remains a significant barrier and phlegm-flinging locals still cough their cacophonous choruses, China is no longer the dour, drab, unfriendly tourist destination it was in the late 1980s. Particularly in the cities the internet generation is all smiles, optimism and enthusiasm for English-language conversation.

Yunnan is included in this book for two main reasons: firstly, because many of the people of southern Yunnan are culturally almost identical to those across the border in Laos, and secondly because Yunnan closes a northern loop between Laos and Vietnam, thus multiplying the possibilities for overland budget travellers. It is also an extraordinarily varied province stretching from the fringes of Tibet to the relatively well-conserved rainforests of Xishuangbanna via traveller favourite Dali and marvellous Lijiang, China's most picturesque old city. And unlike east-coast China it's all possible on a tight budget.

❏ **Country ratings – Yunnan**
● **Expense $$** – it's possible to live very cheaply if you avoid the cities.
● **Value for money** ★★★★☆ Vastly cheaper than east-coast China. Beds are available almost anywhere for $2, or $5 in big cities such as Kunming. Occasionally you will pay more if there's a 'no foreigner' rule in the cheapest places. Food and transport is reliable and cheap.
● **Getting around** ★★★★☆ Buses and minibuses go almost everywhere with considerable frequency, and although roads are slow and winding, they are being rapidly upgraded. The biggest problem is reading the destination characters.
● **English spoken** ★★☆☆☆ OK in Dali, Lijiang and Kunming. Slowly improving elsewhere but still very tough in rural areas. Learn to spot Chinese characters.
● **Woman alone** ★★★★☆ Generally hassle free.
● **For vegetarians** ★★★☆☆ Lots of great food though ascertaining the full ingredients can be tough.

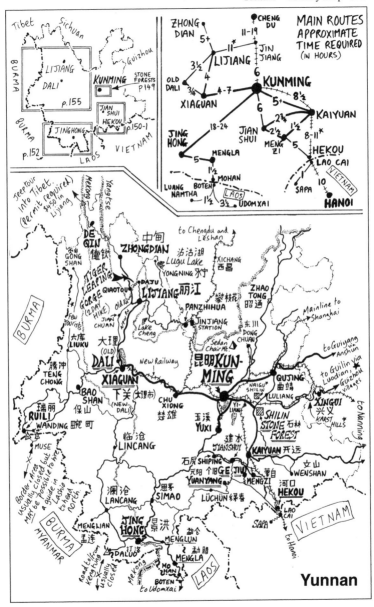

Yunnan

❏ **Essential information for travellers – Yunnan**
● **Visa** Chinese visa required but easy to procure in South-East Asia/Hong Kong.
Around $30 for a one-month stay (valid for three months, takes about four days), or
typically double the price for a same/next day issue. Extensions are generally straightforward. Double-entry visas are often possible for 50–110% extra, worth considering
if you plan an attempt to cross into Burma overland.
● **Currency** Yuan. US$1=8.27Y. Stable. May soon be globally convertible.
● **Time zone** 8 hours ahead of GMT, ¹/₂hr ahead of Thailand and Vietnam, 1¹/₂hrs
ahead of Burma.
● **Religious tone** Mildly Buddhist at heart: Tibetan style in north, Burmese or Thai
in south.
● **Health factors** Increasingly China, including Yunnan, has the infrastructure of a
first-world nation. Even the infamous toilets are improving – well some of them.
Unless travelling in August to very remote areas, malaria is not a serious concern.
● **Special dangers** A few lone trekkers have been robbed in the otherwise idyllic
parks (eg Tiger Leaping Gorge), but generally Yunnan is very safe.
● **Social conventions** Most ethnic groups have their own foibles – be observant
and sensitive. Avoid talking to locals while wearing sunglasses. Shorts and sleeveless
shirts are inappropriate in some areas.
● **Key tips** Don't be put-off by the Chinese script. Even though you can't expect to
learn all the characters, try to spot key differences – it makes finding buses, reading
maps etc much easier. Regional atlases sold cheaply in local bookshops help with
character spotting and asking help reading the place names can make for an easy con-
versational gambit with friendly locals.
   A tent is useful for walks into the mountains. Ad hoc exploration is simple – on
many roads there are between two and eight minibuses an hour so hop-on hop-off visits to random villages don't mean sacrificing a whole day as it would in Laos. If you
don't like a place just carry on to the next.
● **Traveller hubs** Compared to Thailand or Laos, travellers are relatively thin on the
ground with the greatest concentration in Old Dali, certain guesthouses in Lijiang and
Kunming ('Hump' and the Camelia Hotel) plus the Mekong and Lemongrass cafés in
Jing Hong.

HIGHLIGHTS

Lijiang may be swarming with local tourists and surrounded by a soulless mod-
ern city, but the old town remains utterly charming – my favourite place in all of
China. The mountain-tickled views across the traditional rooftops are hard to beat.
And at dawn you'll still see Naxi women washing the cobbled alleyways as their
husbands pop out with the family song bird in a felt-covered cage.
   To the north, **Tiger Leaping Gorge** is a great trek with traveller-friendly hostels midway, you can visit **Tibetan monks** near Zhongdian, see 'Shangri La' at
Deqin and with luck (and a lot of money) you just might even make it across into
Tibet proper. **Dali** is another ancient city and has Yunnan's only real backpacker
enclave but the town is less complete than Lijiang. Nearby **Lake Erhai** is attractive enough, but since there's been considerable building in recent years the villages aren't as scenically backward as you might expect.

❑ Geo-political information – Yunnan

Population: 42 million

Area: 394,000 sq km (ie three times the size of England) of which a quarter is forested.

Capital: Kunming (870,000) but 3.5 million including those in the surrounding county.

Other major cities: Yuxi (350,000 and growing rapidly), Kaiyuan (190,000), Gejiu (163,000), Qujing (140,000), Xiaguan (130,000), Zhaotong (110,000).

GNP per capita: $3600 is the quoted average for China. Seems low – certainly Yunnan appears considerably wealthier than neighbouring Laos or Burma.

Currency history: Yuan/US$1: – April 2002: 8.29Y, May 2001: 8.35Y, Feb 1997: 8.29Y, June 1994: 8.44Y. Stable and liable to strengthen.

Major exports/economy: Minerals (lead, copper, zinc, tin, marble), tobacco, rubber, tropical plants, medicines, sugar, electronics, textiles.

Ethnic mix: Extremely complex with 25 main ethnic groups (Yi, Mao, Bai, Hani, Dai (all over one million), Liso (600,000), Lahu (400,000), Naxi (300,000).

Official language: Putonghua (Mandarin Chinese) but many tribal languages spoken in villages.

Religious mix: Predominantly Buddhist.

Landmarks of Yunnan history: **109BC**: Imperial Chinese armies crushed the two-century-old kingdom of Dian (Kunming) **AD740s/750s**: The principality of Nanzhao (based at Dali) became increasingly powerful and independent. **902**: Nanzhao split by ethnic revolts. **1279**: Dali captured by Kublai Khan, development of Jianshui. **1382** Chinese complete re-conquest of Yunnan, major influx of Han Chinese settlers. **1427**: Battles with the Trân dynasty of Vietnam. **1647**: Kunming became capital of the Southern Ming empire and latterly of the Zhou dynasty following the takeover by military governor Wu San Gui. Only fully re-integrated into the Chinese empire in the 1720s. **1780s** Chinese tussles with Burma and Vietnam backfired as many Imperial soldiers contracted malaria and became addicted to opium taken originally as a palliative. **1839–42** and **56–60** Opium wars as France and Britain forced China to open its ports and legalize the narcotics trade. Meanwhile (**1855–73**) major Muslim and Yi insurrections in Yunnan were brutally repressed with as much as half the population killed!! **1898** China carved into zones of influence by the European powers. **1898–1910** Yunnan dominated by France who had the Kunming–Hanoi railway built. Having stopped short of annexation, the French consul in Mengzi encouraged Chinese republican rebels. **1912**: China declared a republic by Sun Yat Sen. **1915** French influence withered thanks to WWII, Yunnan briefly declared independence. **1927–49** PCC communist forces growing threat to re-united Kuomintang republican China (despite anti-Japanese alliance during WWII). Kuomintang forces eventually pushed back into Yunnan/Sechuan, finally retreating into the Golden Triangle and becoming future drug barons. **1954** Yunnan used as a supply base for the anti-French Viet-minh victory at Dien Bien Phu. **1966–76** Cultural revolution set out to destroy traditional society, large exodus of hill tribes to Vietnam and Laos. **1970** Earthquake killed 15,000!! **1979** Brief border war with Vietnam only formally resolved in 1990. **1989** Tiananmen Square massacre in Beijing. **1990s** Rapid commercialization of China, opening of trade with Burma, Laos and Vietnam, extraordinary modernization of Yunnan's cities and transport infrastructure. **1996** Earthquake killed 228 and severely damaged old Lijiang (since repaired remarkably tastefully).

Leaders: Chinese President is Jiang Zemin, Prime Minister is Zhu Ronji.

Pressing political issues: Drug smuggling from Burma. Democracy versus economic development in China. The strict 'one child' policy for Han Chinese doesn't apply to minority ethnic groups in Yunnan.

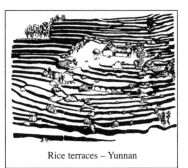

Rice terraces – Yunnan

Bustling **Kunming**, the capital, is not an attraction in itself but while you're applying for Burmese or Lao visas there are some OK cafés near the university and even salsa classes at 'Hump'! **Shilin**, the rather pricey 'Stone Forest' is weird and memorable if you can see it without all the other people, so either stay the night and explore once the tour buses have gone or go to nearby Naigu Shilin instead.

Sweaty southern Yunnan has some very attractive yet accessible '**hilltribe' villages** around Mengla (less kitchy than those of the tourist loop nearer Jing Hong). **Jianshui** is a little-visited historic city with a certain charm and around Yuanyang little hamlets are set amid **impressive rice terraces** – great places to sit and smoke giant bamboo bong-pipes with Miao villagers.

There's great scope for getting well off the tourist circuit – not that there are many Westerners anyway. One tempting route would be the long, reputedly beautiful, dead-end road to Gongshan and beyond – close to the Burmese border.

WHEN TO GO

The tropical forests of southern Yunnan (on the same latitude as Calcutta) are best visited between November and February, when the weather is cool(er) though the hot, humid summers are just about bearable. Rain forests need rain, which can fall at any time, though not usually for prolonged periods. Kunming has cool winter nights and slightly sweaty days. Though Dali and Lijiang are overlooked by high mountains, winters in either are crisp but not as cold as you might think. The travellers' scene remains year-round. Zhongdian is appreciably colder and you can get snowed in for days, from the end of October.

The best time to attempt the road into Tibet is April: winter snows should be cleared but summer rain has yet to cause landslides. In the south, the 'Water Splashing Festival' (April 15th) is a big tourist circus these days with accommodation prices going through the roof in Jing Hong; it's best to avoid Xishuangbanna the week before and after. However, the festival is not celebrated in the rest of Yunnan except at the 'minorities' university in Kunming.

Practical information

VISAS AND FORMALITIES

Chinese visas are required for most nationals. Conditions vary substantially according to where you apply. On the application form it asks where you'll be going – it's often simplest to write something uncontroversially ordinary like Beijing – certainly don't mention any thoughts of going to Tibet! Nobody checks later what you wrote.

Fortunately, in South-East Asian capitals the visa procedure is generally straightforward and in Bangkok, Kao San Road agencies will do the leg work for you for around 1300B. The same visa costs 1100B in the embassy or at the Chiang Mai consulate (typically open 9–11am Mon to Fri only). The three to four working day waiting period can be reduced if you are prepared to pay a supplement, varying according to how many days you're able to wait (2300B for a next-day service in Chiang Mai). You can apply up to three months before using it so this is the visa to get first. Visas are usually extendable for a further 30 days through the Aliens Department of the Public Security Bureau (located in almost any town or city).

Onward visas

In Kunming's Camelia Hotel you'll find consulates for both Burma (visa 185Y, ready next day) and Laos (400–480Y same day, 270–350Y in three working days, apply in the morning only). The nearest Vietnamese consul is in very distant Guangzhou and takes about 10 days to issue a visa. If you're desperate and wealthy enough, CITS travel agency may be able to deliver your passport for you but you'll have to wait around two weeks.

Permits

A few years ago, much of Yunnan was closed to tourism. Now almost everywhere is fair game. The main exception is the route from Deqin into Tibet via Markam for which permits are necessary and expensive. These can *sometimes* be organized through agencies in Lijiang – a nice place to wait while assembling enough companions to rent the jeep and driver (reckon on \$450/pp including the paperwork).

MONEY

Renminbi (people's money) consists of *yuan* (commonly referred to as *kwai*) which are divided into ten *jiao* (normally called *mao*). The one kwai coin that is common on China's east coast, hadn't filtered much beyond Kunming at the time of writing.

The exchange rate is stable with no black market. In Kunming, Lijiang, Jing Hong and Dali, travellers' cheques give better rates than cash, but elsewhere they can prove difficult to exchange. Outside bank hours, upmarket hotels offer the best hope of changing money in the cities, though usually they will only do so for guests. In border towns such as Mohan and Ruili, restaurants and some shops will change cash for you at poor rates. Trying to sell your Dong, Kip or Kyat anywhere beyond the border zone is a lost cause.

Shops which show Visa/MasterCard signs might only accept locally-issued cards. Ditto ATMs – use only those specifically denoted for foreign cards or you may have the magic plastic irretrievably swallowed.

TRANSPORT
Bus and minibus

In rural Yunnan road improvements are underway at an amazing pace, with new highways being built as well as wide-scale surfacing of unpaved trunk routes. Journey times on certain routes may already be reduced by the time you read this.

The bus and minibus system is extensive with frequent services. Deregulation has resulted in a multiplicity of companies vying for business on major long-distance routes.

That's good news for prices but a little confusing as there may be multiple bus stations in bigger towns to cope with mushrooming demand. In big towns, such as Kunming and Xaiguan (new Dali), each bus station offers any major destination so if there's no convenient departure from one, simply try another!

Long-distance routes are covered by convenient if claustrophobic sleeper buses (*wo pu*). Unlaundered blankets are usually provided, but a sleeping map is recommended to protect your back from protruding springs. Putting your daypack under your knees keeps it safe and also compensates for the lack of leg room. Travelling alone you'll generally have to get cozy with a random bedmate!

The minibus services that have developed over the last decade are a boon for random exploration as they shuttle along almost any major stretch of road with considerable frequency allowing you to jump on and off at any point along the route, confident that another will be along soon (services tend to thin out around mid-afternoon).

Train

Chinese trains have improved amazingly over the last ten years and many mainline express services now have airline-style hostess services with souvenir gifts included in the price.

Within Yunnan, the most useful service is the more rickety Kunming–Kaiyuan–Hekou train (see p150) but if you're heading further into China, the multi-tunnel rail link Kunming–Panzhihua–Leshan–Chengdu is well worth considering if you can find a berth.

There are four classes, of which by far the best deal is 'Hard Sleeper'. Prices vary slightly according to the berth (lower is best as you can secure your baggage – see the diagram below).

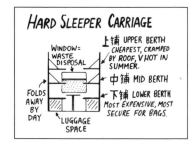

Air

Air travel is not especially cheap but given the distances it can be time efficient: eg it costs 520Y to fly between Kunming and Jing Hong – by bus it would take 18–24 hours. Flying from Jing Hong to Lijiang (daily, China Yunnan Airlines, 620Y) saves two days!

❑ Chinese rail classes		
Class		**Notes**
软卧	Soft sleeper	An unnecessary luxury
硬卧	Hard sleeper	Three-tiered bunks in an open carriage. The uppermost berth is 15% less expensive than the lower one but is cramped and stiflingly hot in summer
硬席	Soft seat	Plus reclining seats
硬席	Hard seat	Your chance to get to know the local farmyard while on the move. Sleeping mats are useful to pad your behind.

❏ **Types of cheap accommodation (for Chinese characters see p146)**
A *zhaodaisuo* is generally the cheapest kind of accommodation available and ranges from a few rooms in a family home above a shop front to large but basic concrete slab buildings. Signs are likely to be marked only in Chinese. In cities where such places are forbidden to foreigners, you'll be forced into the generally much bigger and sometimes very grand *binguan*, *fandian* or *jiudian*.

If the only place available looks very grand don't necessarily be put off. Even some of the plushest hotels have a building B; an annex with festering old rooms at the price you want to pay. Price lists are generally displayed.

Ask first for a *duorenfang* (dormitory). In traveller-primed hotels there seems to be a general policy of putting foreigners in separate dorms from Chinese guests, so if there are no other Westerners (or Japanese) you may have a room to yourself. Sexes are not separated in this way. If the receptionist claims that there are no dorms that may be because they define dormitory differently. It may still be possible to get one bed in a shared triple if prices are quoted *chuangwei* (per bed) rather than *baofang* (whole room). Look closely at the squiggles on the price board. *Danrengfang* (single) rooms are typically more expensive than a triple (*sanrenfang*) as singles are usually luxury rooms with attached toilet and bathroom facilities.

You will have to pay in advance. Often, a Y10 or Y20 deposit is also required – you'll get it back providing you check out by noon and return the room card. This card is held in lieu of a key; show it to the attendant on your floor, and she'll open your door and refill the thermos with boiling water for tea. Lifts stop working late at night and there may be an unofficial midnight curfew.

An interesting international possibility is the Bangkok–Kunming–Jing Hong–Bangkok loop offered for around 8000B in Thailand (note that the BKK–JHG leg operates on Wednesday only in either direction). Kunming to Bangkok tickets bought in Yunnan are considerably more expensive (1250–1560Y from the China Yunnan Airlines office at Camelia Hotel, cash only). You can also fly to Vientiane for $120, Yangon for 2300Y, Nanning daily ex Thursday for 680Y.

The departure tax for an international flight is 90Y and 50Y for domestic.

Bicycle
Cycling is often the easiest way to explore towns and cities and bicycles can be hired from the few back-packer orientated hotels.

Using your own padlock avoids the old bike scam (rare these days and always more common in Beijing than Yunnan) in which the place that lends you a bike uses a spare key to steal it back once you've parked somewhere.

Bicycle parking may require a small fee in central Kunming.

ACCOMMODATION
You'll rarely have to pay more than 10–15Y for a basic bed, except in Kunming where dorms cost from 25Y. Unlike many other areas of China, you're not usually restricted to 'foreigner approved' hotels when travelling in Yunnan, though in certain larger towns away from the tourist circuit, you may find the old ideas enforced. The bigger problem is recognizing that an establishment is a hotel in the first place; see the box above. Once inside, there is almost always a prominently displayed price list which you can learn to decipher using the character list on p146.

Beware that on major Chinese holidays, accommodation can fill up especially in Lijiang – notably around May 1st.

TRAVELLER MEETING PLACES
Several guesthouses and cafés in Lijiang and Old Dali are great traveller standbys. In Jing Hong the traveller scene has died off in recent years but you'll usually find a few backpackers at the Mekong or Lemongrass information cafés. In Kunming, the Kunhu and Camelia hotels still draw plenty of cus-

tom, though Hump (see p148 and the box below) is becoming the new focus for Westerners in the city and there are now several Western cafés around the university where you can meet longer-term visitors and look for temporary work – about the only place in China that casual employment seems tacitly tolerated, albeit actually illegal.

FOOD AND DRINK

Chinese food is the predictable norm in bigger towns. But in the south, don't miss the local Dai cuisine which has many of the fine fruity flavours of Thai cooking without the chilli hot sting. In some villages where traditional Dai houses accept visitors, you are asked (or gesticulated at): 'Eat?' Agreement results in a multi-dish feast well worth the 40Y or so it may cost per person. Of course the Dai is only one of many tribes — each has its own distinct cuisine, which could consist of roots and insects in one place, bamboo shoots and spices in another.

Many places in Dali and Lijiang along with a handful of cafés in Jing Hong and Kunming cater to Western tastes with pizza, banana pancakes, and egg and toast breakfasts.

Locally-made cigarettes are said to be the best in China; better ones have flower petals ground in for fragrance. The 'alternative' smoking scene in Jing Hong that gave the town a slightly hippy air in the mid-1990s seems to have been stamped out.

SHOPPING

Weekly hill-tribe markets such as Menghun's (Sunday mornings) are similar colourful spectacles to those of north Thailand, and offer tempting if useless souvenir fodder.

STAYING IN TOUCH

The internet is increasingly accessible. The best and cheapest connections are typically through China Telecom at 3–4Y/hr. There are a few traveller cafés with English-speaking helpers and a little more ambience though these typically charge 10–15Y.

FURTHER INFORMATION
Books

These days Yunnan's a relatively easy place to explore without a guidebook at all. Bradt produces a *China – Yunnan Province* guide. Lonely Planet includes much improved coverage of the area in its well updated 2002 edition of *South West China*. The Guides Bleu *Chine du sud-ouest* is a very good alternative, especially for cultural aspects, if you happen to speak French. None of these is easy to find in South-East Asia, however.

A Chinese phrasebook is a worthy investment.

For background, read anything by Joseph Rock, a biologist who lived in Yunnan. Compare Samuel R Clarke's 1891 *Among the Tribes in South-West China* with Zhong Xiu's 1983 *Yunnan Travelogue: 100 Days in Southwest China* which is sold fairly widely throughout China.

Maps

Xinhua bookshops sell Yunnan road atlases (*Yunnan Sheng Shiyong Dituce*) for 18Y. These are all in Chinese but useful nonetheless – and friendly locals are usually delighted to help translate. Note that 'normal' county names, 'xxxx'zhan (noted at the bottom of each page), are four characters long. However, ethnic minority areas are named according to the 'autonomous' tribal groups present, so the longer the county name, the more likely it is that the area has an interesting cultural mix and that it could be a good place for random exploration.

Many varieties of Yunnan and Kunming city maps are sold by vendors outside Kunming's main railway station, generally for a *kwai* more than the printed cover price. The very detailed, bilingual *Cross-Border Communications* map includes northern parts of Laos, Vietnam, Thailand and Burma as well as Yunnan – useful for onward travel. If you can figure out the Chinese, it also lists major air and train timetables in the back and gives tourist information.

❏ **Stop press**
Reportedly, as we go to press, Hump (see top of page) had been closed for violations of that very rule on hiring foreigners! Hopefully it will re-open quickly.

❏ Meeting the locals

● The people Yunnan has a very diverse mix of colourful, hill tribes. As Nanzhou it was the original home of the Thai people who emigrated south especially after the 13th-century Mongol raids. Their close relatives, the Dai remain.

Tribal people still wander fairly freely between Yunnan, Laos and Burma. Kunming and the cities are predominantly Han Chinese mellowed by the warmer climes.

Young Chinese are increasingly keen to meet foreigners and learn English – you may be surprised by the 'trendy' side to Kunming. However, in tourist spots remember that most of the Chinese themselves are likely to be on holiday so the best places to meet the real locals is around the universities, or in smaller more remote towns and villages.

● Language In cities the business language is Chinese. This tonal language is hell to pronounce but remarkably easy in terms of grammar. The daunting script would take an age to master but getting a feel for how to differentiate characters is not as hard as it might seem. See the guide on pp144-5. Reading from the 'pin yin' Latin transliterations of Chinese, also requires a little coaching – notably 'q' is pronounced 'ch', and 'i' is often a kind of grunt.

Most tribal groups have their own language. These overlap with the languages of Laos and northern Thailand so Lonely Planet's *Thai Hill Tribe Phrasebook* can prove very useful.

Chinese Numerals

1	2	3	4	5	6	7	8	9	10	100	1000	10,000	100,000,000
一	二	三	四	五	六	七	八	九	十	百	千	万	億

29,481 would be 二万九千四百八十一 ie 2x10,000 + 9x1000 + 4x100 + 8x10 + 1

Useful websites

Select the Kunming Scene option on 🖥 www.china-friend.com/ to read about the latest pizzerias, bars etc in Kunming. The site also has a useful but incomplete flight timetable.

🖥 www.redflag.info/yunnan.htm is a good starting point for links to other Yunnan travel sites of which the most practical is, predictably enough, Passplanet (www.passplanet.com/China/sw/frame_yunnan.htm).

🖥 www.hbpage.com/ is a very useful site with good listings and clickable descriptions of a variety of local festivals, minority groups etc.

🖥 www.sinohost.com/yunnan_travel/ has a wide range of travel information and background.

Looking at Chinese Characters

Aaaaaagh! Help! A perfectly normal reaction to the beautiful but daunting squiggles is panic. When you know nothing about the language, 梅 looks pretty much like 海 and is frighteningly close to

Don't worry. There's no need to try and learn the 5000+ characters. Even locals can't read a newspaper till their late teens! A simpler, more achievable aim is to learn to differentiate one character from another, so you can see that your bus is really heading where you'd hoped. But first learn these two, unless you plan to be constipated throughout your stay in China:

WOMAN 女   MAN 男

Horrifying as it may sound, the best way to come to grips with the characters is to write them out. Count how many pen strokes each one takes. Locals can show you the 'correct' way which is important if you want to learn calligraphy. However, you may find it easier to devise your own counting system. One extra stroke or dot can make all the difference, though not always as simply as between 1, 2 and 3:

一 二 三 十 土 上 止 正 工 王 玉 羊 兰
ONE TWO THREE TEN GROUND UP STOP CORRECT WORK KING GEM SHEEP ORCHID

As with **up** and **ground** (above) check whether two lines meet or actually cross one another:

日 月   目 耳   田 毌   夕 女 夂
SUN MOON EYE EAR FIELD MUM EVE WOMAN WINTER
(DAY) (MONTH)

Also note carefully which way a line bends:

九 力   手 毛
NINE POWER   HAND HAIR

Look again at the toilet markers (man/woman) above. You may notice that **man** is a combination of **power** and **field** squeezed into one letter. In fact characters become much easier to cope with once you understand that MOST are made up of such smaller elements or 'radicals'. Historically, perhaps, men were indeed the 'power in the field' and the link between **tree**, **wood**, and **forest** (below) is easy to see. But don't expect most of the characters to make sense in this way…

木 林 森   口 平 呼   女 子 好
TREE WOOD FOREST MOUTH PEACE CALL WOMAN CHILD LIKE

Many of the smaller radicals don't exist independently and may be as simple as carefully placed dots:

皿 血   大 太 犬 夭   日 白   目 自 貝
DISH BLOOD BIG WIDE DOG PIER SUN WHITE EYE SELF SHELL

Others sit on top like little 'hats' or 'capes' and look confusingly similar. They're worth remembering:

卜 冖 冂 宀 ⺍   亠 艹 爫   人 𣥂 𣥂   厂 广

Some important 'no hat'/'hat' pairs:

丁 宁   子 学   云 会   车 库
AREA TRANQUIL CHILD STUDY CLOUD MEET CAR STORE

Many more radicals like to snuggle into the side of a character. Compare **sea** 海 and **plum** 梅 Both show **mum** 母 in a 'hat' 宀 but with different 'sides': 氵 / 木

Some easily confusable 'sides' include:

氵 冫 亻 彳 木 禾 忄 扌 阝 钅 车 歹 石 己 弓

Don't worry unduly what locals consider to be 'real radicals' - historically there are 214 including 'sides', 'hats', 'capes', 'legs', 'boxes' and even the odd 'dragon' but all that really matters is that you can chop up any character into bite sized pieces that look less frightening. Hopefully by now you'll be able to spot the differences between the first characters in the Chinese place names **Xian**, **Sichuan**, and **Jiuquan** (below). The last characters of **Sichuan** and **Quanzhou** are also different (those three little dots are important). But the *quan* in both **Jiuquan** and **Quanzhou** is the same. The *an* (second character of **Xian**) is *not* woman thanks to the little hat she's sporting!

XIAN — 西安 — WEST SAFE
SICHUAN — 四川 — 4 RIVER
JIUQUAN — 酒泉 — ALCOHOL SPRING
QUANZHOU — 泉州 — SPRING PROVINCE

Town and province names have at least two characters. Don't assume that spotting just one of the two is enough as the same character has an underhand tendency to show up in others, often nearby!

西安 西宁 宁海 上海 海安 梅州 广州 广海
XIAN XINING NINGHAI SHANGHAI HAIAN MEIZHOU GUANG-ZHOU GUANG-HAI

As in English, always read from left to right or from top to bottom.
Xian 西安 and **Anxi** 安西 are entirely different cities.

The good news is that in any given Chinese language each character has only one standard pronunciation. If that sounds obvious try learning Japanese where each character has a multiplicity of readings. There is, however, a difference in pronunciation - though not in meaning - between, say, Mandarin and Cantonese or other Chinese languages.

If the letters look complex, they're not half as bad as they used to be. The communist regime 'simplified' many of the most outlandishly lavish morasses of squiggles into somewhat more manageable shapes. This is something you may only appreciate if you visit Taiwan or Hong Kong where no such simplification occurred. However, once in a while you'll see the old forms used, perhaps on town welcome signs which are trying to evoke a sense of history or class.
Here are some examples of old/classic radicals followed by their 'simplified' versions:

糸→纟 訁→讠 金→钅 車→车 貝→贝 魚→鱼 馬→马 鳥→鸟 島→岛
THREAD WORD GOLD CAR SHELL FISH HORSE BIRD ISLAND

Don't worry. Even if you get the readings entirely wrong, just attempting to battle your way through a few signs on a timetable is likely to impress or at least amuse the locals and help you make a few friends. And you might even catch the right bus!

Chinese words and phrases

Locals are unlikely to understand your attempts at pronouncing Chinese. Even if you speak fluently many seem to assume you're speaking English and so don't listen. Buy a phrase book with Chinese characters: show people the written words. If you have no phrase book our selection of words will be most useful if you first make a couple of photocopies. Cut these up and paste together the words you need to make pidgin Chinese sentences (eg 'cheapest double room, private shower'). For all its other complexities, Chinese is grammatically very simple, so you have a fair chance of hitting on a sentence that someone understands. As we've tried to show (see 'Verbs' below) pasting in an extra character is all you need to change tenses, negatives etc.

PRONOUNS

我 I/ME — wǒ
你 You — nǐ (你)
他 HE/HIM — tā
她 SHE/HER — tā
它 It — tā
Add 们 for plural - eg 他们 men
我们 WE/US — wǒ men (*TO SHOW RESPECT)

VERBS

EAT↘ MEAT↘
我 吃 肉 — wǒ chī ròu — I EAT MEAT (AM EATING, WILL EAT, DO EAT)

↙NOT
我 不 吃 肉 — wǒ bù chī ròu — I DON'T EAT MEAT

↙CAN
我 不 能 吃 肉 — wǒ bù néng chī ròu — I CANNOT EAT MEAT

↙HAVE
我 吃 了 肉 — wǒ chī le ròu — I ATE MEAT

IN PAST↘
我 吃 过 肉 — wǒ chī guò ròu — I HAVE EATEN MEAT (Once upon a time)

↙NOT (PAST)
我 没 吃 肉 — wǒ méi chī ròu — I DIDN'T EAT MEAT

↙TODAY
我 今 天 吃 肉 — wǒ jīn tiān chī ròu — TODAY I (WILL) EAT MEAT

我 明 天 吃 肉 — wǒ míng tiān chī ròu — TOMORROW I WILL EAT MEAT

QUESTIONS

你 吃 肉 吗 — nǐ chī ròu ma? — DO YOU EAT MEAT? (←QUESTION MARKER)

我 吃 — wǒ chī — YES. (I EAT)

我 不 吃 — wǒ bù chī — NO. (I NOT EAT)

ALTERNATIVELY
你 吃 不 吃 肉 — nǐ chī bù chī ròu? — DO YOU EAT MEAT (OR NOT)? (NO "MA")

QUESTION WORDS

~ ~ 什么 — ~ ~ shén me — WHAT IS ~ ~

~ ~ 几点 — ~ ~ jǐ diǎn — WHAT TIME IS ~ ~?

~ ~ 在 哪儿 — ~ ~ zài nǎr — WHERE IS ~ ~?

多少钱 — duō shǎo qián — HOW MUCH (COST)?

TIME

点 — diǎn — HOUR/O'CLOCK
五点四十分 — wǔ diǎn sì shí fēn — 5:40 MINUTE
今天 — jīn tian — TODAY
明天 — míng tian — TOMORROW
昨天 — zuó tian — YESTERDAY
星期一 — xīng qī yī — MONDAY ("one") 2 FOR TUESDAY, 3 WED...ETC EXCEPT SUNDAY

月 — yuè — MONTH
一月 — yì yuè — JAN.
二月 etc. — èr yuè — FEB.
DAY (SUN)
五月十日 — wǔ yuè shí rì — MAY 10TH
一星期 — yì xīng qī — ONE WEEK (c.f.)
星期日 — xīng qī rì — SUNDAY

1	一
2	二
3	三
4	四
5	五
6	六
7	七
8	八
9	九
10	十
11	十一
12	十二

HOTEL

Cheapest type
招待所 / — ZHAODAISUO
宾馆 — BĪNGUAN
酒店 — JIǓDIAN
饭店 — FANDIAN

ROOMS

多人房 — duō ren fang — DORM ROOM
单/双/三人房 — dān/shuāng/sān ren fang — SINGLE/DOUBLE/TRIPLE ROOM
床位 — chuáng wèi — PAY PER BED
包房 — bāo fáng — PAY FOR WHOLE ROOM
MOST↘ ↙CHEAP
最便宜(房) — zuì pian yi (fáng) — CHEAPEST (ROOM)

(私人) 浴室/淋浴/厕所 — (sī ren) yù shì / lín yù / cè suǒ — (PRIVATE) BATH/SHOWER/TOILET

热水 — rè shuǐ — HOT WATER

我可以看看房间吗 — wǒ kě yǐ kàn kàn fáng jiān ma? — MAY I LOOK AT THE ROOM?

HANDY WORDS

太谢谢你了
(tài) xiè xiè (nǐ le)
THANKS (V. MUCH)

对不起
duì bù qǐ
SORRY

仁慈的
rén cí de
KIND

良好的
liáng hǎo de
GOOD

幸福的
xìng fú de
HAPPY

很美的
hěn měi de
BEAUTIFUL

很有意思
hěn yǒu yì sì
INTERESTING

非常的
fēi cháng de
UNUSUAL

朋友
péng yǒu
FRIEND

我不懂
wǒ bù dǒng
I DON'T UNDERSTAND

高价的
gāo jià de
EXPENSIVE

TRANSPORT
Bus or Train

卧铺
wò pu
SLEEPER

上/中/下铺
shàng/zhōng/xià pu
UPPER/MID/LOW BERTH

硬/软席
yìng/ruǎn xí
HARD/SOFT SEAT

到
dào
ARRIVAL

开
zǒu
DEP.

行李寄存处
xíng lǐ jì cún chù
LEFT LUGGAGE OFFICE

慢/直快/特快/国联车
màn/zhí kuài/tè kuài/guó   chē
SLOW/FAST/EXPRESS/INTL TRAIN

售票处
shòu piào chù
TICKET OFFICE

定票处
dìng piào chù
RESERVATION OFFICE

问讯
wèn xùn
INFO

我只要…张硬卧铺去～
wǒ   yào…zhang yìng wo pu qu
I'D LIKE (NUMBER) HARD SLEEPER TIX TO～

我只要租一辆自行车
wǒ   yào zū yí lang zì xíng chē
I'D LIKE TO RENT A BICYCLE

MAPS

我想买一张(市/交通)地图
wǒ xiǎng shi yí zhang (shì/jiāo tōng) dì tú
I WANT TO BUY A (CITY/TRANSPORT) MAP

Map Kanji

江/河 RIVER 湖 LAKE 岛 ISLAND
山 MOUNTAIN 峰 PEAK 山口 PASS
村 VILLAGE 县 RURAL COUNTY/COUNTY TOWN
公园 PARK 物 ZOO 古城 OLD TOWN

PLACES
Street Names:

路
lù

街
jiē

大街
dà jiē

道
dào

大道
dà dào

广场
guǎng chǎng
SQUARE

北 běi
～～北路
～～beilu
= THE NORTH SECTION OF ～～ ROAD

西 xī W-N·E-S 东 dong
南 nán

教堂
jiào táng
CHURCH

寺院/庙
sì/yuàn/miào
TEMPLE

清真寺
qīng zhēng sì
MOSQUE

博物馆
bó wù guǎn
MUSEUM

书店
shū diàn
BOOK SHOP

(中国)银行
(zhōngguó) yín háng
BANK (OF CHINA)

领事馆
lǐng shì guǎn
CONSULATE

大使馆
dà shǐ guǎn
EMBASSY

公安局外事科
gōngan jú wài shí kē
P.S.B. (FOR VISA EXTENSION)

邮局
yóu jú
POST OFFICE

存局候领栏
cún jú hòu lǐng làn
POST RESTANTE

飞机场
fēi jī chǎng
AIRPORT

汽车站
qì chē zhàn
BUS STATION

火车站
huǒ chē zhan
TRAIN STATION

码头
mǎ tóu
FERRY PIER

With its confusing plethora of vowels and its four tones, Chinese is a nightmare to pronounce. There is an increasing use of 'pinyin' (Chinese words in Western letters, as used below the characters on these pages), but the letters don't correspond exactly with their equivalents in Western languages. Most different are:

c - ts   *ie* - like yeah!   *j* - ds   *q* - roughly ch   *x* - roughly SH
e - sounds like the grunt you might make after being punched gently in the stomach.
i - similar to e in some words but is normally a more conventional ee sound.

Accent markers over vowels graphically show the tones: flat, falling, rising, falling+rising.

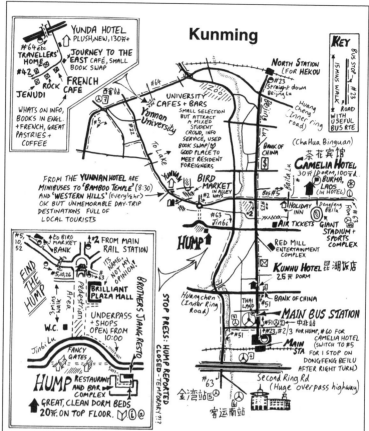

Kunming

KEY — BUS STOP / 15 MINS WALK / #23 / ROAD WITH USEFUL BUS RTE

YUNDA HOTEL PLUSH, NEW, 130元+
TRAVELLERS HOME #64 etc / #42
JOURNEY TO THE EAST CAFÉ, SMALL BOOK SWAP
FRENCH CAFÉ / **ROCK** / **JENUDI**
WHATS ON INFO, BOOKS IN ENGL. + FRENCH, GREAT PASTRIES + COFFEE

UNIVERSITY CAFES + BARS SMALL SELECTION BUT ATTRACT A MIXED STUDENT CROWD, INFO SERVICE, USED BOOK SWAP, GOOD PLACE TO MEET RESIDENT FOREIGNERS

Yunnan University
#64
To Lake
#22

NORTH STATION [FOR HEKOU] #23 Straight down Beijing Lu

Huang Cheng (Inner ring) road

(Cha Hua Binguan) 茶花宾馆
CAMELIA HOTEL 30元/DORM, 100元↓ BURMA, LAOS (IN HOTEL)
BANK OF CHINA

FROM THE **YUNNAN HOTEL** ARE MINIBUSES TO 'BAMBOO TEMPLE' (8:30) AND 'WESTERN HILLS' (every ½ hr) OK BUT UNMEMORABLE DAY-TRIP DESTINATIONS FULL OF LOCAL TOURISTS

BIRD MARKET IN ALLEY WAYS

#63 Jinbi
HUMP

HOLIDAY INN Dongfeng Beilu #63
AIR TICKETS / **GIANT STADIUM + SPORTS COMPLEX**
RED MILL ENTERTAINMENT COMPLEX
bus #5

KUNHU HOTEL 昆湖饭店 25元 DORM

FIND THE HUMP
#5, 10, 52 — To BIRD MARKET / BANK
#5,10,26
#2 FROM MAIN RAIL STATION
ITS NAME, NOT MY OPINION!
Pedestrian Area
3 mins
BRILLIANT PLAZA MALL
UNDERPASS + SHOPS OPEN FROM 10:00
W.C.
BROTHERS JIANG RESTO
Jinbi Lu
FANCY GATES
HUMP RESTAURANT AND BAR COMPLEX
GREAT, CLEAN DORM BEDS 20元 ON TOP FLOOR

STOP PRESS: HUMP REPORTED CLOSED - TEMPORARY?!?

Huangchen (Inner Ring Road)
THAILAND #51
BANK OF CHINA
MAIN BUS STATION 中北站 #51客运
#23, #2/3 FOR HUMP, #60 FOR CAMELIA HOTEL (SWITCH TO #5 FOR 1 STOP ON DONGFENG BEILU AFTER RIGHT TURN)
MAIN STA
#63
金湾站
Second Ring Rd (Huge overpass highway)
客运南站

Since the mid-1990s Kunming has demolished almost all of its once charming older neighbourhoods. The gleaming, modern metropolis nonetheless makes a pleasant, lively hub city, and the new '**Hump**' complex offers a great backpacker alternative to the trusty Kunhu and Camelia hotels. The Camelia houses helpful **Lao & Burmese consulates**, visas usually available within 24hrs. But there's no Vietnamese representation: the nearest consulates are in Nanning or Guangzhou - both painfully slow for visas.

Arriving by bus in Kunming you might find yourself at any one of 8 different terminals! Most are clumped within walking distance of the main railway station and/or the 51/northbound 63 bus routes. More awkward are [7] (bus #23 to centre) and [8] (on the 2nd ring, way out at the east end of Dongfeng Beilu, eastbound bus 63). Departing is easier. As almost all terminals offer the same range of destinations, the best idea is to head for the relatively calm **main bus station** (time-tabled departures, computerised tickets). If there's no service that suits you, try nipping next door to [3] (departures when full). For a better range of short-hop routes within Kunming province, try [5] or [6].

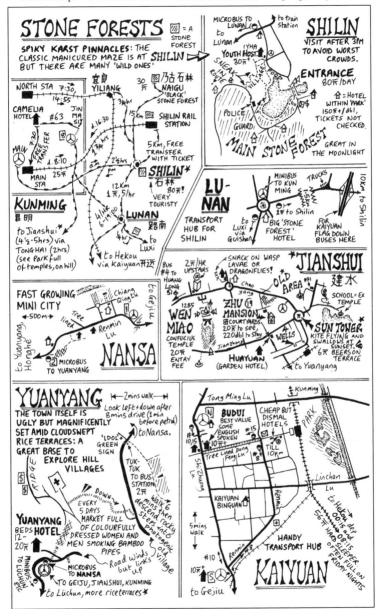

SHIPING 石屏
to Simao via Mojiang
Yitong Lake
2/HR
1¼ Hrs

TUANSHAN
QUAINT OLD HOUSES INC.
ZHANG 1km JIA MINJU

HUANGLONG-SI = YELLOW DRAGON TEMPLE
18. STONE CUTTERS
17 ARCHES
SHUANG LONG QIAO

JIANSHUI 建水
ANCIENT GARRISON TOWN. 13 TEMPLE AND OTHER HISTORIC MONUMENTS

K V.FREQ BY DAY, 5HRS + SEV
22:00-23:20
60.5元

DIRECT TO DALI (XIAGUAN) 13:30

开远
KAIYUAN

SWALLOW CAVE
EASY WALK FROM ROAD
1 hr

2 per hr
7:30-15:30
5-6 Hrs +
K 20:30

10KM

dep 22:55, arr Kunming 7:25 (NORTH STA) [BUT DELAYS FREQUENT]

H 14:00

#10 #15
N
S
#8

H 30元, ≈7HRS
dep 6, 6:30, 7:30, 8:30, 10:30
ret 9, 10:15, 11:40. OR GO VIA MENGZI

2½hr 3/hr
Last 18:00

2½hrs 3-5/hr 17:50
10.5元

2½hrs 3/hr
Last 17:45

MENGZI 蒙自
"MOM-TSU"
CENTRE FOR POLITICAL INTRIGUES IN 1907 AS THE FRENCH CONSUL INITIALLY HELPED CHINESE REPUBLICAN SUN-YAT-SEN.

H 7:30

1½hrs
3-7/hr

2½hrs 3/hr
Last 17:30

1½hrs
5-9/hr
Last 19:30
18元

K 2-3/hr
+ 18-20:00

个旧 GEJIU 个旧
'TIN CITY' HAS A SURPRISINGLY ATTRACTIVE 'GENEVA' SETTING

FREQ
卡房 KA FENG

1/day
9:40

PING BIAN 屏边 IN MIAO HILL TRIBE AREA

7 KM

5HRS
1-2/HR TILL 13:00

HONG 红河 HE

南沙 NANSA

SHO 十蔓措 MANTI

HUAN SAN BA
MINIBUSES STOP ≈10 MINS

5 HRS ≈ hourly in a.m.

FRENCH BUILT 1910 'TONKIN RAILWAY'. GREAT SCENERY. TRAINS OFTEN FULL ON FRIDAY (SOUTHBOUND) AND SUNDAY (NORTHBOUND)

7/day
Last 12:30 from Gejiu

MAIYU TIAN 10km 玉田

5HRS
1-3/hr Last 14:00
22元

TO CONTINUE CHANGE IN HUAN SAN BA VILLAGE

SUSPENSION FOOTBRIDGE, TINY HAMLET OF MUD HOMES

5-6 HRS 7,8,9,10 6:15,15:30 8:15,15:30

RICE TERRACES ≈ 1HR, AS FULL

MARBLE CARVING VILLAGE

1/DAY K dep 18:40 (OR WHEN FULL!)

YUANYANG 元阳

20KM, GREAT RICE TERRACES EG NEAR HUAN MAU LIN, LAO MONG, SHENG-CUN (last ret) ≈ 17:30)

2-3/hr in morning +13:30 20元

河口 HEKOU
CALM BORDER TOWN EXCEPT SAT. NIGHTS (THEN: YUNNAN'S SIN CITY)

金平 JINGPING
CENTRE FOR VISITS TO RELATIVELY UN-EXPLORED HILLTRIBE AREAS

2/day dep 6:40, 7:40

K d8:45+ Sev 18:30-20:00

SHORT STROLL

5/DAY to GEJIU, early a.m., 1-2/hr to Nansa, to Kunming

Back route via Simao to Xishuangbanna

LÜCHÜN 绿春

VIETNAM

RICE TERRACES

1-1½ hrs 25,000đ

3 mins 5000đ moto

CHEAPER TO WALK

5 mins 5-10,000đ moto

To Hekou
Rice terraces and borderlands

K = to Kunming
H = to Hekou
= bed bus svc.

★ SAPA
NORTHERN VIETNAM'S HUB FOR TRAVELLERS
COLOURFUL HILL TRIBE VILLAGES + SAT 'LOVE FEST'

LAO CAI
10hours to Hanoi
dep 18:45, 10:20
The weekly through train is more expensive

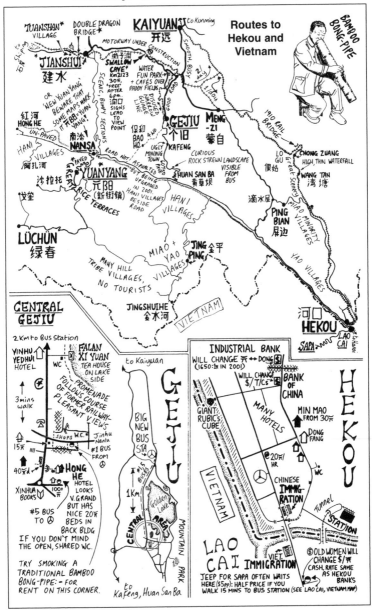

Routes to Hekou and Vietnam

BAMBOO BONG-PIPE

TUANSHAN VILLAGE
DOUBLE DRAGON BRIDGE
KAIYUAN 开远
To Kunming
MOTORWAY UNDER CONSTRUCTION
SMOOTH, BUSY
JIANSHUI 建水
SWALLOW CAVE Km21/23 30元 'FREE' AFTER 6pm.
WATER FUN PARK + CAFÉS OVER PADDY FIELDS
SCENIC BUMPY SECTIONS
DISUSED NARROW GUAGE LINE
OR 'NEW YUAN YANG' BEWARE THAT SOME MAPS MARK IT FOR YUAN YANG.
GOOD ROAD
GEJIU 个旧
MENG-ZI 蒙自
1910 RAIL BRIDGE
红河 HONG HE
UN-PAVED
HANI VILLAGES
南沔 NANSA
阿扎河
BAO HE
UGLY MINING TOWN
KAFENG
4 WD
CURIOUS ROCK STREWN LANDSCAPE VISIBLE FROM BUS
LO GU 俚姑
CHONG ZUANG HIGH, THIN WATERFALL
GREAT SCENERY
WANG TAN 湾塘
沙拉托
YUANYANG 元阳 (新街镇)
GREAT RICE TERRACES
ROAD NOT ASPHALTED
HUAN SAN BA 黄草坝
- BUT BEING UPGRADED IN 2001
HANI VILLAGES BESIDE ROAD
HANI VILLAGES
MIAO MINORITY VILLAGES
PING BIAN 屏边
滴水屋
怯堂
LÜCHÜN 绿春
MIAO + YAO TRIBE VILLAGES
JING PING 金平
YAO VILLAGES
MANY HILL VILLAGES, NO TOURISTS
JINGSHUIHE 金水河
VIETNAM
河口 HEKOU
SAPA
LAO CAI
To Hahoi

CENTRAL GEJIU

2 Km to Bus Station
YINHU YEDHUI HOTEL
FALAN XI YUAN TEA HOUSE ON LAKE SIDE
WC
PROMENADE FOLLOWS COURSE OF FORMER RAILWAY - PLEASANT VIEWS
3mins walk
SHOPS W.C.
Jinhu Nanlu
15元
#1 BUS FROM
40元
HONG HE HOTEL LOOKS V. GRAND BUT HAS NICE 20元 BEDS IN BACK BLDG
XINHUA BOOKS
100+元
#5 BUS TO
IF YOU DON'T MIND THE OPEN, SHARED WC.

TRY SMOKING A TRADITIONAL BAMBOO BONG-PIPE: - FOR RENT ON THIS CORNER.

GEJIU

to Kaiyuan
BIG NEW BUS STA
BUSES
1Km
Golden Lake
CENTRAL AREA
MOUNTAIN PARK
to Kafeng, Huan San Ba

HEKOU

INDUSTRIAL BANK WILL CHANGE 元 ↔ DONG (1650:1元 IN 2001)
WILL CHANGE $/T/Cs
BANK OF CHINA
GIANT RUBIC'S CUBE
MANY HOTELS
MIN MAO FROM 30元
DONG FANG
VIETNAM
@ 20元/HR
WC
CHINESE IMMIGRATION
Tunnel
STATION
$ OLD WOMEN WILL CHANGE $/元 CASH. RATE SAME AS HEKOU BANKS

LAO CAI
VIET. IMMIGRATION
JEEP FOR SAPA OFTEN WAITS HERE ($5pp) HALF PRICE IF YOU WALK 15 MINS TO BUS STATION (SEE LAO CAI, VIETNAM MAP)

Xishuangbanna

Xishuangbanna (西双版纳) is an appealing patchwork of rainforest, rubber plantations and sturdy Dai villages that are conspicuously better-off than similar hill-tribe hamlets across the Lao border. Many once quaint villages are somewhat kitschily over-groomed for the myriad Chinese tour groups (eg those marked ❑). Many, many more, particularly around Mengla, remain barely visited (some easily accessible examples are marked ❒). Booming Jinghong has lost most of its Dai character but it's still a handy hub with traveller cafés like the helpful, down-to-earth Lemongrass where you'll find good maps and plenty of alternative excursion ideas.

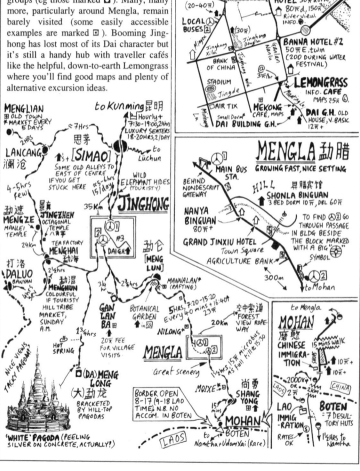

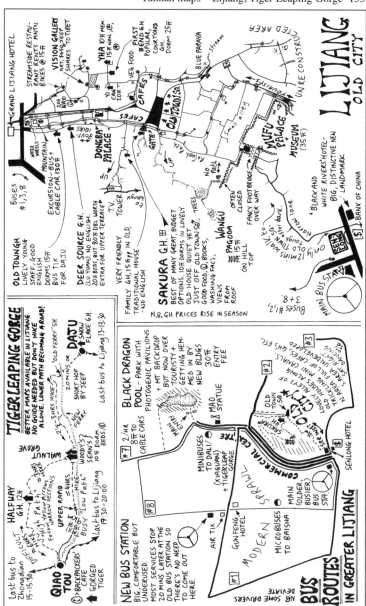

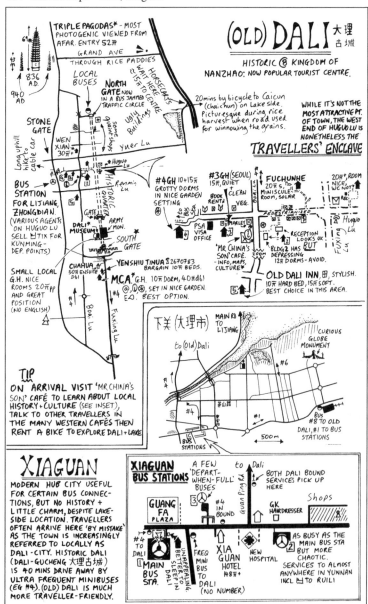

(OLD) DALI 大理古城

HISTORIC ⑧ KINGDOM OF NANZHAO: NOW POPULAR TOURIST CENTRE.

TRIPLE PAGODAS* - MOST PHOTOGENIC VIEWED FROM AFAR. ENTRY 52元

GRAND AVE THROUGH RICE PADDIES

6元
836 A.D.
940 AD

LOCAL BUSES

NORTH GATE NOW IN A BUS JAMMED TRAFFIC CIRCLE

HORSECARTS WAIT HERE 1元 IST TO CENTRE

Ugly Buildings

STONE GATE

WEN XIAN 30元*

Long uphill hike to cable car

Some quaint shops

Yuer Lu

20mins by bicycle to Caicun (chaicun) on Lake side. Picturesque during rice harvest when road used for winnowing the grains.

WHILE IT'S NOT THE MOST ATTRACTIVE PT. OF TOWN, THE WEST END OF HUGUOLU IS NONETHELESS THE

TRAVELLERS' ENCLAVE

Huguo Lu

Renmin Lu

BUS STATION FOR LIJIANG, ZHONGDIAN. (VARIOUS AGENTS ON HUGUO LU SELL 火 TIX FOR KUNMING- DEP. POINTS)

HISTORIC QUARTER

GATE 1

DALI MUSEUM

ARMY MON.

SOUTH GATE

#4GH 10+15元 GROTTY DORMS IN NICE GARDEN SETTING

to Bus Sta

#3GH (SEOUL) 15元, QUIET

BOOK RENTAL

CLEAN VEG.

PSA VISA OFFICE

MARLEY

'MR CHINA'S SON' CAFÉ -INFO, MAPS, CULTURE*

FUCHUNHE 20元 s. MINISCULE ROOM, SOLAR

20元+, ROOM NICE, WC NOT元?

PEDESTRIANIZED

RECEPTION LOOKS OK BUT BLDG2 HAS DEPRESSING 12元 DORMS - AVOID.

Fuxing Lu

Huguo Lu

OLD DALI INN, 田, STYLISH. 10元 HARD BED, 15元 SOFT. BEST CHOICE IN THIS AREA.

SMALL LOCAL G.H. NICE ROOMS 20元pp AND GREAT POSITION (NO ENGLISH)

CHAHUA* G.H. 50元 ENSUITE Dbl

YENSHIU TINUA ☎2670783 BARGAIN 10元 BEDS.

MCA* G.H. 10元 DORM, 40元dbl @, ⊕⑧, SET IN NICE GARDEN. E.O. BEST OPTION.

#4

Boai Lu

Fuxing Lu

下关 (大理市)

MAIN RD TO LIJIANG

to (Old) Dali

#4

CURIOUS GLOBE MONUMENT

#6

苍山峰

#4

#1

BUS #8 TO OLD DALI, #1 TO BUS STATIONS

BUS STATIONS

500m

TIP

ON ARRIVAL VISIT 'MR CHINA'S SON' CAFÉ TO LEARN ABOUT LOCAL HISTORY + CULTURE (SEE INSET), TALK TO OTHER TRAVELLERS IN THE MANY WESTERN CAFÉS THEN RENT A BIKE TO EXPLORE DALI + LAKE

Xiaguan

MODERN HUB CITY USEFUL FOR CERTAIN BUS CONNEC- TIONS, BUT NO HISTORY + LITTLE CHARM, DESPITE LAKE- SIDE LOCATION. TRAVELLERS OFTEN ARRIVE HERE 'BY MISTAKE' AS THE TOWN IS INCREASINGLY REFERRED TO LOCALLY AS DALI · CITY. HISTORIC DALI (DALI-GUCHENG 大理古城) IS 40 MINS DRIVE AWAY BY ULTRA FREQUENT MINIBUSES (EG #4). (OLD) DALI IS MUCH MORE TRAVELLER-FRIENDLY.

XIAGUAN BUS STATIONS

A FEW 'DEPART- WHEN-FULL' BUSES

to Dali

BOTH DALI BOUND SERVICES PICK UP HERE

GUANG FA PLAZA

#4 IN BOUND

Guan Ping Rd

GK HAIRDRESSER

Shops

#4 TO DALI

MAIN BUS STA.

UNAPPEALING, BETTER TO SLEEP IN DALI

FREQ MINI BUS TO DALI (NO NUMBER)

XIA GUAN HOTEL 48元+

NEW HOSPITAL

AS BUSY AS THE MAIN BUS STA BUT MORE CHAOTIC. SERVICES TO ALMOST ANYWHERE IN YUNNAN INCL 巴 TO RUILI

BURMA (MYANMAR)

Introduction

Burma's gentle peoples, infectious smiles and rich history make it one of Asia's most fascinating destinations. Breathtaking Shwedagon Pagoda, the awesome extent of Bagan, sunsets through U-Bein's teak bridge, misty sunrises on Inle Lake, the mysterious Golden Rock, are all memorable in themselves. But more than anything, Burma is picture-book Asia. Ubiquitous white-and-gilded pagodas tower above the encroaching jungle, palm-edged paddies, and dusty wheat-fields where ox carts plod between timeless low-rise villages. And the towns ooze an atmosphere of faded glory.

But faded it is. The country is a loose union of disparate regions, with much of the nation only tenuously under central control. Borders and border areas are closed. Democratic elections, won in 1990 by 'the Lady' (opposition leader Aung San Suu Kyi), were quashed by the self-named State Law and Order Restoration Council (SLORC – 'Slor-awk') with the complicity of the armed forces (Tatmadaw). Renamed Myanmar by its military dictators, Burma is reckoned to be one of the world's worst abusers of human rights. Whole towns have been wiped out at the government's whim and thousands of people are press-ganged into forced labour units. Some of the tourist infrastructure has been built by such slaves.

❑ **Country ratings – Burma (Myanmar)**

● **Expense $$$** The cost of living is low, but you must fly in and change $200.

● **Value for money ★★★★☆** $5 single rooms are available in most places ($2–3 if regulations are being flouted). Rural hotels ($15–20 for a double) are often brilliant value but paying less, the quality drops disproportionately. With some effort, it is possible to do a four-week trip on the $200 that you have to exchange on arrival. Souvenirs are a bargain, gin/whisky costs less than $0.50 a bottle (and only a little more in restaurants!), buses are cheap (if overcrowded). But trains incur big tourist surcharges. And steep entry fees for places of tourist interest are charged in $/FECs.

● **Getting around ★★☆☆☆** Ropey. Trains are unreliable and overpriced. Express buses can be good but mainly run at night so you see very little. Local buses and pick-ups (P/Us) are so packed you'll dangle off the back.

● **English spoken ★★★☆☆** Former British colony – surprisingly many locals can speak English, even in rural areas.

● **Woman alone ★★★★☆** Some minor gropings reported in Yangon.

● **For vegetarians ★★★☆☆** Any Burmese spread has a meaty centre-piece but plenty of vegetarian side dishes including the ubiquitous 'tea-leaf salad'. Great choice of Chinese fare if you eat fish/seafood.

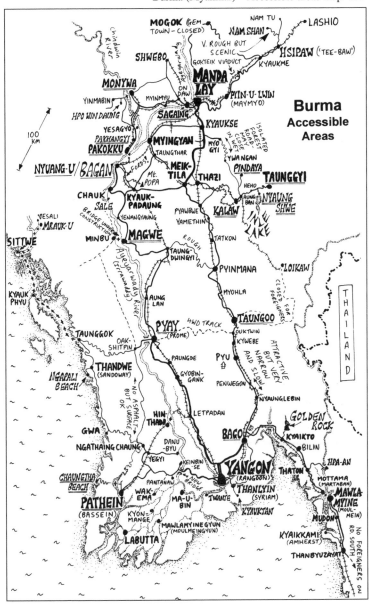

❏ **Essential information for travellers – Burma (Myanmar)**

● **Visa** Required. A four-week visa valid for two months is issued in 24 hours for around $20; a two-week extension is usually possible in Yangon (Rangoon).

● **Currency** US$1 = 1150Ky at street rates and tumbling daily: Website 💻 www.irrawaddy.org/ has the updated figures. Unbelievably it's officially only US$1 = 6.72Ky, a rate ignored by real people but used by some banks, credit cards and utility companies.

● **Time zone** 6½ hours ahead of GMT, ½hr behind Thailand, 1hr ahead of India, 1½hrs behind China).

● **Religious tone** Deeply Buddhist country coping with less than spiritual military government.

● **Health factors** Don't drink the tap water. There's a real risk of malaria throughout most of the country and some of cholera.

● **Special dangers** Insurgency in some outlying areas. Rebel groups don't seem to target foreigners and you're unlikely to be allowed anywhere near a 'problem' area anyway. The undercover police are more likely to cause trouble for the people you meet than for yourself.

● **Social conventions** Standard Buddhist conventions apply. Wear long skirts/trousers (not shorts) for visits to all monasteries and remove shoes before entering the grounds (bring a bag to carry them or pay the shoe-attendant).

● **Traveller hubs** Nyuang U (Bagan), Nyaung Shwe (Inle Lake), White House hotel (Yangon), Hsipaw. Total backpacker numbers are relatively miniscule.

● **Key tips** On arrival in Yangon collect as many maps as possible (eg free from Myanmar Tours and Travels; MTT). Be very aware that visiting people's homes and staying in unlicensed accommodation can get your hosts into very serious trouble after you've left. Just because you don't see police doesn't mean that you're not being watched. Consider splashing out on hiring a driver and car for some of your trip as a safer way to meet the locals. Know the day of the week on which you were born.

BOYCOTT BURMA?

Given the repressive regime, many feel you 'shouldn't visit Burma until democracy does'. The idea is to choke off the hard currency that tourism brings. Visiting does, however, give locals a sense that they're not forgotten by the world outside. To minimize how much of your cash gets into government coffers:

● **Avoid taking trains** Foreigner pricing funds the regime – many of the rail lines were built and repaired using forced labour, and anyway the service is unreliable.

● **Stay in non-government hotels where possible** Most of the best cheap ones are private anyway. However, be careful about using unlicensed hotels or accepting hospitality from families. After you leave, your hosts may be arrested for their troubles, though you won't get to hear about it.

● **Try to avoid changing money at the airport** (See Money p165).

If you do boycott Burma, you may consider it morally consistent to boycott Laos as well. In Burma at least the opposition exists, albeit disgracefully emasculated. In Laos the opposition has never been allowed to organize at all.

❏ **Geo-political information – Burma (Myanmar)**
Population: 42–46 million according to different sources, 35m (1983), 30m (1975).
Area: 658,000 sq km.
Capital: Yangon (Rangoon), 4 million but very widely spread.
Other major cities: Mandalay (1,060,000), Mawlamyine (367,000), Bago (228,000), Pathein (220,000), Taunggyi, Sittwe/Akyab, Monywa (160,000), Meiktila, Mergui (150,000), Lashio, Pyay (130,000). These official figures are deceptive – only Mandalay really feels like a city at all (much more so than Yangon).
GNP per capita: $1500 estimates seem optimistic.
Currency history: Kyat/US$1 – Official rate Jan 2001: 6.60Ky, Jan 1997: 5.4Ky, 1994: 5.9Ky, 1991: 6.3Ky, 1986: 7.3Ky. The real/black market rate is vastly higher.
Major exports/economy: Gemstones, timber, agriculture, illicit drugs.
Ethnic mix: Extremely complex: Burmese/Burman 68%, Shan (9%), Karen (7%), Chin, Kachin (3%), Mon (2%), Chinese (2%), Indian (2%).
Official languages: 'Myanmar'/Burmese (also spoken are Chin, Kachin, Karen, Kayah, Mon and others).
Religious mix: Buddhist (89%), Muslim (4%), Christian (2%), Hindu (2%).
Landmarks of national history: **849**: Pagan founded. **1287**: Mongol invasion. **1826, 1852** and **1885**: Wars with British India resulted in progressive annexation of the Burmese kingdoms. **1857**: Capital of upper Burma moved to Mandalay from Amarapura. **1890**: Shan States became British. **1948**: Independence. **1989** Names changed. Burma became Myanmar **27 May 1990**: Election (won by Aung San Suu Kyi, daughter of Independence leader) ignored by SLORC (the State Law and Order Restoration Council) – the ruling military Junta. **1991**: Nobel Peace Prize for Aung San Suu Kyi but 'the Lady' remained under house arrest for most of the 1990s. **1997** SLORC renamed the State Peace and Development Council (SPDC).
Leaders: General Than Shwe is Prime Minister, Minister of Defence and chairman of the SPDC. Secretary #1 Khin Kyut and Secretary #2 Tin U also wield considerable power.
Pressing political issues: International outcries against human rights abuses, fudged democracy. Drafting of a new constitution which the SLORC abolished in 1974; a new constitution has been planned since 1993. Democracy groups in 1996 announced plans to formulate an alternative constitution, which the SLORC made a criminal offence (punishable by 20 years in jail) a few days later.

HIGHLIGHTS

Shwedagon Pagoda (see the box on p171), timeless Inle Lake, the peaceful ruins of former capital Awa, the surreally-perched Golden Rock, U Bein's bridge (Amarapura/Taungmyo) at sunset (the world's longest teak bridge), river boat trips, towns that tourists overlook such as Taungoo and Kyaukse, the feeling of 'South-East Asia as it used to be', padding barefoot around any town's central pagoda (Paya), waiting at a river-boat terminal with a $0.30 flask of gin and mango.

WHEN TO GO

The coolest time is between October and February. Yangon is pleasantly warm during these months but you'll need a sweater at night in the interior of the country, and perhaps a jacket at night at higher altitudes (eg at Kalaw which is positively frigid after dark, though sweltering by day).

❏ **Old and new names**

Pointing out (correctly enough) that many place names were colonial anachronisms, the SLORC set about renaming everything. The country is now officially the Union of Myanmar (reasonably enough as the Burmese are just one group within a complex ethnic jigsaw), the people now speak 'Myanmar' language (less politically correct as this refers to Burmese), colonial names have been dropped, and other names have been given standardized spellings which may look different, but are simply different transliterations of the same Burmese letters rather like Peking becoming Beijing (eg Rangoon > Yangon). Certain of the old names remain in everyday use, and several Burmese democracy groups suggest people continue using them as a sort of anti-government protest. In the list below * marks the name that unscientifically seemed to be in most common usage. Everyone knows the old names, so their use shouldn't cause much confusion.

Town names

Old	New	Old	New
Akyab	Sittwe*	Moulmein	Mawlamyine*
Amherst	Kyaikkami*	Pagan	Bagan*
Ava/Awa*	Inwa	Prome	Pyay ('Pee')*
Bago*	Pegu	Rangoon	Yangon*
Bassein	Pathein*	Sandoway	Thandwe*
Maymyo*	Pyin U Lwin	Syriam*	Tanyin/Thanlyin

State names

Old	New
Arakan	Rakhine
Karen	Kayin

River names

Old	New
Irrawaddy	Ayeyarwady
Salween	Thanlwin

COLOUR SECTION (following pages)

● **C1** *Top* Timeless Bagan (see p184). *Bottom left* Mingun: would have been the world's largest stupa. Now it's just a huge pile of bricks. *Bottom right* Smears of *thanaka* keep sunburn at bay in Burma.

● **C2** *Top* Petronas Towers, Kuala Lumpur. *Bottom left* Wat Arun, Bangkok. *Bottom right* Ya Taw Me Paya, Taunggyi.

● **C3** Angkor (see p108): *Top* Angkor Wat's unfashionable east end. *Bottom left* Tree-strangled Ta Prohm *Bottom right* The inscrutable face of the Bayon.

● **C4** Transport: *Clockwise from top left* 1) Pick-ups can get very full. 2) Approaching Bagan by chartered boat from Pakokku. 3) The Siem Reap–Phnom Penh boats are frequently overloaded – the best views are from a precarious perch on the roof. 4) The hard life of a cyclo driver. 5) Overloaded pick-up. 6) Speedy and erratic, Cambodian moto drivers wear caps but you'll soon wish you had a helmet. 7) Antique tuk tuk, Thailand.8) Nam-Ou river boats at Muang Ngoi.

● **C5** You may leave home to see places but it's the people you meet while you travel that you'll remember when you return.

● **C6** Food: *Top left* The ubiquitous Burmese tea-leaf salad, usually served with palm wine and jaggary. *Top right* Fried locusts: a tasty snack on the streets of Bangkok (© BT). *Middle left* Durian seller (© BT). *Middle right* Drying rice noodles (see p183). *Bottom left* Fast food Burmese style, Aungban market. *Bottom right* Piles of rambutan and other delicious local fruit you should try. (© BT).

● **C7** *Top* South-East Asia has every kind of beach to offer, from tourist beaches (top left: Batu Feringghi, Malaysia) to deserted pristine sands (top right: Komodo, Indonesia)(© BT). *Middle left* Upmarket beach hut, Koh Phi Phi (© BT). *Middle right* Even in some 'open' areas of Burma you can expect occasional passport checks as here on the Pyay–Pathein road. *Bottom left* Sakura Hostel, old Lijiang (Yunnan). *Bottom right* View from Room 12, Saysong GH, Vang Vieng (Laos).

● **C8** Bangkok: *Top* Long-tailed boats on the Chao Phraya river, Banglampoo. *Bottom left* Statue at the Royal Palace (© BT). *Bottom right* Familiar signboards on the handy but much-derided Kao San Rd.

All photographs © Mark Elliott unless otherwise indicated (BT = Bryn Thomas)

IMMIGRATION CHECK

The peak tourist season is in December, with January and February also being popular (dry, less hot). March to May is the hot season and it's really hot! Transport is packed the first two weeks of March (end of the school year) and even fuller than usual during *Thingyan* (the New Year water festival in March/April, see below and p22) so the only thing to do is relax for a week wherever you are stuck and join in the splashing (hotels remain open, though most restaurants close). Schools reopen from the last week of May and buses are packed full again.

The monsoons begin in early June bringing lower temperatures but higher humidity. The rain isn't too bad in Mandalay and the north, but the Ayeyarwady/Irrawaddy delta becomes one giant rainstorm and the Gulf of Martaban region isn't much better. Many roads get washed out and even the road access to Bagan can be difficult. You can get stuck for days even on major routes. The west coast may become unreachable altogether. However, boat trips are faster with higher water and the dust-bowl winter fields are transformed into magical emerald greens. Around late September the monsoons begin to fade away, though not always in a hurry – it rained a little even in mid-November during one visit to Bagan.

❑ Calendar and festivals

Events are based around the Burmese lunar calendar, with many festivals year-round (see below). While businesses take weekends on Saturdays and Sundays, markets and rural workers still observe full, new and half moon days as their weekly rest days.

Burmese month (and its Western equivalent) plus what happens

● **Tagu (March–April)**   *Thingyan* water spraying mayhem everywhere for the Burmese new year. The festival lasts for three or four days depending on astrologers' decrees, but the holiday is longer: 90% of restaurants are closed but hotels stay open. However, you'll be stuck for days as transport is full for a week before and after.

● **Kason (April–May)**   Pouring water on the roots of bodhi trees on full moon ('Buddha') day.

● **Nayon (May–June)**   Mt Popa festival

● **Waso (June–July)**   Start of the three-month 'Buddhist lent', Sangha monks go into retreat. Full moon is the day of Buddha's conception with cakes and flowers offered to images.

● **Wagaung (July–Aug)**   Several *nat* festivals

● **Tawthalin (Aug–Sept)**   Boat racing on Inle Lake and/or the Royal Lake in Yangon.

● **Thading-yut (Sept–Oct)**   The end of the Buddhist 'lent' is celebrated at full moon with a festival of light: lamps and candles illuminate pagodas signifying Buddha's return to earth. A popular time for weddings.

● **Tazaung-mon (Oct–Nov)**   *Kahtein* festivals: '*Pantthagu*' offerings plus weaving contests between unmarried women to create the best ceremonial robes for monks and Buddha images. Taunggyi hotels are over-full during the full moon hot-air balloon festival.

● **Nadaw (Nov–Dec)**   More *nat* festivals to placate the local spirits. *Sarsodaw* literature day.

● **Pyatho (Dec–Jan)**   Traditional month of equestrian festivals, but nowadays mounted bowmen are rare!

● **Tabodwe (Jan–Feb)**   *Htamanei* harvest festival with rice-coconut 'cake'-making competitions.

● **Tabaung (Feb–Mar)**   *Pujayanti* (pagoda rededication) ceremonies. Sand mini-pagodas on riverbanks.

An optimist's overview of possible border crossings

At present the only sure way to visit Burma proper is to fly in to Yangon (or possibly to Mandalay, if approved). However, there are a few chinks in the armour. If rules are relaxed and the security on roads to the border zones improve, things might change suddenly so it's always worth asking. Below I'll summarise the present situation by border post (letters refer to routes marked on the map opposite).

A, **B** and **D** usually allow day passes for visitors to cross from Thailand. You leave your passport with the Thai immigration office in Ranong, Sangkhlaburi or Mae Sai respectively. They'll give you a special paper (you'll need passport photos) that you take to the Burmese frontier point who'll charge you $5 for the right to wander into the border town. However, you're not allowed beyond a radius of a few kilometres. Without your passport that would not be wise, anyway.

If you're coming the other way and have flown to Kawthoung or Tachilek or somehow made it from Yangon to the border by truck (dodging all the road blocks and bandit ambushes en route), you are theoretically still not allowed to cross out of Burma without a permit and an officially approved 'guide'. In reality few have tested this but suitable palm greasing may well get you through. Recent reports suggest that groups of Thai visitors are already crossing on route **B** and continuing to Mawlamyine and beyond, so it's worth asking carefully as to whether Westerners are yet being allowed to join them.

C Crossing here is unlikely for the foreseeable future following a major outbreak of fighting in 2001, with Mae Sot town shelled from the Burmese side.

D, **E** and **F** In the mid-1990s a plan was signed to build an important new road from Thailand to China via Mae Sai and Daluo (points **D** and **F**) but as yet there's little sign that any real construction has been achieved. From time to time, agencies in Mae Sai have been allowed to run excursions to Kengtung. These are reported to be fascinating if uncomfortable, but typically cost from around $200 per person. You'll be expected to return to Mae Sai afterwards rather than being free to take the $76 flight on to Heho and Burma proper. Rumours of a route **E** into Laos are mostly apocryphal. Chinese citizens can cross border point **F** but there are no reports of success from other foreign travellers.

G There have been sporadic successes crossing between Muse and Ruili. Southbound was always tough, despite rumours of travellers joining Chinese tour groups ex-Kunming. Northbound it was possible in the late 1990s to hire a guide in Lashio to get you through the formalities. This cost around $100, though some bargained to as little as $40. Recently, however, the success rate seems low to nil, and Burmese visas issued in Kunming are specifically stamped 'No Land Entry'. But it's always worth a try!

H The Burma-India border region is closed and sensitive on both sides, and there is little semblance of a road. The WW2 era track from Myitkyina to Ledo has disappeared into the jungle. Even if there is a trail from Kalewa to Imphal, the chances of being allowed to use it are slimmer than having Scottie teleport you via the Enterprise.

Burma
Borders, states and
divisions

Practical information

VISAS AND FORMALITIES

One-month tourist visas are readily issued at Myanmar embassies usually within 24–48 hours. Visa extensions are not so easy, are issued in Yangon only and require a **recommendation letter**. For a **two-week extension** such a letter is available in one or two working days from Myanmar Tours and Travels (MTT) beside Sule Pagoda. It costs $2, requires three copies of your passport/visa, one copy of an FEC voucher proving that you really did change $200 into Monopoly money and a letter from your guesthouse proving you're staying in officially-approved accommodation.

For a **two- to four-week extension** (tough) take the same paperwork to the Ministry of Hotels and Tourism (1st floor up the unmarked second wooden staircase south of MTT, turn right into a Kafka-esque office of antiquated desks whence you should be ushered into the office of the friendly director for a little chat to check your non-political credentials). If all goes well and the minister approves, you should get the letter in three to four working days for 5FEC+500Ky. Armed with the letter and two photos, the immigration office on 37th St should take another one to two working days to issue the extension.

If you're likely to overstay your visa by less than four days it is possible to simply pay a $3/day fine on exit. Longer overstays are likely to get you into trouble.

For long stays you could try for a three-month business visa, with the possibility of a three-month extension but you'll need serious contacts in Burma. If you really plan to study Buddhism, your monastery will be able to get you a long stay pilgrim's visa – but this is also for serious applicants only!

Onward visas

It is only possible to get an onward visa in Yangon.

China 1 Pyidaungsu Yeiktha St, Mon to Fri, 9–11am. In 24 hours $60, two working days $40, four working days $30.

Laos Taw Win St near Pansea Hotel, Mon to Fri 8:30–12 noon. Three working days $38–50. Available the same day for $10 extra. Must enter within one month of issue.

Vietnam 36 Wingbar St, Mon to Fri 8–11:30am, 1–4pm. $50. Fixed entry dates. Takes one week to issue but you can leave a copy of your passport for processing while travelling then collect your visa when returning to Yangon.

Cambodia Your visa starts from the issue date so there's no real point applying here.

Bangladesh 56 Kaba Aye Paya Rd. Apply between 10am and 12:30pm Mon to Fri and collect the same afternoon. UK£40, US$45.

Permits and off-limit areas

Beyond the tourist circuit, much of the country is only tenuously in government hands (if at all) and 'for your protection' you are not allowed to visit several areas. Border zones, especially the frontier with India and the long thin tentacle of land stretching south along the Thai border, are typically the most sensitive and the police will turn you back if they find you there.

Chin state is out of bounds, though at the time of research tickets for the slow boat to the gateway town Kalewa *were* available from the port office in Monywa; staff seemed uncertain whether or not they were 'suitable' for foreigners.

It can be an amusing challenge to 'go for it' and try to reach the more outlying regions. If you're stopped and turned back it seems to be OK for you to plead ignorance (honestly in most cases). But there's a fair chance that the driver of whatever bus or car you were in will suffer more severely, especially if it's a blatant infraction.

There are 'brown zones' which may or may not be out of bounds. The exact rules regarding where tourists can and can't go are constantly changing, but if anything the open areas have reduced of late. Notably Laikaw (home of the Padaung 'giraffe' women) and Mogok (the gem-mining town) have recently closed. However, this seems to be a commercial ploy as you can still visit those areas with a government-approved (ie expensive) tour. Indeed with sufficient money and contacts you could get almost anywhere!

Similarly if you want 'land border exit clearance' (ie a legal permit to leave Burma overland having arrived by air) there are big fees, guide requirements and you'll also need a letter from the Immigration office in Yangon. Even then you're not totally assured success and, for the adventurous, it might prove cheaper to try simply paying your way through step by step!

Site fees

Archaeological zones – Bagan, nearby Salay, Sri Ksetra (Pyay), Inwa/Ava, Mingun – and the Inle Lake area require foreigners to buy site tickets ($3–10). This often covers a wide area including whole villages so there are sometimes opportunities to avoid payment.

MONEY

This is rather confusing. For years the official currency (the *Kyat* pronounced 'chat') has been artificially set at between 5Ky and 7Ky to the US$. As a cheap meal costs about 600Ky, Burma would appear to be very pricey. Fortunately even official money changers recognize a 'real' exchange rate that is vastly better – it fluctuates constantly but as we go to press is roughly US$1 = 1150Ky. That's right, nearly 200 times the official rate!

Given the instability of the kyat, many tourist services (notably train and air tickets, airport tax, and tourist-registered accommodation) are priced in US$. But you can also pay in FECs (Foreign Exchange Certificates). The latter are 'monopoly dollars'. Independent visitors are forced to buy 200 FECs on arrival at Yangon airport (for US$200). Since you can't legally reconvert them this means you are effectively forced to spend at least $200 during your stay, putting cash directly into the government's dirty wallet. However, if you have a 'package tour' visa the compulsory exchange rule is waived. Many politically-aware travellers try to avoid buying the 200FECs at the airport. You can attempt this by claiming that you are only staying a few days and/or offering a small 'gift' to the airport desk. Don't offer too big a gift or it'll be self defeating!

There have been sporadic rumours that the funny money may be withdrawn leaving traders with bundles of useless paper. It wouldn't be the first time in Burma that money was withdrawn: the 15, 25, 75 and old 100 'Bank of Burma' notes were demonetarized overnight in 1988. With the FEC worth some 10–20% less than the US$, hotels (understandably) have started to become reluctant to accept them (ie to accept 5FEC for a '$5' room). But for now most will and the FEC system continues. Check carefully with other travellers whether the system has broken down.

Kyat can be used for shopping, food and bus tickets. FECs can be changed for kyat. Should you find that you've blown all 200FECs (possible if you rent a car/take trains or internal flights) it is possible in a few places to buy more FEC using kyat that you've previously bought at a better rate using real US$. Or buy FECs for US dollars direct at around 1.1:1.2/1, eg from certain moneychangers in Mandalay, Yangon, and Inle (I won't endanger them by listing who – ask around). This gave as much as $1 = 1.26FEC in 2001, rather less in 2002.

Note that exchange rates vary from town to town, with the best deals in Yangon, small discrepancies in Mandalay, Bagan and Nyaung Shwe (Inle Lake) and generally much lower rates in other towns or with taxi drivers. A very few banks (open Mon to Fri, 10am–2pm) will change US$ travellers' cheques but they'll give you FECs at 1:1. The Foreign Exchange Bank in Yangon also gives US$ credit card cash advances but charges 6% commission and still gives you FECs. Some shops and restaurants also take plastic but make quite certain that you'll be billed in a hard currency before you charge anything. One traveller rashly charged a 45000Ky purchase that would have cost him less than $40 in black market cash. It was billed via the official rate at US$6521.74. And legally so!

TRANSPORT
Pick-ups/Linega

Pick-ups ('*Linega*' literally 'line bus') with makeshift plank seats in the back are the commonest form of short and medium distance public transport. Don't expect them to leave until they are so overloaded that the front wheels are lifting off the road. Women are almost always squeezed inside (with little or no view), while the last dozen or so (male) passengers are left clinging to a side railing with toes hooked onto a few precious inches of bumper – exhausting for a kilometre or two, a major physical ordeal on longer distances. Sitting on the roof would be easier, but the covering frame may not be strong enough and collapsing it onto the passengers below could cause serious harm as well as embarrassment.

Some linega drivers don't like taking foreigners – 'You move around too much,' one told me. An assurance that you'll behave is usually enough and will win you respect if you can keep it. Alternatively for about 50% more you can sit in a real seat in the front with the driver. As a foreigner it is possible you'll be charged about 50% more anyway. This is pure pragmatism; you take up about 50% more space.

Buses

Local buses are extremely cheap but infrequent and so packed that sardines prefer to be canned. In contrast the best 'express' services (most notably *Kyaw* and *Leo* on the Yangon–Mandalay route) do offer a pretty decent service, guaranteed seats, meal stops and there have even been tales of punka-wallah girls fanning you in lieu of air-conditioning. But even good express buses buck and bounce uncomfortably thanks to the dismal state of the roads, and as most travel by night you miss much of the best scenery.

Despite a sometimes wide selection of companies on main routes, almost all choose the same departure times (designed to arrive around dawn). If you stop part way you'll

often be asked to pay the same fare as if you were going to the bus's final destination. And once you're in an intermediate small town, it can be difficult to get any onward seat reservation so you may be stuck on pick-ups or local buses. In tourist centres it can be well worth paying the small commission to have guesthouses or agencies book your buses for you.

Leave plenty of time to reach the bus station which may be as much as 20km (Yangon) from the town centre. If buying express bus tickets from Nyaung Shwe/Inle beware that you'll actually be picked up from the Shwe Nyaung junction where nerve-racking long waits are common – it can be more reassuring to go all the way to Taunggyi bus station where all the services originate anyway (see map p179).

Train

Burmese trains are slow, expensive and often unreliable with very frequent delays especially on newer lines thanks to subsiding, uneven track (much of it laid by forced labour). Bring a bed-roll to pad the wooden slat seats – even for the once up-holstered 'first class' ones whose only real advantage is the easier chance of reservations. There are a few sleeper trains including a couple of private services which are more comfortable but little more punctual.

At most stations, tickets for foreigners are sold at an inflated tourist rate. Tickets from Mandalay and Yangon are doubly expensive as foreigners may only buy double cost 'first class' tickets. However, in areas that are 'off limits', travelling by train can make sense as your ticket can qualify as a quasi-official permit to pass through. Rail enthusiasts enjoy the precipitous Maymyo–Mandalay ride for its unusual, if not particularly spectacular series of switch-back directional reverses, and the Maymyo and Hsipaw run for the remarkable Gokteik viaduct.

The train timetables are available online at 🖥 www.yangonow.com/eng/transportation/train/schedule.html.

Air

Flying is usually the only way into Burma with the cheapest flights generally on Biman

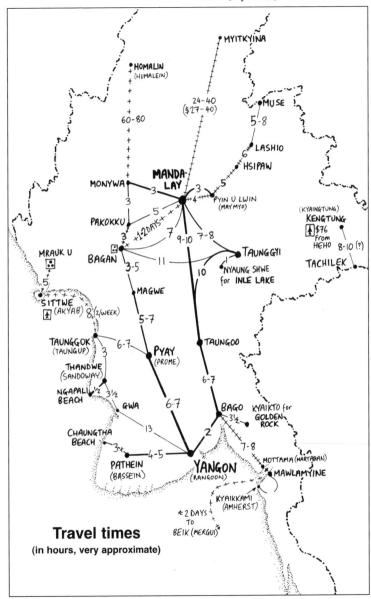

Travel times

(in hours, very approximate)

Bangladesh Airlines (eg as a stopover between Calcutta, India, and Bangkok).

There are three Burmese airlines with Air Mandalay (6T) and Yangon Airlines (HK, 🖥 www.yangonairways.com) generally considered safer than Myanmar Air (UB). Air Mandalay has two confusingly similar websites, 🖥 www.airmandalay.com and 🖥 www.air-mandalay.com – only the latter allows you to reserve online though prices are marginally higher than I found within Myanmar (despite its claims to the opposite).

Flying is the only permitted way to reach certain towns eg Kengtung/Kyaingtung (the cheapest is $73 from Heho near Inle Lake). Yangon–Tachilek costs $110 but to exit into Thailand you'd still need a guide/tour plus a $10 border fee/permit (issued in Yangon via MTT, takes a week or more). All in all that certainly isn't a way to save money over a normal Bangkok–Yangon return ticket. Direct Chiang Mai–Mandalay hopper flights are restricted to package-tour groups. If you buy a Chiang Mai–Mandalay ticket as an individual ($180 r/t) you'll actually arrive in Yangon and then be put onto a connecting flight to Mandalay,

Note that Mandalay's new airport is much further out of town than the old one; the latter is still marked on most maps. The international departure tax is US$10 or FECs.

Boat

The most popular boat trip with tourists is downstream from Mandalay to Bagan. 'Fast' boats leave Mandalay at 6am on Monday, Tuesday, Thursday, Friday and Saturday; they arrive at 3pm if the water level is high, but 5pm or later in January/February when the water is lower. In the reverse (upstream) direction it takes more like 15 hours. The Wednesday and Sunday slow boat takes 24–36 hours. A clever alternative is to go by road from Mandalay to Pakokku, then hire a private boatman to take you the three hours or so into Bagan. This is a wonderful way to arrive at sunset and may even save money as you arrive without falling into the gleeful hands of MTT and may be able to avoid baying ing the $10/per person Bagan entry fee.

Dozens of slow boats ply the inland waterways of the Ayeyarwady (Irrawaddy) Delta, most popular amongst tourists being Yangon–Pathein. Ideas for the adventurous include Pathein–Labutta and Monywa–Kalewa–Homalin/Humalein (at least three nights up river in an area that's closed to visitors travelling by road).

Renting bikes and cars

In most cities of tourist interest it is possible to rent bicycles. Not, however, in Yangon where such rentals have been banned 'for your protection'. There is no organized motorbike rental, and although a few travellers have managed to get 125cc bikes for $12/day from shops in Yangon, the shops don't want to advertise this. Taxis are inexpensive; $0.20 for a 10-minute ride, around $0.50 for an hour's hire.

Even if you could arrange it, self-drive car hire would be very awkward given the numerous, confusing roadblocks, the trouble of finding petrol (see below), and all the tolls and bridge fees. Renting a car with driver, however, is heartily recommended even if it takes you above the normal backpacker budget: rates are about $28–50/day including fuel, driver's accommodation and food, tolls etc. It works out cheaper for longer rentals on agreed routes assuming that you'll spend some of those days doing relatively few kilometres. Many drivers speak excellent English and can give great insights into the culture, food and political dilemmas as well as showing you the country. A highly-recommended agency is Myanma Smile (☎ 1-704255; 📠 553547 🖥 smilelan@mptmail .net.mm; open 12–5pm – I paid $580 for 24 days (half in FECs). Their office is a long way out of Yangon but once you call they will come and meet you.

Getting petrol Getting a beer in Iran is easier than finding a gas station in Burma. And when you do find one you will be allowed at best a hilariously minuscule ration – maybe just two litres after queuing up for half an hour. That is then formally written and stamped into a log book to stop you coming back again the same day. Or in some cases, the same month!! Certain towns only sell to residents of that town. And each car is allowed a pitiful monthly maximum. Over 96 litres and you may not buy petrol at all. Anywhere! Well anywhere official. Fortunately there is a black market. But drivers are reluctant to use it: not just because the petrol is five times the price, but also as the quality is unreliable and a bad batch may damage the engine. So if you do have your own wheels be aware that plans, prices and possibilities will revolve around petrol procurement. If you want to change your plans, offer to pay the difference and warn the driver well in advance so that the petrol puzzle can be resolved for the new route!

ACCOMMODATION

The government is increasingly strict on making foreigners sleep in registered tourist hotels. Competition in tourist hubs like Nyuang U (Bagan) and Nyaung Shwe (Inle) means that there are some real bargains, though there is a plan to enforce a new minimum price of $5/FECs per person: a way to push up tax revenues. In reality, many hotels are likely to maintain their old prices if you ask quietly and don't publicize what you actually pay. Mandalay and Yangon are generally much more expensive anyway, albeit with a couple of traveller favourites while certain towns have only one or two registered hotels, allowing them to push up prices.

In towns where there is no authorized accommodation, you 'might' be able to stay in local hotels (in which case conditions are fairly dismal, but prices are minimal and quoted in kyat). However, this could cause difficulties for the hotelier who may need to cover his back by reporting you to the police who in turn *might* just demand that you charter a taxi to the nearest town with authorized accommodation. And that could be very costly. Staying with locals is not really fair on your hosts – however hospitable they'd like to be, there is a real chance that they'd be arrested after you depart.

Note that the room prices quoted on the maps are those that I or other travellers have managed to bargain, not the price initially offered. Bargaining is almost always possi-

ble and how much you pay will depend on the season, the time of day you show up (prices are potentially cheapest in the early evening if space remains), and on how long you plan to stay.

Hotels marked with the symbol (!) are government owned or associated companies like the November Group. While a few of these are old colonial places worth visiting (not staying in), value for money is generally relatively low and your cash goes you know where.

FOOD

The main cuisines on offer are Myanmar (Burmese), Chinese (often very high quality and with English menus, and dishes from 600Ky), and Indian (common in Yangon and Mandalay). A typical Burmese meal is *hin* – an oily stew usually using mutton, fish or chicken, though commonly translated in local English as 'curry'. Ordering *hin* usually results in the magical appearance of a plethora of side dishes which are often more photogenic than palatable. This always includes the ubiquitous fermented *lappe* tea leaf salad which is a national passion but very much an acquired taste.

The standard breakfast meal is a form of rice pudding or *mohinga* (rice noodles with fish gravy) sold by roving hawkers as well as street stalls and restaurants from 5am until about 9.30am. The dish comes with different garnishes in the different regions.

The Burmese will be curious if you dare to order a dinner of *ngapi* (rice with fish paste) and after you've smelt it you might wish you hadn't. Other common dishes include: *amehnat* (roast beef cooked with sugar, onions and garlic), *myinkuayuet* (a side dish of leaves with roots, salad, ground nuts and garlic), *bangoki* (fried cauliflower), and *gobido* (fried vegetables with eggs, potatoes or beans). On an English menu, ordering 'white mustard' gets you Chinese Cabbage and 'fish cakes' usually stand for crispy shrimp crackers. Street snacks include appealing *moonlekau* (deep fried bracelets of sticky rice dipped in jaggary sauce) and the offputtingly black, gelatinous *bamageris*. For dessert, you can try *sawin-ma-kin*.

> ❏ **Superstition or facts of life?**
> Eight is the lucky number of the opposition, thus the 8th of the 8th month, 1988 was
> chosen as the beginning of a pro-democracy strike, and it started at eight minutes past
> 8am. SLORC strong man Ne Win's lucky number is nine, thus in the 1990s the coun-
> try started using 90Ky and 45Ky bills (both being divisible by nine and having digits
> which add up to nine). Being a former British colony, the Burmese used to drive on
> the left side of the road; until, the story has it, Ne Win was told that his right side was
> his lucky side and ordered everyone to change. With most vehicles bought second-
> hand from Thailand or Japan, the steering wheel is very frequently on the 'wrong' side.

DRINK
A flask of green tea (*akaiye*) usually comes
free with a meal. Coffee and Indian-style tea-
with-milk (*lappeye*) are commonly available
[pronounce this carefully or you'll get *lappe*
tea-leaf salad]. Both are served outrageously
sweet – ordering your drink *jah-neh-neh*
(with less sugar) might help. Safe bottled
water (*ye*) is available everywhere: typically
$0.10 for a litre though as little as $0.06 in
certain shops. Though relatively hard to find
(ask specifically), the potent Mandalay 'red'
beer is much better than the more common
Mandalay 'blue' (weak and gassy) or
Myanmar brands.

In Pyin U Lwin/Maymyo market you
can find several varieties of over-sweet fruit
wines, while all over the country locally-pro-
duced gin (great with mango soda) and
Myanmar whisky (in an obvious Johnny
Walker lookalike bottle) cost next to nothing.
In a bar, order them by '*fingers*' (shots) or
you'll end up being served a whole bottle!
Palm wine is drunk in villages and converted
into tasty *jaggary* sugar.

Tequila Sunlight, Grass Sofa
(Grasshopper) and Run Sour are amongst the
delightful entries on one famous hotel's care-
lessly-spelt cocktails menu.

STAYING IN TOUCH
Mail
Using black market kyat, the postal services
are perhaps the cheapest in Asia. Sending
mail is surprisingly efficient, especially from
Yangon. One traveller was advised to make
all mail look as worthless as possible and
even urged to sign the front of his postcards
to keep someone from ripping off the picture
(to be pasted on another piece of cardboard

and re-sold)! That said, all my mail arrived
safely in Europe and the US within 10 days
or less.

Telephone
International telephone calls are reasonable
from Mandalay but are difficult to place elsewhere. Foreigners are not allowed to carry
mobile phones so should you have one you
must leave it at Yangon Airport on arrival
and pick it up again on departure!

International country code: +95.
Yangon: 1, Mandalay: 2, Pyay: 53.

Email
Direct web access is simply not allowed.
Sending emails (and receiving replies) is
possible from a very few hotels plus a
money-changer on 27th St in Central
Mandalay, see map on p181. In each case
prices are outrageously expensive and use a
fixed mail provider. That means that web-
based servers like Hotmail/Yahoo are inaccessible. Warn people that you'll be offline
for the duration of your stay.

SHOPPING
Burma is hard to beat for handicrafts. While
much is artificially aged to look antique, old
and new laquerware alike is incredibly good
value, textiles are cheap and a whole range of
tempting gift items and art is available in
shops, markets and from hawkers at tourist
sites.

Some of the best prices for tea/tobacco-
boxes were at the Inle lakeside markets,
especially when things are packing up and
the tour groups have left. Visiting craft workshops is fascinating but prices tend to be
higher.

ACTIVITIES
Hiking
There is a great potential for hiking but at present it's only really sanctioned from Kalaw and Nyaung Shwe (Inle) where guides can take you into the attractive if heavily deforested hills and through disturbingly poor tribal villages.

Buddhism
Buddhist meditation courses are available in several monasteries but to get the long, pilgrim/monastic visa you'll need to make arrangements in advance or leave the country to change visa type.

The **Vipassana Centre** (☎ 1-39290, Burma Dhamna Joti, Nga Htat Gyi, Pagoda Rd, Bahon Township, Yangon) runs 10 or 11-day retreats twice a month.

Panditarama (☎ 531448, 📠 527171, 80-A Than Lwin Road, Shwegondine PO, Bahan, Yangon) offers longer, intensive Vipassana meditation retreats for experienced meditators under Sayadaw U Pandita and can arrange placement in the Hse Mea Gong forest monastery. Write well in advance.

The Aung Tha Pyay/**Swedaw Meditation Centre** near Taunggyi (☎ 081 22719), with its curiously kitschy tower and working 1950s Chevrolet, accepts tourist meditators for a donation and has a sub-monastery in Washington State, USA. One hundred thousand monks converge here at the March full moon.

Language
Several Yangon schools offer Burmese language studies, ask at MTT (see below).

Martial arts
Classes are held at the Yangon YMCA (3.30–5.30pm on Tue, Thur and Sat).

FURTHER INFORMATION
Information offices
Myanmar Tour and Travels (MTT) is the official tourist office cum travel agency. MTT's offices in Yangon (☎ 1-75328, 📠 1-82535) beside Sule Pagoda, plus a booth at

---

❏ The Shwedagon Pagoda
Totally dominating Yangon, this stupendous stupa is the holiest in Burma. It was established around 500BC by King Okkalapa, supposedly to house eight magical hairs which the Buddha personally gave to two Burmese trading brothers. However, one monk told us that this notion was in fact a terrible misunderstanding. 'Shwedagon houses only seven hairs' he insisted. 'The eighth is in a different pagoda across town. Your book must get this right!'

Expanded to its current vast size in the 13th century, the pagoda has a long political significance too as the central gathering point for anti-government resistance, both to colonists and to the current military junta.

But more than anything, it's fantastically beautiful. Surrounded by a forest of lesser shrines and images, the gleaming central *zedi* is covered with three-quarters of a tonne of gold and tipped with 5448 diamonds and 2317 rubies. It is at its most impressive viewed from a reasonable distance: eg from the Maha Wizara Pagoda terrace, across the Peoples' Park, floodlit at night, distantly glimpsed across Kadawgyi Lake or glowing at sunrise above the eastern access road. The latter is by far the best approach as you climb barefoot with pilgrims up a vast, ornate teak-covered stairway lined with colourful booths selling flowers, charms, votive candles, lucky papier-mâché owls, and shiny Buddha images.

Entry to the uppermost level for foreigners costs 5FEC (plus 3FEC for cameras) but before 6am it is rarely charged to those who act suitably pious (ie no photos!). Another plus of visiting at dawn is that there are many fewer tourists so the atmosphere is noticeably more reverent.

❏ Weights and measures
Markets can be confusing with prices often marked in Burmese numerals, volume measured in *nobizu* (0.283litres) and weights in *vis* (1.68kg), *ngazeda* (1/2 vis) or *taseda* (1/10 vis). Gold is weighed in *tical* and rather than 'carats' uses the *kittle* system in which 16 is pure gold and 1.8 is just copper.

---

the airport) give away maps when asked directly and are helpful if commercially biased with travel tips. The Mandalay office is a much smaller affair that charges for 'free' maps.

Maps and books
DPS produces excellent maps of Yangon, Bagan and Mandalay in various, regularly updated versions. They also print an OK country map. These are all generally available free at MTT in Yangon (worth stocking up) but will cost around 200Ky elsewhere. You can also access the maps on 🖥 www.dpsmap.com/.

Inwa Books (Yangon) sells the very accurate Nelles map of Burma at 2600Ky and a passable phrase book for 900Ky while Pagan Books (also Yangon) has the best selection of English-language books on Burmese history and culture.

At the time of writing, guidebooks to Burma are relatively poor. The 7th edition Lonely Planet guide is severely out of date but remains the most commonly used and can be found in a couple of Yangon bookshops. The Guide de Routard (French)

misses out Pathein and the delta area.

For trips off the beaten track, guidebooks from the 1960s and 1970s often offer the most comprehensive coverage of areas now officially closed – copies are occasionally available second-hand in Yangon.

Several books have been written about current political happenings. *Freedom From Fear* by Aung San Suu Kyi (Penguin, 1991) is an excellent read, as is Bertil Lintner's *Outrage* (White Lotus, 1990) which details the 1988 democracy uprising, and Edith Mirante's *Burmese Looking Glass: A Human Rights Adventure and a Jungle Revolution* (Grove, 1993).

Shelby Tucker's *Burma: The Curse of Independence* and David Steinberg's prohibitively expensive *The State of Myanmar* take starkly contrasting views on the roots of Burma's problems but share a sense of hopelessness as to their solution.

The classic colonial account is *Burmese Days* by George Orwell (Penguin, first published in 1934) whose descriptions of places and people read as if they were written yesterday. Most of the books listed are available in Bangkok.

Useful websites
🖥 www.yangonow.com/eng/ is a promising new site with everything from Burmese pop to helpful transport timetables, written in endearingly imperfect English.

🖥 www.passplanet.com/Myanmar/ offers Passplanet's usual high standard of straight-talking personal reviews, detailed practical information and helpful opinion polls.

🖥 http://private.addcom.de/asiaphoto/burma/burmapage.htm is one way into a gorgeous photo tour of Burma with plenty of travel notes and background information.

🖥 www.dpsmap.com. is the website of Myanmar's excellent free tourist-map company which allows you to download maps for free.

🖥 www.burmaproject.org/ is one of many sites offering compiled news reports from Burma.

❏ Meeting the locals

● **The people** The Burmese are naturally friendly and kind, but fraternizing with foreigners can be a very dangerous business for locals, facing possible arrest if they are suspected of passing on anti-government views. So it isn't a good idea to push the reluctant to discuss politics! Many young monks are eager to expand their linguistic and general knowledge as part of their religious devotions, and they can often be the most interesting source of deeper conversation. In areas not under government control, people are contrastingly very free with their opinions. An introduction might begin 'I am a Karen rebel, my name is.......'

Note that many Burmese students learn how to write English without necessarily having the confidence to speak it so a pen and paper can help you through the language barrier.

● **Lifestyle peculiarities** Across the social spectrum you'll see Burmese faces (notably women) ghoulishly plastered with what appears to be swirls of white paint. In fact this is a natural sunscreen made by grinding *thanaka* sticks (sold in any market) or bought as a conveniently pre-prepared cream from supermarkets.

Archetypal peasant villagers smoke chunky *cheroots* – artisanal cigars. Especially in the delta area, many blacken their teeth and redden their spittle by chewing leaf-wrapped parcels of betel nut pasted with lime and spices. Fascinating *yesa* (literally 'lick-eat') candies wage full-blown ammoniacal assaults on the senses in the guise of digestive aids. With so little investment in modern industry, Burma has more traditional craftsmen than anywhere else in the region and visits to workshops (laquerware, paper-making, metal crafts, embroidery etc etc) are fascinating and rarely involve any sales pressure.

● **Burmese celebrities**: Everywhere you'll see the name and statues of **Aung San** (Bogyoke), he was the hero of Burmese independence. However, mentioning his daughter, the 'Lady' (opposition leader Aung San Suu Kyi) is best avoided till you know someone pretty well and you're sure that you're not being overheard!

You're on much safer ground admiring actress **Tata Mo-U**, or actor **Luin Moe** (who looks a little like a Burmese Will Smith). They are ubiquitous, appearing in more than half of all TV and print advertisements. **Kyaw Hein** is arguably the most famous actor of all and you're unlikely to find someone who doesn't like him. **Zaw Ping** ('So Bai'), is a 'Chris Rea-rocker', but his big 2001 hit *Min-ne-ma Chidabi*, had his fans unwittingly singing along to the tune of Ronan Keating's *When you say nothing at all*. **Leh Pyu** mixes ballads with Scorpions-style guitar hero antics on the excellent 'Fansidar' CD. **Acid** are Burmese rappers using Western pop hooks while **Ni Tuh** is altogether more gentle.

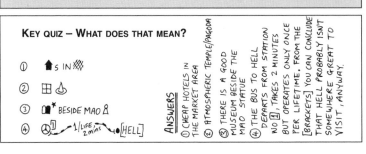

KEY QUIZ – WHAT DOES THAT MEAN?

① 🏠s IN 卐

② 田 ⚓

③ 📷* BESIDE MAO 尺

④ 🕐—1/LIFE 2mins—•[HELL]

ANSWERS
① CHEAP HOTELS IN THE MARKET AREA
② ATMOSPHERIC TEMPLE/PAGODA
③ THERE IS A GOOD MUSEUM BESIDE THE MAO STATUE
④ THE BUS TO HELL DEPARTS FROM STATION NO ①, TAKES 2 MINUTES BUT OPERATES ONLY ONCE PER LIFETIME. FROM THE [BRACKETS] YOU CAN CONCLUDE THAT HELL PROBABLY ISN'T SOMEWHERE GREAT TO VISIT, ANYWAY.

BURMESE

THE BEAUTIFULLY ROUNDED SCRIPT IS RATHER HARD TO READ. AS IN THAI, VOWELS CLUSTER AROUND ROOT CONSONANTS (SEE EXAMPLES →) BUT BURMESE VOWELS CAN LOOK CONFUSINGLY LIKE CERTAIN CONSON'TS.

EXAMPLES

CITY = myou = Modifier, Root Con., Y = see box

The . is a tone marker

NOODLES = hkau hswe = Modifier, Root Consonants, see box

ROOT CONSONANTS

B B C/Ch D D D D D G G H* Hk Hp Hs Ht Ht J(=G+Y) K Ky(=Ch/C) L L

M N N N(at end of syllable) P "Q"(or long vowel) S T Th W* Y(R) Y Z Z(Sy)

Ng Ny C

* CONSONANTS THAT MODIFY OTHERS:
H* (HATU) eg
Hm
W* [SEE "U"] Zw
Y*
eg see J, Ky above

SIMPLE VOWELS

Pronounced after the consonant ■, even if written before or around it:

A (CF "D") (CF "Y*") E Ei I O Ou U

TONE MARKS (JUST IGNORE THEM AT FIRST) TONE 1 None TONE 2 TONE 3

→ NOTE THAT ■ || IS NOT "U": I¯ MARKS THE END OF PHRASE
→ COMPARE (U) WITH (H*)

VOWELS IN DISGUISE

A (like "K") Ai (like "K") A' (like "He") Ain An Au Ay (= long I)

Aun E' Ei Ein I' In Ou

Oun U' (Same as a "W" modifier) Un

WHERE ■ = ANY CONSONANT

TOILET (EINDA) MARKERS

ma (meima) WOMEN'S
chā (yaucha) MEN'S

Burmese Numerals
1 2 3 4 5 6 7 8 9 10

❏ Language

There are many distinct tribal tongues but the national 'Myanmar Language' (Burmese) is spoken in most areas you're likely to reach and English remains surprisingly well understood. While spoken Burmese has its origin in Central Asia, the curvaceous script comes from South India and is similar to the Sinhalese writing found today in Sri Lanka. It's devilishly complex to learn with sneakily morphing modifiers like the *Hatu* which can wreak major pronunciation changes with the smallest of strokes. To have any chance of reading spidery handwritten characters you'll need to learn the correct stroke order for each letter.

It takes a lot of practice to start hearing the difference between the many similar vowel sounds (eg *ka* = dance, *kaa* = catch, *kaar* = car; good luck with *kaun* and *kaung*). Several pairs of consonants (eg B and P, K and G,Th and T) are also easy to confuse. Further confusion springs from the different transliteration systems: the first letter of Yangon is often transliterated as R, hence the confusion between Yangon and Rangoon, which are simply alternative Latin renderings of the same Burmese word. Ky is pronounced 'ch', Gy is 'j' and a long 'i' sound is usually transliterated as 'ay'.

Burmese numerals are often used for local transport (eg bus numbers and time tables) and in market pricing, but Western numbers are generally understood.

Some phrases in Myanmar/Burmese:

Hello – *mingala ba*
Thank you – *chizu timbade*
Don't have/
  not possible – *mishibu*
(A polite way to turn some one down) – *ahnah-bareh*
It tastes good – *salo-kounde*

Some phrases in Palaung
(Spoken in some 'trek' villages around Kalaw)

Hello – *mekka*
Good-bye – *auru wee yu*
Thank you – *la'da !ggu*
  (more formally *lada gong gai jun*)
Beautiful – *m'chik a'sow*
Longhouse – *tai yow*

Some phrases in Karen

How are you? – *na-aw hsaw-ha?*
(reply...) – *mwe*
Thank you (very much)
    Tabyu (do-lor)
    or
    hsa-khawn
    in Pho Karen

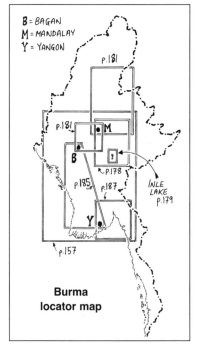

B = BAGAN
M = MANDALAY
Y = YANGON

p.181

p.181

M

B

p.178

p.185   p.187

INLE LAKE p.179

Y

p.157

Burma locator map

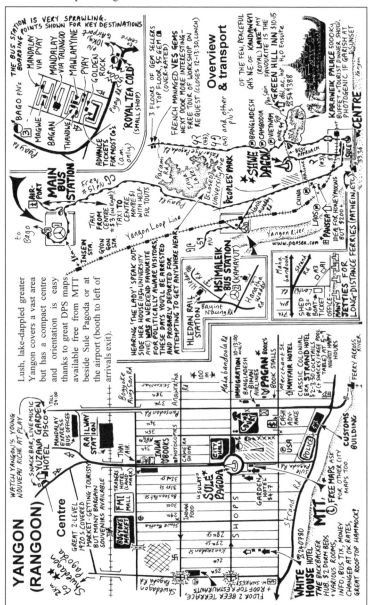

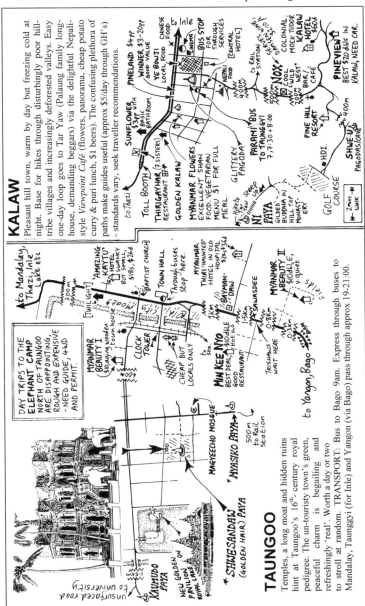

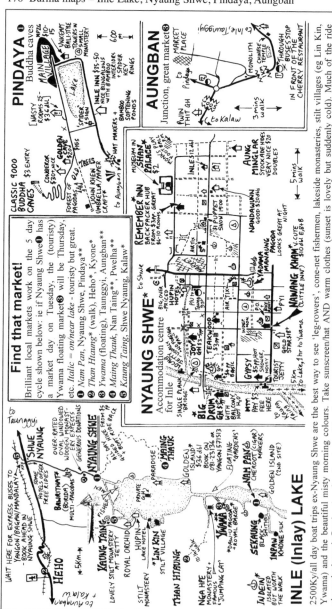

PINDAYA — Buddha caves

AUNGBAN — Junction, great market

NYAUNG SHWE — Accommodation centre for Inle

INLE (Inlay) LAKE

Find that market!

Brilliant local markets work on the 5 day cycle shown below: ie if Nyaung Shwe❶ has a market day on Tuesday, the (touristy) Ywama floating market❷ will be Thursday, etc. Italic = on/near lake - touristy but great.

❶ Nam Pan, Nyaung Shwe, Pindaya**
❷ Than Htaung* (walk), Heho*, Kyone*
❸ Ywama (floating), Taunggyi, Aungban**
❹ Maing Thauk, Nan Taing*, Pwelha**
❺ Kaung Taing, Shwe Nyaung, Kalaw*

2500Ky/all day boat trips ex-Nyaung Shwe are the best way to see 'leg-rowers', cone-net fishermen, lakeside monasteries, stilt villages (eg Lin Kin, Ywama) and the beautiful misty morning colours. Take sunscreen/hat AND warm clothes (sunset is lovely but suddenly cold). Much of the ride channels through floating 'gardens' and marsh/reeds - most maps draw the lake misleading big. Boatmen want to take you to various craft workshops: DO GO ALONG - these are mostly very interesting and have zero sales pressure. The 3FEC site fee for the lake area is valid 1 week. Several stilt hotels make tempting splurges, but you pay the boat taxis on top. Cheap accommodation in Nyaung Shwe except Oct festival.

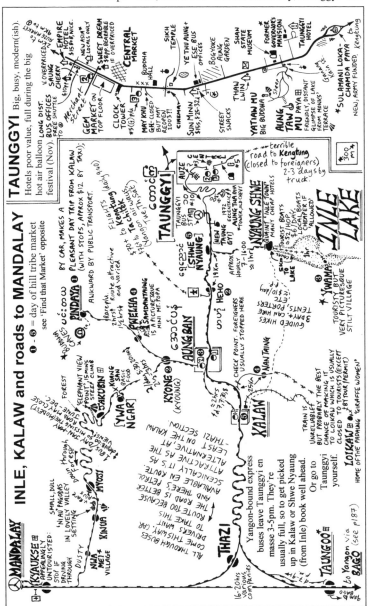

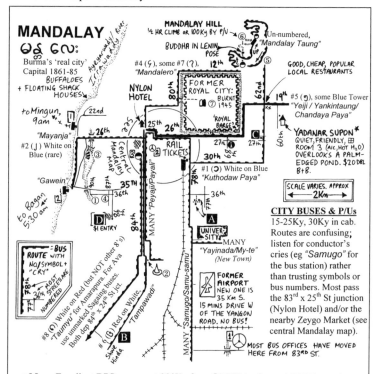

MANDALAY

ဗန္ဒေလ:

Burma's 'real city'
Capital 1861-85
BUFFALOES
+ FLOATING SHACK
HOUSES

to Mingun,
9am

"Mayanja"
#2 (၂) White on
Blue (rare)

"Gawein"

to Bagan
5-30 am

MANDALAY HILL
½ HR CLIMB OR 100Ky BY P/V
BUDDHA IN LENIN
POSE

#4 (၄), some #7 (?),
"Mandalero"

NYLON
HOTEL

22nd

26th

25th

35TH

36th

FORMER
ROYAL CITY:
BURNT
1945

'ROYAL
BARGE'

26th

27th

30th

RAIL
TICKETS

Central Mandalay map

#1 (၁) White on Blue
"Kuthodaw Paya"

36th

Un-numbered,
"Mandalay Taung"

GOOD, CHEAP, POPULAR
LOCAL RESTAURANTS

19th #5 (၅), some Blue Tower
"Yeiji / Yankintaung/
Chandaya Paya"

YADANAR SUPON
QUIET, FRIENDLY,
ROOM 3 (A/C, HOT H₂O)
OVERLOOKS A PALM-
EDGED POND. $20 DBL
B+B.

SCALE VARIES. APPROX
◄——— 2Km ———►

<u>CITY BUSES & P/Us</u>
15-25Ky, 30Ky in cab.
Routes are confusing;
listen for conductor's
cries (eg *"Samugo"* for
the bus station) rather
than trusting symbols or
bus numbers. Most pass
the 83rd x 25th St junction
(Nylon Hotel) and/or the
nearby Zeygo Market (see
central Mandalay map).

:BUS
ROUTE WITH
No/SYMBOL +
"CRY"

MOST STREETS ARE
NUMBERED

$1 ENTRY

UNIVER-
SITY

MANY
"Yayinada/My-te"
(New Town)

FORMER
AIRPORT
NEW ONE IS
35 KM S.
15 MINS DRIVE W
OF THE YANGON
ROAD. NO BUS!

#8 (၈) White on Red (but NOT other 8's)
"Taunryu" for Amarapura. For Ava
use unmarked Sagaing buses.
Both dep 84th x 24th St jct.

"Peyaji/Payal"

"Tampawadi"

9 (၉) Red on White

MANY "Samugo/Samu-samu"

Shwe Hinda

MOST BUS OFFICES HAVE MOVED
HERE FROM 83RD ST.

● <u>Maps</u> Excellent DPS maps cost 200Ky from ❶MTT (or free at MTT Yangon).
● <u>Craft Workshops</u> are low key and remarkably interesting. **A** ***Gold leaf
pounders (within block 78-77th x36th) easy to miss shacks, totally uncommercial.
B **Bronze Buddha foundary (☎23182, Shwe Hinda Rd). **C** *Typical 'stuffed'
embroidery (Sandar Tun shop, 62nd [26-27th]). Avoid the hassly gem market **D** .
● <u>Favourite pagodas</u>: ① **Shwe-In-Bin**: wooden, free entry, peaceful,
② **Peyaji** (Mahamuni Paya): bustling atmosphere, many wood carvers in precinct.
4FEC to approach the sacred inner sanctum (men only) where Buddha is spongily
bulbous with the centuries of gold leaf. Spy the statue from afar without paying.
③ **Chan Thraya**: little visited, picturesque seen across pond with wooden bridge.
④ **Masoe Yein Taik**: free, visually unimpressive but monks have interesting views.
⑤ Popular with tourists but more crowded and commercialised are a group of
pagodas at the base of Mandalay Hill. Includes a) **Sandamani Paya** (forest of
white stupas) and **Kuthodaw** ("world's biggest book" marble slabs) 5FEC for the
two, b) **Shwenandaw Paya** (wooden), 5FEC, c) **Kyauktawgyi Paya** (giant
Buddha carved from single piece of marble), 2FEC. **Mandalay Hill** ⑥ is over-
rated (3FEC to enter upper levels). Sunset on top is most memorable for the many
English-speaking locals who converge there to find conversation practice.
● Behind the <u>vast moat and walls</u> that dominate central Mandalay the **palace** ⑦
is a modern concrete reconstruction. Very mixed reviews. 5FEC

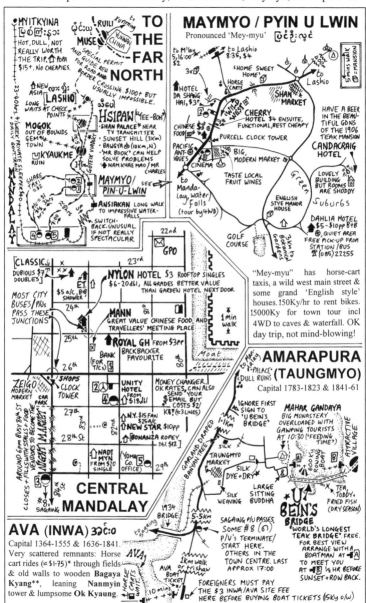

"Mey-myu" has horse-cart taxis, a wild west main street & some grand 'English style' houses. 150Ky/hr to rent bikes. 15000Ky for town tour incl 4WD to caves & waterfall. OK day trip, not mind-blowing!

MONYWA

Quietly attractive river town.

MONYWA HOTEL, $30dbl, POOR
GOOD FRIED NOODLES
RAUNG SAN
170Kg

SHWE TAUNG TAN
$5pp B+B

CHERRY G.H.

CLOCK TOWER

NEW BUS STA.

BOAT TICKETS

PASSENGER BOATS. Locals cross river for 10Ky. Foreigners must charter boat @ 500Ky

MYO MYAT G.H.

only 300 m

1.5Km

5 MINS WALK

RAISED PROMENADE

CAR FERRY

MINGUN

Ring the world's 2nd largest bell (Moscow's is bigger but cracked!) See what would have been the world's biggest stupa had 18/19th century King Bodawpaya finished it. Now a truly gigantic, quake-cracked pile of bricks.

1 MIN WALK
HUGE BELL IN HERE
HSIN BYU MEH PAYA
IRRAWADDY

INFIRMARY

RUINED 'CHINTHE' GUARDIAN DRAGON/LIONS

MINGUN PAYA*

HILL TOP MONASTERY

TICKET BOOTH (SITE FEE 3FEC)

DEAD END

VILLAGE

'DOGS'

CLIMB OVER SMALL FENCE

TOURIST BOAT, 13:00ish

to Mandalay

THIS TRACK GIVES A NICE APPROACH TO THE GREAT MINGUN PAYA AND A CHANCE TO AVOID PAYING!

PAKHANGYI

to Monywa

3FEC combined entry ticket for the museum Ⓐ plus the wooden monasteries of Ⓑ Chaung Dogyi & Ⓒ Pakhan Ngeh (supposedly the world's largest).

OLD PAGODAS IN TREES

POTTERY

AIYUA VILLAGE
2Km

19th CENTURY, BRICK

SCHOOL Ⓒ

CITY WALL FRAGMENTS

Hike 6Km

Ⓐ

Approx 500 m

Ⓑ

OLD PAGODAS IN FIELD

RED/GOLD GATEWAY

SITU SHIN PAYA 1118 AD

to Pakokku

SAGAING

Capital city 1315-64 & 1760-64. Now a pilgrimage centre with dozens of monasteries on the hills and alleys away from the town's disappointing centre.

to Monywa

KAUNG MUDAW 1636 PAGODA $2FEC ENTRY, VISIBLE FROM RD.

SILVER SMITHS EN ROUTE

Ticket booth and access Rd (cars) for SAGAING HILL, 2Km DRIVE BEYOND. $4 P.P.

SAGAING HILL PAGODAS

1.3Km

AUNG SAN STATUE

HAPPY HOTEL $8pp fan, shared squat. $15-25 en suite

LOVELY AREA WITH ALLEYS, MONASTERIES AND 'LESSER' PAGODAS. NICE STROLLING AND NO ENTRY FEE

MARKET IN UGLY BUILDING

TRI-SHAWS

CINEMA

TOWN CENTRE

to Mandalay

PAKOKKU

Pleasantly green, long Irrawaddy river town.

to Monywa

BUSES TO MONYWA 5,10,14:00

THA PYO G.H.

MARKET AREA, NOT VISIBLE FROM MAIN STREET.

Plus to local villages

PARK

SMALL BRIDGE

to Kanma village

BUSES TO MANDALAY (5+10 am) AND YANGON (7am, 2300Ky)

BICYCLE REPAIR SHOP

TEH HO SHIN PAYA (1117 AD)

BAKHURAI MONASTERY

'ROYAL WALK'

GOOD FOOD @ 250Ky/meal

TRI-SHAWS

SANDY TRACK

Naga St.

Teho shin

Alternative accommodation at MYA YA THANAR
☎ 62 21457

SMALL GREEN SIGN IN TREES

FREIGHT BOATS

PASSENGER BOATS ACROSS RIVER + TO NUANG U (BAGAN) AT 6,9,13:00

MANDALAY-BAGAN FERRY STOPS HERE
CAR FERRY - ASK AT RESTAURANTS TO CHARTER BOAT TO BAGAN

to Bagan. Beware - wide ford can take 1-2hrs in wet season. Taste palmwine/Saagang en route

Kyauk-Padaung 16mi

to Myingyan

Mt POPA

Home of the 'Nats' (spirits) and myriad monkeys. Free entry but looking AT the shrine on its abrupt rocky knob is nicer than the views gained by climbing the 700 steps to the top!

MMS $7pp COLD H₂O EN SUITE

PRIVATE GH

MT POPA RESORT $150++

ZAY YAR THEIN $15/20 cold H₂O, $20/30 hot with A/C

Mt POPA

SEVERAL BASIC RESTAURANTS

plus to K'Pathaung + BAGAN (13-13:30)

LEAVE SHOES

SCHEMATIC: V. ROUGH SCALE 300m≈

Mandalay – Bagan tactics. Direct Mandalay-Bagan boats provide a popular and relaxing way to while away a day (or two if you take the slow boat going upstream). But views aren't particularly spectacular and, especially if you have a car, it's more interesting to drive via Sagaing to Monywa then continue to Pakokku where by chartering your own boat at around 4pm, you can arrive idyllically in Bagan at sunset. And as MTT won't be expecting you, you might be able to avoid the $10 Bagan site fee too! Note that Pakhangyi & Myinmyu are only mildly interesting. Nice brief stops when driving, but they have no hotels and you might get stuck if you try to stop off using public transport. Note also that south bound drivers will want you to arrive in Pakokku by 1pm to reserve a place on the last car ferry.

Ava/Inwa is best visited as a day trip from Mandalay, combined with a trip to Amarapura/U Bein Bridge. If you visit Mt Popa as a day trip from Bagan, your Bagan site-fee tickets will be examined on returning (or else you'll have to buy a new one).

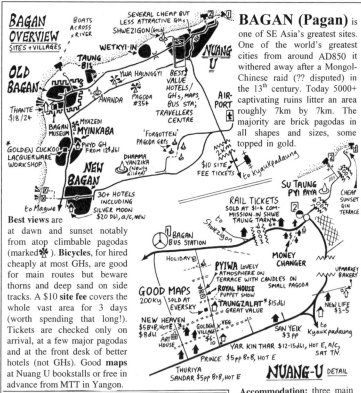

BAGAN (Pagan) is one of SE Asia's greatest sites. One of the world's greatest cities from around AD850 it withered away after a Mongol-Chinese raid (?? disputed) in the 13th century. Today 5000+ captivating ruins litter an area roughly 7km by 7km. The majority are brick pagodas in all shapes and sizes, some topped in gold.

Best views are at dawn and sunset notably from atop climbable pagodas (marked ✹). **Bicycles**, for hired cheaply at most GHs, are good for main routes but beware thorns and deep sand on side tracks. A $10 **site fee** covers the whole vast area for 3 days (worth spending that long!). Tickets are checked only on arrival, at a few major pagodas and at the front desk of better hotels (not GHs). Good **maps** at Nuang U bookstalls or free in advance from MTT in Yangon.

Accommodation: three main areas. Travellers congregate in **Nuang U** which also has the bus and boat stations, market, many cafés, good cheap GH's and is not at all bad for cycling to the ruins. Atmospheric **Old Bagan** is set right amongst the best temple grouping, but the cheapest rooms are $18s/24d (at the Thante, originally built for Edward VIII's 1930s visit, nice riverside terrace). **New Bagan** (Myothit) is for those who want clean, new en-suite GHs ($15-20 dbls) and don't mind transport inconvenience, the dull atmosphere and lack of affordable dining options.

BAGAN–PYAY–YANGON
plus West Coast alternatives (very limited transport).

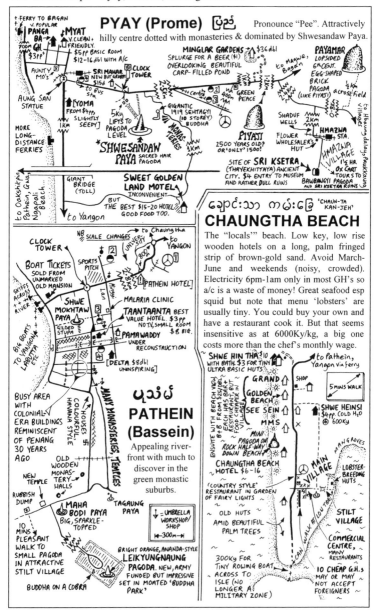

PYAY (Prome) ပြည်

Pronounce "Pee". Attractively hilly centre dotted with monasteries & dominated by Shwesandaw Paya.

ကျောင်းသာ ကမ်းခြေ 'CHAUN-TA KAN-JEH'
CHAUNGTHA BEACH

The "locals'" beach. Low key, low rise wooden hotels on a long, palm fringed strip of brown-gold sand. Avoid March-June and weekends (noisy, crowded). Electricity 6pm-1am only in most GH's so a/c is a waste of money! Great seafood esp squid but note that menu 'lobsters' are usually tiny. You could buy your own and have a restaurant cook it. But that seems insensitive as at 6000Ky/kg, a big one costs more than the chef's monthly wage.

ပုသိမ်
PATHEIN (Bassein)

Appealing riverfront with much to discover in the green monastic suburbs.

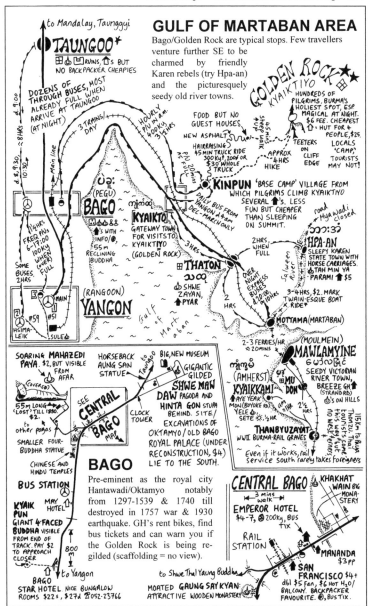

GULF OF MARTABAN AREA

Bago/Golden Rock are typical stops. Few travellers venture further SE to be charmed by friendly Karen rebels (try Hpa-an) and the picturesquely seedy old river towns.

to Mandalay, Taunggyi

TAUNGOO
⊞ RUINS, 's BUT NO BACKPACKER CHEAPIES

DOZENS OF THROUGH BUSES, MOST ALREADY FULL WHEN ARRIVE AT TAUNGOO (AT NIGHT)

d. 8, 9.30, ~8HRS
~9.00
Main line
3 TRAINS/DAY
HOURLY PIU IN AM. 400kγ 3-5HRS
d. 9.30, 10.30

GOLDEN ROCK
KYAIKTIYO
HUNDREDS OF PILGRIMS. BURMA'S HOLIEST SPOT, ESP MAGICAL AT NIGHT. $6 FEE. CHEAPEST 🏠 HUT FOR A PEOPLE,$25.

steep walk
steep walk
TEETERS ON CLIFF EDGE

LOCALS 'CAMP', TOURISTS MAY NOT!

APPROX 4 HRS HIKE

FOOD BUT NO GUEST HOUSES
NEW ASPHALT
HAIRRAISING 45 MIN TRUCK RIDE 300kγ, 200γ OR $30 WHOLE TRUCK

p/u only
p/u 20min

KINPUN 'BASE CAMP' VILLAGE FROM WHICH PILGRIMS CLIMB KYAIKTIYO SEVERAL 🏠's. LESS FUN BUT CHEAPER THAN SLEEPING ON SUMMIT.

road Myawadi closed

BAGO (PEGU)
🏠's WITH INFO/⊞, 55m RECLINING BUDDHA

KYAIKTO GATEWAY TOWN FOR VISITS TO KYAIKTIYO (GOLDEN ROCK)
DAILY BUS FROM YANGON d. 6am DEC-MARCH ONLY

3 HRS

1¼HRS FREQ PIUS 5-17:00 100kγ WHEN (OVER) FULL
SOME BUSES, 2HRS

THATON
SHWE ZAYAN, 🏠 PYAR
OVER NIGHT EXPRESS BUSES 6.00, 7.00, ½ HR

2HRS, WHEN FULL

2 HRS

HPA-AN
SLEEPY KAREN STATE TOWN WITH HORSE CARRIAGES. 🏠 TAH MIN YA 🏠 PARAMI $5

3-4HRS, 2 MARK TWAIN-ESQUE BOAT RIDE

Salween river

(RANGOON) **YANGON**
Gulf of Martaban

MOTTAMA (MARTABAN)

2-3 FERRIES/HR ≈ 20 MINS

(MOULMEIN)
MAWLAMYINE
SEEDY VICTORIAN RIVER TOWN, BREEZE GH (STRAND RD) 🏠's ON HILLS

(AMHERST) **KYAIKKAMI**
🏠 AYE YEAK
MON (BOYOKE) YELE 🏠
SETE 🏠, ½HR

🏠 MU DON

THANBYUZAYAT WWII BURMA-RAIL GRAVES
Even if it works, rail service south rarely takes foreigners

115km to Baya Thanzu. Then tourists some this way but...

SOARING **MAHAZEDI PAYA**, $2, BUT VISIBLE FROM AFAR
(COVERED)
55m LONG 'LOST' TILL 1880. $2.
to other payas
SMALLER FOUR-BUDDHA STATUE
CHINESE AND HINDU TEMPLES
BUS STATION
KYAIK PUN GIANT 4 FACED BUDDHA VISIBLE FROM END OF TRACK. PAY $2 TO APPROACH CLOSER
KYAIK HOTEL MAY
800 m
to Yangon
BAGO STAR HOTEL NICE BUNGALOW ROOMS $22s, $27d ☎052-23766

HORSEBACK AUNG SAN STATUE
Taungoo
SEE CENTRAL BAGO MAP
CLOCK TOWER

BIG, NEW MUSEUM
GIGANTIC GILDED **SHWE MAW DAW** PAGODA AND **HINTA GON** STUPA BEHIND. SITE/ EXCAVATIONS OF OKTAMYO/OLD BAGO ROYAL PALACE (UNDER RECONSTRUCTION, $4) LIE TO THE SOUTH.

BAGO

Pre-eminent as the royal city Hantawadi/Oktamyo notably from 1297-1539 & 1740 till destroyed in 1757 war & 1930 earthquake. GH's rent bikes, find bus tickets and can warn you if the Golden Rock is being re-gilded (scaffolding = no view).

to Shwe Thal Yaung Buddha
MOATED **GAUNG SAY KYAN** ATTRACTIVE WOODEN MONASTERY

CENTRAL BAGO
KHAKHAT WAIN BIG MONASTERY
3 mins walk
EMPEROR HOTEL $4-7, 🏠 200kγ, BUS TIX
RAIL STATION
MANANDA $3 pp
SAN FRANCISCO $4+ dbl $5 fan, $6 HOT H₂O/ BALCONY. BACKPACKER FAVOURITE. 🏠, BUS TIX

SINGAPORE

Introduction

Clean, safe, efficient, modern, convenient, helpful and orderly. Maybe too orderly. Singapore has none of that 'Asian mayhem' which adds the atmosphere and the hassle to travel elsewhere on the continent. It's a truly international city – you might be in Europe except that the people look smarter and richer. Come here to re-charge your batteries with the great selection of food (from S$5 a meal at hawker stalls). Forget about chewing gum, jay walking, dropping litter (S$1000 fine) and, of course, drugs.

Free alternatives to shopping include strolling along Little India and Arab Street or a visit to the botanical gardens. For S$1 visit the attractive orchid garden there, or invest S$20.60 for the surprisingly impressive Night Safari at the zoo. Sentosa Island has enough themed attractions to keep you busy and bankrupt for days. For events listings check *Singapore This Week*.

❑ **Country ratings – Singapore**
● **Expense $$$$** Slightly less than the USA and a real shock coming from Indonesia.
● **Value for money ★★★☆☆** Food is OK value but the budget accommodation is almost unanimously terrible.
● **Getting around ★★★★★** The public transport system is extremely efficient and extensive, particularly now that the MRT extends to the airport.
● **English spoken ★★★★★** English is an official language, spoken along with Chinese, Malay, Tamil.
● **Woman alone ★★★★★** Trouble-free, like everything else in Singapore.
● **For vegetarians ★★★★☆** A wide variety of food available for all tastes.

❑ **Essential information for travellers**
● **Visa** A visa-free two-week stay is plenty for most. Immigration requires an onward ticket or sufficient funds, but officials rarely check.
● **Currency** Singapore dollar. US$1=S$1.83.
● **Time zone** 8 hours ahead of GMT (1hr ahead of Thailand, Java, Sumatra; same as Malaysia, Borneo).
● **Health factors** The tap water is clean and malaria has been eradicated.
● **Typical traveller destinations** Restaurants, zoos, theme-parks and shopping malls.
● **When to go** It's always hot and humid and short rainstorms are common, especially from November to January. The weather makes little difference to a city that consists largely of air-conditioned shopping malls.

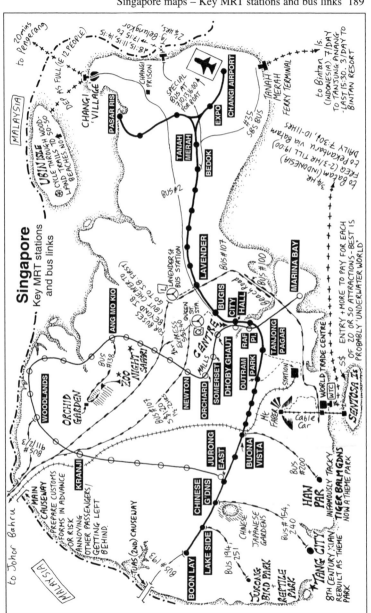

❏ **Geo-political information – Singapore**
Population: 4.3 million (2001), 3.4m (1997), 2.7m (1990), 2.5m (1984).
Area: 637.5 sq km (expanding through land reclamation).
GNP per capita: $26,500 (1994) – world's fifth highest.
Currency history: S$/US$1 – April 2002: S$1.83, Jan 2000: S$1.72, Feb 1998: S$1.72, Jan 1996: S$1.41, Jan 1995: S$1.46, Jan 1994: S$1.61.
Major exports/economy: Financial services, oil refining and chemicals, manufacturing and electronics, trans-shipment, ship repair, tourism.
Ethnic/religious mix: Chinese (76.7%) mostly Buddhist/Daoist, Malay (14%) mostly Muslim, Indian (7.9%) majority Hindu or Sikh.
Official languages: English; however, 37% speak Chinese dialects as a first language. Malay and Tamil are also spoken.
Landmarks of national history: **1819**: Leased from the Sultan of Johore by Stanford Raffles. **1867**: With Malacca (now in Malaysia) and Penang became the Straits Settlements British crown colony. **1942**: Invaded by Japan (defence bungled by Churchill, Australasian casualties). **1959**: Self government. **1963–65**: Part of Malayan Federation. **1965**: Independence.
Leaders: President S R (Sellapan Rama) Nathan, elected September 1999.
Pressing political issues: Money-laundering issues.

Practical information

MONEY
Travellers' cheques are accepted in some stores, are easy to exchange and get a better rate than for cash. There are plenty of ATMs, and credit card advances are straightforward and commission free.

TRANSPORT
Now that it extends to the airport, Singapore's metro (MRT) is more handy than ever. Fares are S$0.80–1.80 and stations are well integrated to the phenomenally extensive bus networks, on which cash fares are S$S0.60–1.20 (exact sum required). Save money ($S0.05–0.20) and hassle by buying a stored-value farecard. The **Singapore Explorer Ticket** allows unlimited travel on all public transport and comes with a free map: $7 for one day, $15 for three.

Singapore Tourist Promotion Board (STPB) publishes the useful planner pamphlet *See Singapore by Bus*. If you know where you want to go, the site 🖥 http://transit.smart.lta.gov.sg will tell you which bus/MRT to take, the time and the fare. Most services run 6am–midnight.

If that's not working, as sometimes seems to be the case, you can use 🖥 www.tibs.com.sg/busguide/. The site also gives links to the websites of the various urban transit operators.

ACCOMMODATION
Tourist brochures don't admit to any hotels under S$40/night, but 'crash pad' dorms do exist for as little as S$8–15 (Bencoolen St, Beach Road etc) or for S$18 (see the 'inncrowd' website, p192). A park bench might be more comfortable than some which might invite you to sleep on the floor or even in the bathtub! Several such places have been closed in recent months and I've heard first-hand reports of bed bugs. All in all you're really advised to get recent personal recommendations before checking in (eg 🖥 www.lonelyplanet.com's Thorn Tree). For a comprehensive if slightly dated review of the cheapest places read 🖥 www.passplanet.com/Singapore/.

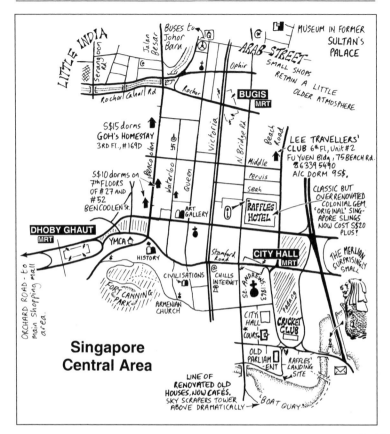

Singapore Central Area

LITTLE INDIA

Buses to Johor Baru

ARAB STREET
MUSEUM IN FORMER SULTAN'S PALACE
SMALL SHOPS RETAIN A LITTLE OLDER ATMOSPHERE

Serangoon Rd
Jalan Besar
Ophir
Rochor Canal Rd
Rochor
BUGIS MRT

S$15 dorms
GOH'S HOMESTAY
3RD FL., #169D

Bencoolen
Waterloo
Queen
Victoria
N. Bridge Rd
Middle
Beach Road

LEE TRAVELLERS' CLUB 6th Fl, Unit #2
FU YUEN Bldg, 75 BEACH Rd.
86339 5490
A/C DORM 9S$.

S$10 dorms on 7th FLOORS OF # 27 AND # 52 BENCOOLEN St.

Pervis
Seah

ART GALLERY

RAFFLES HOTEL

CLASSIC BUT OVER RENOVATED COLONIAL GEM. 'ORIGINAL' SINGAPORE SLINGS NOW COST S$20 PLUS!

DHOBY GHAUT MRT

YMCA

HISTORY
CIVILISATIONS

Stamford Road

CITY HALL MRT

THE MERLION SURPRISINGLY SMALL

ORCHARD ROAD - to main shopping mall area.

FORT CANNING PARK
ARMENIAN CHURCH

@ CHILLS INTERNET
St. Andrew's

CITI HALL COURTS

CRICKET CLUB

Parking

OLD PARLIAMENT

RAFFLES' LANDING SITE

LINE OF RENOVATED OLD HOUSES, NOW CAFÉS.
SKY SCRAPERS TOWER ABOVE DRAMATICALLY

'BOAT QUAY'

For those who can clear the psychological hurdle of spending around S$25 for a dorm bed, the **YMCA** (☎ 6336 6000, 🖹 6337 3140) is an excellent choice with a weight room, swimming pool and kitchens. It's worth booking well in advance.

STAYING IN TOUCH

Singapore is a reliable though not particularly cheap place from which to send parcels home. The best value **international phone calls** are from the various Telecom centres, eg on Victoria Road. Nearby, **Chills Internet Café** (36 Stamford St) is open 9am–midnight

daily. Curious Singaporean rules ban cyber-cafés from operating too near schools, require those under 18 to stop surfing by 8pm and ban under 16 web-café users altogether unless accompanied by an adult guardian!

International country code: +65. There are no city codes.

SHOPPING

Singapore is often touted as a shoppers' paradise. It's true that there's a tremendous range available, especially for electronics. But it's not necessarily going to be at bargain

❏ **Hide that blowpipe**
Should a Borneo Dayak family be kind enough to honour you with a present of a spear and blowpipe (unlikely, sure, but it happened to me!) do appear suitably awed: hand-drilled blowpipes are the fruit of hours of extraordinarily skilled labour. However, you can expect trouble at borders where they may be impounded as illegal weaponry. The paperwork to retrieve mine from the Singapore customs and firearms department was annoying enough that on continuing my journey a disguise seemed in order. I bought a detachable toilet brush head, inserted it into one end of the blowpipe, then made quite a spectacle of myself as I left Singapore into Malaysia. 'What's that?' demanded a bemused customs inquisitor. I simply shrugged – 'It's from Indonesia!'. 'Oh Indonesia, huh!!' laughed the officer. That, it seemed, explained perfectly the mentality behind insanely long, inflexible bog-brushes. And I was waved through, assumed to be harmlessly insane.

prices compared to your home country. For good value, exotic souvenirs it certainly isn't the best place to shop.

FURTHER INFORMATION AND MAPS
A guidebook is unnecessary as STPB offers excellent free information on everything in Singapore – bus maps, transportation schedules and mini-guides to different areas. Their head office (☎ 6736 6622, ▤ 6736 9423) is at Raffles City Tower #36-04, 250 North Bridge Road, but there's a handy branch inside the Raffles Hotel Arcade (toll-free ☎ 1-800-334 1335) at 328 North Bridge Road, open daily 8.30am–8pm. They also have a free 24-hour automated tourist information line (☎ 1-800-736 2000).

New guidebooks for other countries are available at bookshops in Singapore's many shopping malls: there are several on Orchard and Stanford roads. A full listing is available online at ▭ www.mybookstall.com/book stallmain.htm.

Useful websites
▭ www.streetdirectory.com/ will find you detailed maps and the location of a street, business or landmark.

An overview of sites, festivals and practical information is at ▭ www.regit.com/regi tour/spore/regitour.htm.

The official Singapore Online Guide is at ▭ http://www.newasia-singapore.com/ with options in a dozen languages.

▭ www.sg/index.html has an extensive list of official links.

▭ www.nparks.gov.sg/ is for the National Parks – yes there are some!

▭ www.sentosa.com.sg/home.htm for Sentosa Island.

▭ www.gov.sg/ is the government site aimed mainly at residents, but click on the travel bar, bottom right for more useful links.

▭ www.the-inncrowd.com is the website of a great, brand-new backpackers pad in Little India with S$18 dorms.

MALAYSIA

Introduction

Peninsular Malaysia is less exotic than Thailand, less developed than Singapore, and more expensive than Indonesia. Stuck in the middle, somewhat lacking an image, it's often overlooked by travellers. Yet this is a confederation of nine separate sultanates, each with its own character. The country has everything from cyber city to ancient jungle and is host to a variegated rainbow of ethnicities and cultures. Chinese Buddhist shrines and Hindu temples stand shoulder to shoulder with stylish new mosques, gleaming towers and colonial relics of 300 years as the region's main trading centre. And it's all conveniently accessible. East Malaysia (ie Sarawak and Sabah), across the South China Sea on the once-forested island of Borneo, is also modernizing rapidly, but retains a partially-justified wilderness image.

HIGHLIGHTS

Malaysia's highlights include rainforest parks, Kuala Kangsar (a small town with a great palace and mosque), KL's Petronas Towers (whether they are the world's tallest or not they are really impressive), the ease of getting around and talking to locals, night markets (eg Penang), kite flying in Kota Bharu, the vast Niah Caves (Sarawak) and climbing Mt Kinabalu.

WHEN TO GO

Sailors knew Malaysia as 'the land where the winds meet' and when they meet they like blowing-up mischief. The monsoons in Peninsular Malaysia are sup-

❑ **Country ratings – Malaysia**
- **Expense $$$** Malaysia is a relatively-developed country. Budget accommodation is sparingly available but not always a bargain. Food from night markets is affordable but bottled drinking water is rather pricey.
- **Value for money** ★★★☆☆ Not bad, but Thailand is a better deal.
- **Getting around** ★★★★☆ Efficient bus services, good but infrequent trains, hitch-hiking is feasible.
- **English spoken** ★★★★☆ Very wide comprehension. English is compulsory in schools and is often used between different ethnicities of Malaysians themselves.
- **Woman alone** ★★★★☆ Generally no problem. Un-Islamic dress and behaviour can cause raised eyebrows especially on the somewhat more pious north-east coast. Some minor hassles have been reported on the Perhentian Island beaches.
- **For vegetarians** ★★★★☆ Wide variety.

❏ **Essential information for travellers – Malaysia**
● **Visa** Most nationalities are allowed a one-, two- or three-month visa-free stay.
● **Currency** Ringgit (or Malaysian Dollar) US$1=M$3.80 (pegged).
● **Time zone** 8 hours ahead of GMT (same as Singapore; 1hr ahead of Thailand and Indonesia).
● **Religious tone** The official religion is Islam but many others are freely practised – particularly Chinese Buddhism and Hinduism.
● **Health factors** Tap water is technically safe but bottled water makes sense. Very moderate malaria risk in places.
● **Special dangers** 200g of marijuana = trafficking = the death penalty. Very rare but highly publicized cases of tourists being kidnapped by Filipino rebels from diving resorts in Sabah. Piracy in the sea off Sabah. Thefts in Perhentian Islands.
● **Main traveller hubs** Cherating, Tanah Rata (Cameron Highlands), Kota Bharu, Perhentian Islands, Georgetown (Penang), Melaka (Malacca).

posed to come from late May to October on the west coast, and from early November to March on the east. But the monsoons are not always aware of their timetabled regulations. I enjoyed a week in late November on east coast beaches with no more than a single shower. On a December west-coast trip in another year it rained constantly in Melaka but was beautiful in Penang. The standard advice is: if it is raining on one coast, try the other!

Being a rainforest Taman Negara National Park is rarely totally dry, but from November to January the downpours can be miserably continuous. Regardless of the rain, days are usually hot and nights warm, if not unpleasantly sultry. The highlands are, of course, cooler. Borneo is wettest from October to February.

FESTIVALS

With so many different religious groups there is almost always a festival going on somewhere. Probably the most extraordinary is Thaipusam with (according to some reports) over a million people descending on the Batu caves near KL. Hindu devotees in trance-states ask forgiveness of sins from Lord Subramaniam (son of Shiva), by various bizarre forms of self-mutilating penance: piercing their cheeks with spears, dragging carts with flesh-embedded hooks, walking on nails etc.

For extensive listings of the scores of other events a useful website is 🖳 www .emasholiday.com/calendar.html.

Practical information

VISAS AND FORMALITIES

No visa is required for most tourists. Most Westerners get three months, Irish get two months, Portuguese and Greeks get a month. However Israelis, Yugoslavs and women over six-months pregnant aren't welcome at all! Hippie types are also officially banned. The process of identifying 'hippie'ness remains a state secret but it's advisable to be reasonably smart for border crossings. Signs

❏ **Geo-political information – Malaysia**

Population: 22.2 million (2001 est), 17.6m (1991), 13.5m (1980).

Area: 328,500 sq km.

Capital: Kuala Lumpur (KL), though government offices are relocating to the stylish new 'cyber-city' of Putrajaya, 25km south. KL population 1.4 million city, 3.6m metropolitan area.

Other major cities: Johor Bahru (730,000); Ipoh (600,000); Klang (500,000); Petaling Jaya (460,000); Kuching (370,000); Kuala Terengganu, Kuantan, Kota Bharu (290,000); Seremban (270,000); Georgetown (Penang), Taiping, Alor Setar, Sandakan, Kota Kinabalu, (over 200,000); Kluang, Tawau, Shah Alam, Melaka/Malacca (over 150,000), Butterworth (110,000).

GNP per capita: $10,300 (2000 est), $3520 (1994), $2040 (1988).

Currency history: Ringgit (or Malaysian dollar)/US$1 – April 2002: M$3.80 (pegged since 1999), Feb 1998: M$4.29, June 1996: M$2.49, Feb 1996: M$2.56, 1991: M$2.75, 1981: M$2.25.

Major exports/economy: Electronics, natural gas, palm oil (world's largest producer), rubber, wood, textiles, tourism.

Ethnic mix: Malay 58%, Chinese 27%, Indians 8%, indigenous tribes 1%.

Languages: Malay (Bahasa Meleyu, official), English, various Chinese and Indian dialects, several indigenous languages including Kadazan and Iban.

Religious mix: Islam (mostly Malay) 53%, Buddhist (mostly Chinese) 19%, large Hindu (Indian), Dao-ist (Chinese) and Christian (mixed) minorities, animist/shamanist groups in Sabah/Sarawak.

Landmarks of national history: **1511**: The Portuguese took Malacca. **1641**: Dutch took over. **1795**: Start of British rule. **1838**: James Brooke arrived in Sarawak later to become the White Rajah. **1888**: Britain extended rule over Sabah (and Brunei). **April 1946**: Malayan Union formed. **31 Aug 1957**: Independence of Malaya. **1950s and 1960s**: Communist insurgency campaign from southern Thailand. **16 Sept 1963**: Malaysia formed from Malaya plus Sarawak and British North Borneo (Sabah). **Aug 1965**: Singapore left the union. **1970**: Anti-Chinese riots. **1987**: Amnesty finally ended the communist insurgency, **1997**: South-East Asian economic crisis slows the country's 'Tiger' growth.

Leaders: Figurehead Sultan is elected from amongst the nine hereditary rulers of the Peninsular Malay States. Currently Sultan Tunku Salahuddin (since 1999). However, political clout is wielded by the Prime Minister, Mahathir Mohammad.

Pressing political issues: Maintaining dynamic economic growth, repatriation of Vietnamese boat people, ecological concerns over the rapid logging in Sarawak/Sabah, the controversial prime minister.

on arrival are swift to remind you of the mandatory death penalty for drug offences.

MONEY

The Ringgit (M$) is divided into 100sen. Credit card advances are commission free and rates for travellers' cheques are marginally better than for cash. Banks are open Monday to Friday 9am–3pm, Saturday 9.30–11.30am. You're strongly advised to get enough cash exchanged before heading out to islands or small villages where exchange may be at grotty rates or altogether impossible. You're not meant to bring Ringgit in or out of the country.

TRANSPORT
Bus

Malaysia's roads are well paved and the bus system is extensive and reasonably efficient except during monsoons. The main confusion lies in the plethora of different companies which may duplicate services to the same destination at a variety of prices, speeds, quality and by a variety of routes, possibly from different terminals. Air-conditioned buses are generally faster than non-airconditioned ones which allow passengers to get on and off anywhere along their route – handy for spontaneous exploration. If there's no bus, hitchhiking is relatively easy.

Share taxi

You'll usually find a share taxi station close to a town's bus station. However, as Malaysians themselves become increasingly wealthy, it gets decidedly more difficult to find people who need to bother sharing a ride. So unless you have a group of three or four, you may wait longer than for a bus – or have to charter the whole vehicle (still cheaper than a regular taxi, as you won't have to pay the return leg).

Car

Mainland Malaysia is the one place in South-East Asia where renting your own car would be an ideal option were it not rather expensive. Signs are in readable Latin script and despite some frighteningly macho drivers, the high-quality roads give you a considerable freedom to seek out less-visited villages and interesting accommodation options that are inconvenient to reach by public transport.

Train

Note that the splendid old 'Kuala Lumpur' station is no longer the capital's main terminal – that's the new KL Sentral, three minutes away by frequent suburban train. Wakaf Bharu is the station for Kota Bharu, and for Penang you'll use Butterworth station, a quick ferry hop from Georgetown.

Malaysia's mainline trains are generally too infrequent for hopping on and off. However, there are a few useful overnight trains between KL Sentral and:

● Butterworth (from M$37.50, compared to M$20 by bus) [continues to Hat Yai (Thailand)]
● Singapore (from M$37.50 via Johor Bahru)
● Wakaf Bharu (from M$45.50) [destination Tumpat] (via Seremban and Gemas).

There's also a Tumpat/Wakaf Bharu to Singapore sleeper (M$48.50) and three or four more expensive express day trains between KL Sentral and Singapore (under five hours). Note that any transport from Singapore will cost much more (the same figure but in S$!) so northbound it's worth going as far as Johor Bahru by road first.

The fares quoted above are for **ADNS** second-class a/c sleeper, dormitory style along a corridor; **2plus** has an en suite wash

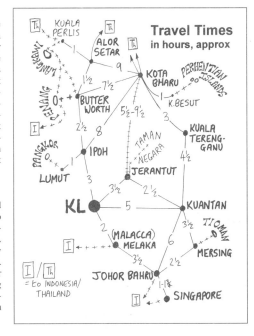

basin in a two-bed compartment and **ADNF** first class even has a private toilet. Timetables are available at 🖳 www.ktmb.com.my and online tickets can be booked 3–30 days ahead with Visa or MasterCard: you must enter your passport number and print out the ticket from the computer.

The cheapest, third-class, non-airconditioned local trains aren't listed on the KTM website, but the timetable for such services on the 'Jungle Train' line is available on 🖳 www.perhentian.com.my.

KL's metro ('LRT') and suburban KTM services run every 8–20 minutes with fares starting at M$1.80. For further information call the KTM help line (☎ 03-2267 1200).

KL's monorail (PRT) marked prominently on several maps and in many guide books, was never built, but since April 2002 there has been a high-speed train connection between KL Sentral and KLIA, the main international airport – if you can afford M$35.

Air
Kuala Lumpur has two airports: the stylish new KLIA deals with international services but the cheaper internal airlines often operate from Subang. These include Air Asia, a ticketless no frills service that has fares as low as M$99 to Kuching; book online at 🖳 www.airasia.com or telephone ☎ 603 7809 6888 (7am–9pm daily).

Hopper flights within Borneo are sometimes cheaper as well as more convenient than road/river combinations and the Miri–Labuan flight at under US$40 can save money especially if you need a visa to cross Brunei.

Flights between East Malaysia and Peninsular Malaysia are usually cheaper if you fly late in the evening.

The international departure tax is M$20 (M$5 to Brunei and Singapore).

ACCOMMODATION
Generally the local population expects much higher standards of accommodation than do travellers. Thus it's only in backpacker hangout areas of KL, Tanah Rata, Cherating, Georgetown, Kota Bharu, Melaka, Tioman, the Perhentian Islands etc that you're likely to find real budget options. In these places you can find basic insalubrious dorm beds for M$6–12. At the lower price you'll often be jammed into virtual cattle pens and may be entering an insect menagerie. It's worth paying marginally more for air-conditioned dorms and checking with other residents about the state of the beds before you pay. Fan rooms may be available from M$20, but figure on at least M$50 for a nicer en suite with hot shower.

In towns with no traveller base it is still generally possible to find a basic room for M$25–35, though the establishment may be rather seedy with flimsy walls and hourly rates.

The best available review of budget accommodation is free online at 🖳 www.passplanet.com/Malaysia; the site is really worth consulting.

Beach accommodation gets packed out at weekends and during holidays, with prices rising correspondingly. In the monsoon season (summer on the west coast, winter on the east) some islands become inaccessible and beach guest houses may close down.

A good waterproof tent is recommended for jungle camping. You are supposed to obtain permission from the Forestry Department before setting up make-shift camping sites in national parks or use official campgrounds.

FOOD AND DRINK
The boundaries between Malay and Indonesian cuisine are blurred, each offering cheap and cheerful *nasi goreng* (fried rice), *mee goreng* (fried noodles), *satay* (barbecued chicken dunked in peanut sauce) and *gado gado* (crunchy cold vegetables and nibbles in spicy peanut dressing). *Laksa lemak* is a spicy coconut-noodle soup that brings a Thai tinge to the tastebuds.

The night markets are great places to snack with Chinese and Indian dishes often more in evidence than Malay specialities. It's a joy to watch the wild dough-juggling that goes into making *roti* (cheap and delicious when dunked in vegetable curry) and the flamboyant milk-hurling that adds an artistic flourish to brewing sweet, Indian chai (tea).

Western fast food is commonly available and virtually everywhere there are convenience stores selling an international selection of snacks and drinks.

STAYING IN TOUCH

The **mail** system is efficient and trustworthy. Poste Restante is arguably more reliable than in Thailand.

The **telephone** system is also efficient and payphones (card or coin) have English-language options and a great 30sen/request directory information service (also English speaking). The international country code is +60; KL: 03, KK: 088, Kuching 082, JB:07, Penang: 04.

ACTIVITIES
Beaches

Malaysia has many glorious beaches. With alcohol consumption curbed by Muslim morals and drugs utterly outlawed, Malaysian beaches offer fewer distractions to scuba lovers who'll find some competitively-priced dives. However, many beaches are 'over-developed', geared to rich locals on package tours, and lacking much in the way of budget accommodation. For cheap chill-outs, you'll need either your own tent and a sense of adventure, or to head to one of the established traveller hubs: eg Cherating, Tioman or the Perhentian Islands. Even these are getting mixed reviews recently as demand outstrips supply in peak seasons. If considering going to the smaller 'resort' islands without a tent, it can work out cheaper to take a tour from a nearby mainland town. Or go to Thailand.

Jungle exploration ideas

Just because 'everyone else' goes there, doesn't mean that **Taman Negara NP** isn't a brilliant experience. Few places make so much 'real' jungle so easily accessible (and at a sensible price). The river trip to get there is great but you can walk for days within the park to really get a feel for the power of nature. You may need to do some planning ahead to book lodges – eg through **MTIC** (in KL ☎ 244 3929) or via the park HQ. And do remember that this is wild rainforest, not a stroll through a country garden.

Isolated **Endau Rompin Park** is said to be spectacular but is expensive and awkward to reach – you might get a group together in Mersing.

The '**Jungle Train**' line, from Kuala Lipis to Tumpat (near Kota Bharu), is touted

---

❏ Coliseum Café, KL

In an otherwise unspectacular main street in KL's unexotic Chinatown, the delightfully-faded Coliseum Hotel is worth a visit for the time warp of its old saloon café. The décor is an improbable intermarriage of Horta Art Nouveau and wild-west brawl bar. In the upmarket restaurant section next door, Lea and Perrins' sauce bottles sit uneasily, looking underdressed on the starched white tablecloths. But the bar itself makes no such pretences. The wood and whitewash walls are enlivened by fuse boxes interspersed with Gerald Scarfe style cartoons of the regular customers. But they're irrelevant as the customers are all present and correct; a perfect microcosm of Malaysia's ethnic diversity. Sikh, Chinese and Hindu are dining together, gulping down mouthfuls between mobile phone calls. A Tamil with wild hair is picking at a plate of minute fried fish in scarily lurid chilli-&-lime sauce. An increasingly sozzled Malay is holding forth in English to a Sikh while chugging away on a M$9.50 'Carl's Reserve' draft beer, before shuffling off around the vinyl-edged bar giving one-armed hugs to all in reach. The one dishevelled-looking European wanders out only to be replaced by an earnest pair of dark-jacketed Mormons and their Filipino lady friend. There's a framed yellowing article about the place itself, suggesting that tourists might once have been on the manager's mind. But not for a long time...

for its wonderful, effortless forest views glimpsed from the train window. Personally I didn't find it very exciting. Maybe the best went by after I'd nodded off.

The **Borneo Jungles** of Sarawak have been subject to intense logging. Some remote, majestic forests do remain but they'll be expensive to reach by river or air. Once you're there you'll find that the famous longhouse lifestyle has been largely abandoned by most locals – who don't necessarily like the ideas of backpackers poking round their houses, anyway. That's what the museum longhouses are for!

FURTHER INFORMATION

Tourism Malaysia and regional equivalents maintain offices in most major towns offering colourful brochures and useful free maps. The country maps and KL city plans are especially good, though certain other town plans are not at all to scale.

Tourist offices are typically open Monday to Friday (and possibly Saturday morning) with longer midday breaks on Fridays (for prayers). Coming from Singapore, there's a useful branch on the Johor Causeway.

There are many English-language bookshops but Georgetown (Penang) is the best place to look for second-hand guides.

❏ **Meeting the locals**

● **The people** 'Don't mess with the Chinese – only their hair is straight' joked one Malay businessman playfully. There may be a little tension between the politically-powerful Malay majority (about 60%), the wealthy Chinese middle classes and the marginalized Borneo forest tribes. But, despite the complex ethnic and religious tapestry, everyone seems to get along pretty well and the country, one of the world's most multi-racial, remains a showcase of multiculturalism. The Muslim majority follow a fairly low-key form of Islam but it's polite to avoid wearing shorts and sleeveless shirts in more conservative areas.

● **Language** Bahasa (Malay) is the official language and one of the world's easiest. It is worth trying to learn some Bahasa – especially if you're heading to Indonesia where the language is very similar. But by no means all Malaysians are ethnically Malay and between groups many locals use English. Indeed, so many Malaysians use English that travel in Malaysia is easier than anywhere else in the region.

Some phrases in Bahasa Malay: NB Bahasa uses the Western alphabet.

Thank you – *terima kasih*	Excuse me – *maafkan saya* (or simply *ma-af*)	
How are you? – *Apa khabar?*	Good-bye – *selamat tinggal*	

Useful websites

🖳 www.passplanet.com is strong on Peninsular Malaysia.

Malaysia is well geared up to the web with online air ticketing (see p198) and online booking available even for some budget guesthouses (eg 🖳 www.machinta.com.sg/ kancil in Melaka). It's worth making a 🖳 www.google.com search for any town or subject you're interested in, though results may throw up a lot of Malay language sites.

The *New Straits Times* has news in English and a useful searchable archive (though for full access there are fees to pay) 🖳 www.nstpi.com.my/Services.

🖳 www.perhentian.com.my/ is the commercial site for a Kuala Besut travel agency but it remains a very useful, in-depth introduction to East Coast Peninsular Malaysia and the offshore islands.

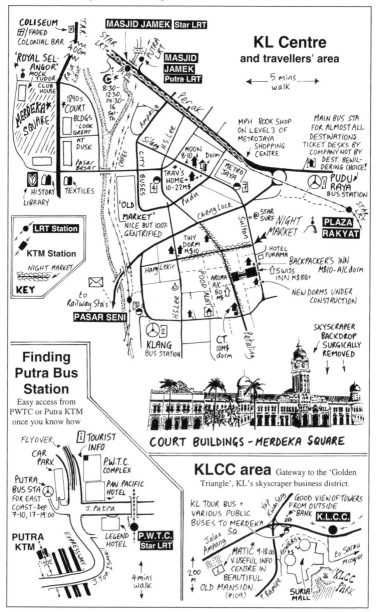

KL Centre
and travellers' area

← 5 mins walk →

COLISEUM
⊞/FADED COLONIAL BAR

MASJID JAMEK Star LRT

MASJID JAMEK Putra LRT

'ROYAL SEL-ANGOR' MOCK TUDOR CLUB HOUSE

STAR LRT
PUTRA LRT
JA. T.A.R.
← 400m

RAJA Laut

Perak

8:30-12:30, 14:30-16 Sat/Thu

1890s COURT BLDGS -LOOK GREAT AT DUSK

MERDEKA SQUARE

Ampang

Silang H.S.Lee

CITY BUSES

CAFES

PASAR BESAR

HISTORY LIBRARY

TEXTILES

MPH BOOK SHOP ON LEVEL 3 OF METROJAYA SHOPPING CENTRE

MAIN BUS STA FOR ALMOST ALL DESTINATIONS. TICKET DESKS BY COMPANY NOT BY DEST. BEWIL-DERING CHOICE!

MOON 8-10 Dorm

METRO JAYA

TRAV'S HOME 10-22M$

Pudu

PUDU RAYA BUS STATION

STAR LRT

'OLD MARKET' NICE BUT 100% GENTRIFIED

Cheng Lock

@ STAR SURF NIGHT MARKET

PLAZA RAKYAT

Sultan

TINY DORM M$10

Hang Lekir

FOOD TALET

AROMA A/C 50 M$

HOTEL FURAMA

BACKPACKER'S INN M$10-A/C dorm

⇧ SWISS INN M$88+

NEW DORMS UNDER CONSTRUCTION

KEY
- ● LRT Station
- ✕ KTM Station
- ▲ NIGHT MARKET

to Railway Sta's

PASAR SENI

H.S.Lee

Petaling

KLANG BUS STATION

CT. 10M$ dorm

SKYSCRAPER BACKDROP SURGICALLY REMOVED

COURT BUILDINGS - MERDEKA SQUARE

Finding Putra Bus Station

Easy access from PWTC or Putra KTM once you know how

FLYOVER

CAR PARK

ℹ TOURIST INFO

P.W.T.C. COMPLEX

PAN PACIFIC HOTEL

J. Putra

PUTRA BUS STA FOR EAST COAST - Dep 7-10, 17-19:00

PUTRA KTM

EXPRESSWAY

J. TUN ISMAIL

LEGEND HOTEL

P.W.T.C. Star LRT

4 mins walk

KLCC area
Gateway to the 'Golden Triangle', KL's skyscraper business district.

KL TOUR BUS + VARIOUS PUBLIC BUSES TO MERDEKA SQ.

Yap Kwan Seng

GOOD VIEW OF TOWERS FROM OUTSIDE BANK

K.L.C.C.

Jalan Ampang

to Saran Mosque

MATIC 9-18:00 V. USEFUL INFO CENTRE IN BEAUTIFUL OLD MANSION. (#109)

200 M

P. Ramlee

AMPANG

KLCC PARK

SURIA MALL

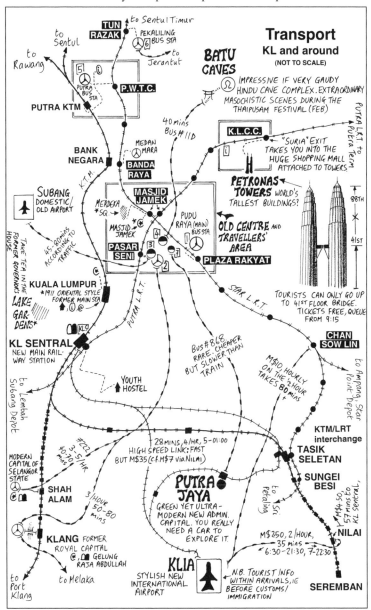

Transport
KL and around
(NOT TO SCALE)

to Sentul Timur

to Sentul

to Rawang

TUN RAZAK

PEKALILING BUS STA

to Jerantut

BATU CAVES

IMPRESSIVE IF VERY GAUDY HINDU CAVE COMPLEX. EXTRAORDINARY MASOCHISTIC SCENES DURING THE THAIPUSAM FESTIVAL (FEB)

PUTRA BUS STA

P.W.T.C.

PUTRA KTM

40 mins BUS #11D

K.L.C.C.

PUTRA LRT to Putra Term

"SURIA" EXIT TAKES YOU INTO THE HUGE SHOPPING MALL ATTACHED TO TOWERS

BANK NEGARA

MEDAN MARA

BANDA RAYA

MASJID JAMEK

PETRONAS TOWERS WORLD'S TALLEST BUILDINGS?

88TH

41ST

SUBANG DOMESTIC/ OLD AIRPORT

MERDEKA SQ.

Masjid Jamek

PASAR SENI

PUDU RAYA (MAIN) BUS STA

OLD CENTRE AND **TRAVELLERS' AREA**

TAKE TEA IN THE FORMER GOVERNOR'S HOUSE

45-80 MINS ACCORDING TO TRAFFIC

PLAZA RAKYAT

TOURISTS CAN ONLY GO UP TO 41ST FLOOR BRIDGE. TICKETS FREE, QUEUE FROM 9:15

KUALA LUMPUR *1911 ORIENTAL STYLE FORMER MAIN STA*

LAKE GARDENS

PUTRA L.R.T.

STAR L.R.T.

CHAN SOW LIN

KL SENTRAL NEW MAIN RAILWAY STATION

to Lembah Subang Depot

BUS #868 RARE, CHEAPER BUT SLOWER THAN TRAIN

M$10, HOURLY ON THE '2 HOUR TAKES 80 MINS +

to Ampang, Star Point Depot

YOUTH HOSTEL

KTM/LRT interchange

TASIK SELETAN

MODERN CAPITAL OF SELANGOR STATE

#ZZ2 3.5/HR 40-70 MINS

28 MINS, 4/HR, 5-01:00 HIGH SPEED LINK: FAST BUT M$35 (cf. M$7 via Nilai)

SUNGEI BESI

to Seremban via M$4.50

SHAH ALAM

3/HOUR 50-80 MINS

PUTRA JAYA GREEN YET ULTRA-MODERN NEW ADMIN. CAPITAL. YOU REALLY NEED A CAR TO EXPLORE IT.

to Sri Petaling

NILAI

KLANG FORMER ROYAL CAPITAL GELUNG RAJA ABDULLAH

M$250, 2/HOUR, 35 MINS 6:30-21:30, 7-22:30

to Port Klang

to Melaka

KLIA STYLISH NEW INTERNATIONAL AIRPORT

N.B. TOURIST INFO WITHIN ARRIVALS, IE BEFORE CUSTOMS/ IMMIGRATION

SEREMBAN

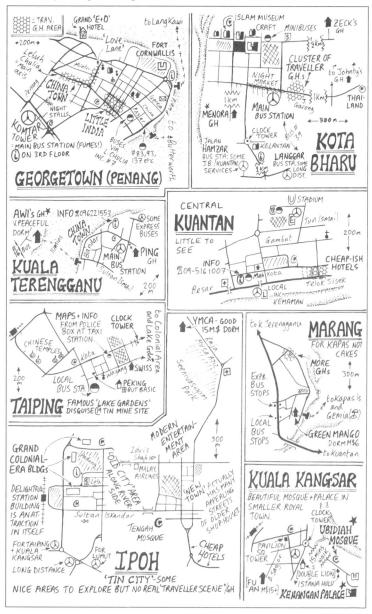

GEORGETOWN (PENANG)

= TRAV. G.H. AREA
GRAND 'E+O' HOTEL
to Langkawi
←200m→
Lebuh Chulia = main axis
"Love Lane"
FORT CORNWALLIS
Penang
Muntri
CHINA TOWN
NIGHT STALLS
KOMTAR TOWER = MAIN BUS STATION (FUMES!)
ⓘ ON 3RD FLOOR
LITTLE INDIA
Penang
Chulia
Green
Cross
to jetty
to Butterworth
BUSES VIA #83, 93, 137 etc INC. L.CHULIA

KOTA BHARU

ISLAM MUSEUM
CRAFT MINIBUSES
ZECK'S GH
½ km
CLUSTER OF TRAVELLER G.H.s
to Johnty's G.H.
THAI-LAND
NIGHT MARKET
1 km
1 km
Gurong
MENORA GH
MAIN BUS STATION
300m
CLOCK TOWER
BUS 39
KELANTAN
LANGGAR BUS STA. SOME LONG DIST.
JALAN HAMZAR BUS STA: SOME J.B./KUANTAN SERVICES
1 km

KUALA TERENGGANU

AWI's GH★ INFO ☎096221553
V.PEACEFUL DORM'
CHINA TOWN
#161 BUS
Umax
Bandar
MAIN BUS STATION
SOME EXPRESS BUSES
PING GH
Sultan Ismail
200 M

KUANTAN

CENTRAL
LITTLE TO SEE
INFO ☎09-516 1007
ⓤ STADIUM
Tun Ismail
200m
Gambut
Mah Kota
Besar
Telok Sisek
LOCAL INC. KEMAMAN
CHEAP-ISH HOTELS

TAIPING

MAPS + INFO FROM POLICE BOX AT TAXI STATION
CLOCK TOWER
to Colonial Area and Lake Gdns
CHINESE TEMPLES
Kota
200 M
LOCAL BUS STA.
Wayang SWISS
PEKING ⊞ BUT BASIC
FAMOUS 'LAKE GARDENS' DISGUISE A TIN MINE SITE

Seenvasagam Park
Jalan Musa Aziz
to K. Terengganu
YMCA - GOOD 15M$ DORM

MARANG

FOR KAPAS NOT CAKES
MORE GHs
300m
EXPR. BUS STOPS
LOCAL BUS STOPS
to Kapas Is. and Gemia (☎)
GREEN MANGO DORM M$6
to Kuantan

IPOH

GRAND COLONIAL-ERA BLDGs
DELIGHTFUL STATION BUILDING IS AN AT-TRACTION IN ITSELF
FOR TAIPING + KUALA KANGSAR
LONG DISTANCE
Padang
Idris Shah
'OLD CITY AREA' ALONG RIVER SIDE
Leila
MALAY AIRLINES
MODERN ENTERTAINMENT AREA
300 M
Sultan Iskandar
TENGAH MOSQUE
FOR LUMUT
'NEW TOWN' ACTUALLY HAS MANY APPEALING STREETS OF OLDER SHOP-HOUSES
CHEAP HOTELS
'TIN CITY'-SOME NICE AREAS TO EXPLORE BUT NO REAL 'TRAVELLER SCENE'/GH

KUALA KANGSAR

BEAUTIFUL MOSQUE + PALACE IN SMALLER ROYAL TOWN.
CLOCK TOWER
UBIDIAH MOSQUE
PAVILION SQ TOWER
15 MIN WALK
[DOUBLE LION]
ISTANA HULU
FU AN M$15
KENANGAN PALACE

Peninsular West Coast

BATU FERINGGHI

SMALL HUDDLE OF GH's - EG ALI's. PARK ROYAL

MUKA HEAD 2HRS WALK FROM T.B.

TELUK BAHANG ⌂'s, ⌂ 'MISS LOH'S HAS DORM.

TITI KERAWAN DIRTY, DRIED UP EX-WATERFALL

QUIETER AREA SOME ⌂ OLDER HOUSES IN TREES- EXPLORE BY MOTOR BIKE (EASY IN GEORGETOWN)

NB MANY REFER TO GEORGETOWN AS 'PENANG' TOWN

BOT. GDNS.

CABLE CAR #93

AYER ITAM

KEK LOK SI-VERY TOURISTY #83

BUILT UP 5km

GEORGETOWN
STREETS OF OLD CHINESE SHOPS, ⌂s, ⊞, ⓘ, 丞, MANY ⌂'s, TRAVELLER FRIENDLY. GOOD NIGHT MARKET

M$0.6 3/HR ¼HR RUNS 24HRS/DAY FREE-QUICKER THAN BRIDGE!

MANY DIRECT BUSES (INCL GH MINIBUSES TO THAILAND) BUT FOR MOST DESTINA-TIONS IT'S QUICKER + EASIER TO HOP ON THE FERRY AND GO FROM BUTTERWORTH

PENANG ISLAND. ⌂'s, ⌂ RIDES, OVER-RATED ☼'s

See Thailand Chapter

BUTTERWORTH
BUS STA/ RAIL STA/ + FERRY ALL CLOSE TO EACH OTHER

to Tanah Rata 8:30,14:30

to KL: 1-2/HR 5-6 HRS 8-00:30

*BUKIT LARUT REST HOUSE M$15

¾ HR HOURLY ON THE HOUR

1½ HRS

TAIPING FAMOUS GARDENS

KAMUNTING EXPRESS BUS STA.

CENTRE ¼HR, #8 BUS

2km LAKE

1¼ HRS, 2/HR TILL 18:00

DIRECT BUSES 9:30,14:30, 18:00 OR VIA IPOH

2HRS d7 9,12,4 14,17:00

FREQ 2-2½ HRS

PERAK BUDDHA CAVES ☸

2-3/HR 6-21:00

KUALA KANGSAR
⌂⌂☪⌂

1HR, 2-5/HR TILL 21:00

DAY+NIGHT BUS TO KOTA BHARU

TELOK NIPAH ☼ HAS THE CHEAPEST G.H.'s EG JOE'S ⌂, CORAL BEACH ⌂, BUT YOU NEED A ⊕/☼ TO AVOID THE 'TAXI MAFIA' (NO BUS)

TELOK DALAM

1km JUNGLE

½ HR, UP TO 3/HR

LUMUT
6/DAY

1HR, 1-2/HR

IPOH
SOME GRAND COLONIAL BLNS + INTERESTING CHINESE SHOP HOUSES

1HR, 2-5/HR

PASIR BOGAK MAIN HOTEL AREA ⌂/⌂ 25M$ MIN. HOURLY BUS FROM PANGKOR TOWN

BERAGGLED DUTCH FORT

PANGKOR TOWN ⊕/☼

PANGKOR ISLAND
NICE BEACHES (w) EXPENSIVE TAXIS

[KAMPAR]

25Mins 2-3/HR

3 - 3½ HRS 2/HR

CAMERON HIGHLANDS
TANAH RATA IS THE HUB FOR BACKPACKERS EG TWIN PINES⌂, FATHERS'⌂ ETC HAVE M$8+ DORMS, ⊕ @...

- COOL,GREEN, TEA HILL HIKES, ENGLISH COUNTRY HOUSES'- EG 'OLD SMOKE HOUSE'

TAPAH
⌂'s. NB. BUSES LEAVE FROM VARIOUS POINTS. GETTING TICKETS ON LONGER DISTANCE BUSES CAN BE AWKWARD AT SHORT NOTICE BUT YOU CAN BOOK FROM TANAH RATA.

TAPAH INTER-CHANGE: CAN HOP OFF IPOH→ KL BUS HERE + TRY TO HITCH TO CAMERON HIGHLANDS - BUSES PASS EVERY 1½ HRS

8/DAY, 2HRS

KL
☿ !

4½ HRS, 4/DAY

UBIDIAH MOSQUE

KUALA KANGSAR

Jungle train timetable

Wau	Ord	Tumuran	Ord	Kenali	Ord	Ord	Station	Ord	Ord	Ord	Kenali	Ord	Wau	Timuran
16	84	14	94	18	92	58		57	93	91	19	83	17	15
Daily	Daily	Daily	Daily	Fri, Sat,	Daily	Daily		Daily	Daily	Daily	Fri, Sat,	Daily	Daily	Daily
7:45	12:30	9:45	17:30	19:05	22:10		**TUMPAT**		3:45	5:10	8:25	13:20	18:20	20:05
7:31	12:06	9:30	17:09	18:47	21:54		**WAKAF BHARU**		4:02	5:36	8:44	13:43	18:38	20:23
6:19	10:20	8:8	15:31	17:16	19:53		**KUALA KRAI**		5:23	7:27	10:15	15:22	19:48	21:31
5:30	8:01	7:18	14:03	16:22	17:56		**DABONG**		7:00	9:00	11:06	17:04	20:37	22:22
4:28	5:10	6:12	12:20	15:18	16:39	21:20	**GUA MUSANG**	7:00	9:20	10:46	12:09	19:30	21:43	23:28
3:05		4:46		13:48	14:30	19:13	**KUALA LIPIS**	7:33		14:16	13:46		23:13	0:57
					11:27	18:15	**TEMBELING**	8:39		15:24				
2:09		3:51		12:50	11:10	18:00	**JERANTUT**	8:53		15:40	14:38		0:11	2:15
0:03		1:17		10:44	7:48	14:42	**BAHAU**	12:01		18:46	16:46			4:25
23:28		0:40		10:09	7:00	14:00	**GEMAS**	12:46		19:25	17:55		3:45	5:05
		22:33				12:01	**KLUANG**	14:44						6:31
		21:12				10:20	**JOHOR BAHRU**	16:22						7:57
		20:10				9:6	**SINGAPORE**	17:30						8:50
21:19				8:14			**SEREMBAN**						19:34	5:17
20:00				7:00			**KL SENTRAL**						20:58	6:56

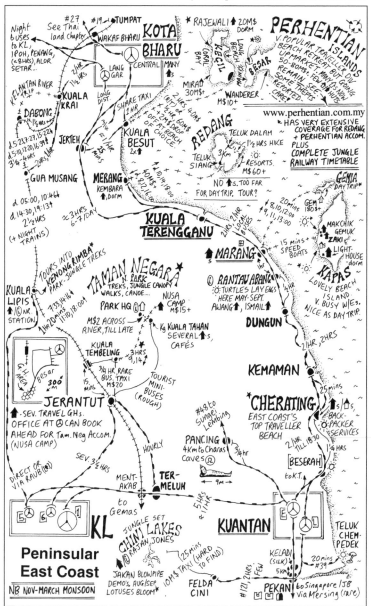

Peninsular
East Coast

NB NOV-MARCH MONSOON

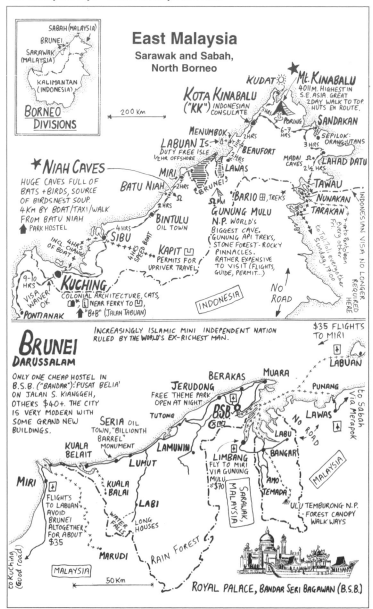

BORNEO DIVISIONS

SABAH (MALAYSIA)
BRUNEI
SARAWAK (MALAYSIA)
KALIMANTAN (INDONESIA)

East Malaysia
Sarawak and Sabah, North Borneo

200 Km

KUDAT

★ Mt. KINABALU
4011M. HIGHEST IN S.E. ASIA. GREAT 2DAY WALK TO TOP. HUTS EN ROUTE.

KOTA KINABALU ("KK") INDONESIAN CONSULATE

3 HRS

PORING 6-7 HRS

SANDAKAN

SEPILOK: ORANG-UTANS

MENUMBOK
2 HRS

LABUAN Is. DUTY FREE ISLE ½HR OFFSHORE

BEAUFORT

3 HRS

MADAI CAVES 2½ HRS

LAHAD DATU

★ NIAH CAVES
HUGE CAVES FULL OF BATS + BIRDS, SOURCE OF BIRDSNEST SOUP. 4 KM BY BOAT/TAXI/WALK FROM BATU NIAH
▲ PARK HOSTEL

MIRI

LAWAS
2 HRS

BRUNEI

TAWAU

BATU NIAH
2 HRS

BARIO ⊞, TREKS

NUNAKAN

BINTULU OIL TOWN

2 HRS

GUNUNG MULU N.P. WORLD'S BIGGEST CAVE. GUNUNG API TREKS, STONE FOREST - ROCKY PINNACLES. RATHER EXPENSIVE TO VISIT (FLIGHTS, GUIDE, PERMIT...)

TARAKAN

INDONESIAN VISA NO LONGER REQUIRED HERE

to Tol/Tul everywhere every other Sunday 17.00

4 HRS INCL. CHANGE OF BOAT

SIBU

4 HRS

KAPIT ⌂ PERMITS FOR UPRIVER TRAVEL

4 HRS SPEED BOAT

No ROAD

9-10 HRS

KUCHING

VISA WAIVER OK

COLONIAL ARCHITECTURE, CATS, ⌂ ℹ NEAR FERRY TO ⌂,
▲ "B+B" (JALAN TABUAN)

INDONESIA

PONTIANAK

BRUNEI DARUSSALAM

INCREASINGLY ISLAMIC MINI INDEPENDENT NATION RULED BY THE WORLD'S EX-RICHEST MAN.

$35 FLIGHTS TO MIRI

LABUAN

ONLY ONE CHEAP HOSTEL IN B.S.B. ("BANDAR"): PUSAT BELIA' ON JALAN S. KIANGGEH, OTHERS $40+. THE CITY IS VERY MODERN WITH SOME GRAND NEW BUILDINGS.

BERAKAS

MUARA

JERUDONG FREE THEME PARK OPEN AT NIGHT

PUNANG

to Sabah via Merapok

TUTONG

B.S.B.

LAWAS

SERIA OIL TOWN, "BILLIONTH BARREL" MONUMENT

LABU

No ROAD

KUALA BELAIT

LAMUNIN

LIMBANG FLY TO MIRI VIA GUNUNG MULU $70

BANGAR

LUMUT

MALAYSIA

MIRI

KUALA BALAI

AMO
TEMADA

FLIGHTS TO LABUAN AVOID BRUNEI ALTOGETHER FOR ABOUT $35

LABI

SARAWAK, MALAYSIA

ULU TEMBURONG N.P. - FOREST CANOPY WALKWAYS

WATER FALLS

LONG HOUSES

to Kuching (good road)

MARUDI

RAIN FOREST

MALAYSIA

50 Km

ROYAL PALACE, BANDAR SERI BAGAWAN (B.S.B.)

ISLAND SOUTH-EAST ASIA

The glorious archipelago nations of the Philippines and Indonesia are beyond the scope of a book on mainland South-East Asia. To cover them in sensible depth would almost double the size (and weight) of this book which would be annoying for readers who don't plan to leave the mainland. Visiting either nation I'd suggest buying a country-specific guide book, but I have provided an at-a-glance overview to each, and also to Brunei and East Timor, to help with planning. Also note that there is a useful regional planning map on p31.

Brunei Darussalam

2001 was 'Visit Brunei Year' but this fascinating, increasingly Islamic mini-state remains cautious about how much tourism it really wants, afraid to undermine its 'strong traditional values'. With its significant oil wealth it can afford to be choosy. Dotted all over with attractive new mosques and festooned in conspicuous wealth, the towns are modern yet retain large areas of 'water village' (ie stilt houses). And there's a surprising amount of untouched forest hinterland.

❏ **Geo-political information – Brunei**
Population: 344,000
Area: 5770 sq km.
Capital: Bandar Seri Begawan (BSB), pop 75,000
Other cities: Kuala Belait (27,000); Seria (23,000), Tutong (17,000)
GNP per capita: $24,600
Major exports/economy: Crude oil, natural gas, income on external investments
Ethnic mix: Malay 67%, Chinese 15%, Iban/Dayak and Kelabit 6%.
Official languages: Malay, English
Religious mix: Muslim (67%, official religion, increasingly strict), Buddhist (13%), Christian (10%), traditional/animist (10%).
Landmarks of national history: **15th C**: Nominally the entire island of Borneo controlled by the Brunei sultanate. **1841** Civil war quashed with the help of the British, Sarawak given away as a reward. **1846** Labuan Island also became British. **1888** Brunei itself became a British protectorate. **1929** First commercial oil strike. **1962** Sultan ruled by decree, annulling election in which the outright winning party proposed his removal (shades of Burma 1991?!). **1984** Independence, the Sultan became the world's richest man.
Leader: Sultan Sir Hassanal Bolkiah (since 1967).
Pressing political issues: Diversification of the economy. Growing Islamic fundamentalism. Repairing financial mismanagement.

The main worry for budget travellers is expense. If you're on a really slim budget your best bet may be to take a hopper flight and avoid it altogether. It is just about possible to cross the country in a day (take a ferry from Labuan to Bandar Seri Begawan, then a bus to Seria and from there to the border, and finally to Miri): but it's tight! Better still hitch-hike and make local friends.

VISAS AND FORMALITIES
Without a visa, Americans can stay 90 days; Brits, Germans, Greeks, Singaporeans and Malaysians can stay for 30 days; several other nationalities (including Swiss, French, Benelux, Swedish, Danes, Italians, Kiwis, Norwegians, Spaniards, Canadians, Japanese and Koreans) get 14 days.

Aussies, Irish, South Africans, Finns, Portuguese and most other nationalities need a visa. If flying in these nationals may be allowed a 72-hour transit pass, but NOT when arriving overland. Visas aren't expensive (typically B$15) but theoretically you'll need to show an onward ticket to get one. As the country is in two unconnected chunks, you may need a double or multi-entry visa.

Website 🖳 www.brunet.bn/homepage/tourism/formiss/formiss.htm gives a listing of all Brunei's missions abroad.

Note that alcohol isn't sold in any shop in Brunei and if you bring any in with you (up to two bottles of wine/12 cans of beer) you have to declare it!

MONEY
The Brunei dollar is on a par with the Singaporean dollar which can be used interchangeably. Travellers' cheques get better rates than cash.

ACCOMMODATION
There is only one **budget accommodation** option – the nice B$10 air-conditioned dorms at Pusat Belia Youth Hostel/Sports complex (☎ 229 423, Jl Sungei Kianggeh), near the Sheraton in BSB. You may require an IYHA membership or a student card and the place is rather touchy about who it lets in (no long hair, strictly single sex dorms).

To find the next cheapest place walk past the Belia, turn right then right again, for Capital Hostel (☎ 223 561, Jl Tasak Lama), which costs from B$60 a single.

FURTHER INFORMATION
For free maps there's a new tourist information office in the main post office building whose *Explore Brunei* pamphlet is useful.

Useful websites
🖳 www.backpackasia.com/brunei/brunei.html has a traveller-view approach with highlights and basic details of BSB bus routes.

🖳 www.bruneibay.net/ is a most extensive and useful site, albeit lacking any budget traveller advice.

🖳 www.brunei.gov.bn/ has various news and government information items as well as a listing of the national holidays.

🖳 www.geocities.com/TheTropics/Cove/2636/travel/borneo/diary7.htm is a personal travelogue including Brunei and Malaysian Borneo.

Indonesia

The most populous nation in South-East Asia, Indonesia's rapidly growing population is unevenly sprinkled on the biggest thousand of a 13,667-island volcano-popping archipelago which stretches over 6000km, further than from Madrid to Moscow, or Seattle to Savannah.

Indonesia is a natural paradise of intense greens; emerald rice terraces, ancient rainforests, and lush roadside foliage weighed down with hibiscus flowers and bougainvillea. The claim is of a land 'so fertile that a stick will sprout' – a poetic exaggeration I thought until I saw a Flores fencepost that had indeed grown leaves. The country is rich in history with Hindu, Buddhist and, most recently, Islamic influences coming together over a melting pot of diverse animist cultures. The combination has produced some extraordinary architectural splendours, particularly in Java and Bali.

Less attractively, Indonesia has had a spate of social upheavals and the Bali terrorist bombing that made international news. It is also a rapidly industrializing country; the capital Jakarta is a pit worth avoiding and the clearfelling of forests that I saw in Kalimantan is shocking.

There is a lot of land to spoil, but the sooner you go the more that will remain for you to savour.

❏ Country ratings – Indonesia
The ratings vary greatly between the many islands in this huge archipelago.
● **Expense $$$** Kalimantan and West Papua tend to be more expensive than the more populated regions; since transport is limited you may have to take internal flights.
● **Value for money ★★★★☆** Cheap and cheerful.
● **Getting around ★★☆☆☆ to ★★★★★** This depends on the region; it's very easy in Java and Bali but very patchy in Kalimantan and West Papua where there are few roads.
● **English spoken ★☆☆☆☆ to ★★★★★** You can always find someone who speaks English in Bali or Java, but in the more isolated regions Bahasa Indonesia is essential; it's easy to master.
● **Woman alone ★★☆☆☆** Women report a noticeable difference between the Muslim and non-Muslim areas. Mild harassment is common but it rarely gets physical – saying you're married may help.
● **For vegetarians ★★★★☆** You'll have few problems, especially if you eat seafood.

❑ **Essential information for travellers – Indonesia**

● **Visa** A non extendable two-month visa-free stay is possible for most nationals at most but not all entry points. An onward ticket is theoretically required.

● **Currency** Rupiah. US$1= Rp9600.

● **Time zone** Sumatra, Java, west and central Kalimantan are 7 hours ahead of GMT (same as Thailand); east and south Kalimantan, Timor, Sulawesi and Bali are 8hrs ahead (same as Malaysia); Maluku and West Papua are 9hrs ahead (same as Japan).

● **Religious tone** Relaxed Islam from Sumatra to Sumbawa; a unique form of Hinduism heavily mixed with local culture in Bali; Christian areas such as Flores and others, particularly central Sulawesi, retain a strong animist feel. West Papua, like neighbouring Papua New Guinea, is home to tribes with various fascinating beliefs.

● **Health factors** Malaria risk in some areas. Drinking the water is not encouraged.

● **Special dangers** Insurgency and sporadic intercommunal violence in Aceh, Maluku, Papua, Central Sulawesi (notably Poso) and Kalimantan coastal cities. Ambon/Maluku is effectively closed to foreigners at the time of writing. Forest fires when serious (as in autumn 1997) can choke the skies and have caused at least one serious air crash. Western interference in Islamic Afghanistan and inaction to aid the Palestinians has contributed to a slight backlash against those who might be mistaken for GIs.

● **Social conventions** Indonesian bathrooms typically have a *mandi* tub rather than a bath or shower; use the scoop to pour water over yourself – don't get in! Especially in Muslim areas (the majority of the country) conservative dress is important – no shorts, bare shoulders etc, except in beach areas. Cover your mouth when yawning or using a toothpick.

● **Key tips** Learn the language – it's so easy. If you can't get a visa extension, consider seeing the country in two loops; two months simply isn't enough to get a feel of more than a small portion.

● **Main backpacker hubs**: Lake Toba, Bukittinggi, Yogyakarta, Gili Isles, Lovina (Bali), Manado.

HIGHLIGHTS

Indonesia is a continent more than a country, it would take months to get just a taste. The following is a list of highlights island by island:

Bali

A unique Hindu-based culture with more temples and shrines than houses. The island has lush mountains and gorgeous rice terraces and charming Ubud is a cultural centre with stylish accommodation and restaurants. The beaches are attractive if tourist-saturated: Lovina offers black sand and the chance to dolphin watch. It is calmer and more backpacker orientated than beery Kuta or package tour

❑ **Overall highlights**
Bali, Sulawesi, Flores, Komodo dragons at Rinca rather than Komodo, Borobudur (the universe as a 9th-century stone metaphor), Prambanan, Mt Bromo (Java), Bukitinggi and Lake Toba (Sumatra), island hopping in the east.

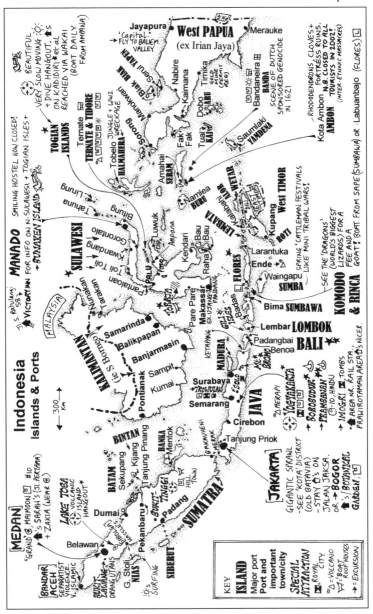

❏ Geo-political information – Indonesia

Population: 228 million (2001), 209m (1997), 179m (1990), 135m (1975).

Area: 1,826,000 sq km.

Capital: Jakarta (10.8 million, 17m+ including satellite cities!)

Other major cities: Surabaya, Bandung (2.8m); Medan (2.1m); Palembang (1.4m); Makassar (Ujang Pandang), Semarang (1.3m); Malang, Bandar Lampung (750,000); Padang, Samarinda, Pekanbaru (600,000); 14 other cities over 400,000 and 90 with over 100,000!!

GNP per capita: $2900 (2000 est), $880 (1994), $475 (1988).

Currency history: Rupiah/US$1 – April 2002: Rp9600, Jan 2001: Rp10,100, Feb 1998: Rp7300, Oct 1997: Rp2905, Jan 1994: Rp2100, Jan 1991: Rp2102, 1985: Rp1125.

Major exports/economy: 80% of earnings from oil/gas, though still a major producer of spices (nutmeg, cloves, pepper) and copra (from coconuts). Also wood, textiles, shoes, rubber, tourism.

Ethnic mix: Reflected in the many languages.

Official languages: Bahasa Indonesia. Though most of the population can speak Bahasa Indonesia, only 15% claim it as a mother tongue. There are 583 other languages including Javanese (45%), Sundanese (14%), Madurase (7.5%) and around two million speakers each of Batak, Micaoc, Buginese, Banjarese and Balinese. Chinese was included in the 17% of 'others' in the census.

Religious mix: Muslim (88%), Christian (8%), Hindu (2%, in Bali), Buddhist (1%).

Landmarks of national history: **7th century**: Palembang became the Buddhist centre of the Srivijaya empire. **9th century**: Borobudur and other Buddhist temples constructed. **1292–1398**: The Majapahit empire created an Indonesian identity. **1520s**: Portuguese and Spanish raced to the spice islands (Moluccas). **16th century**: Islam spread through seaborne commerce while Dutch colonialism took root. **1619**: Genocide of Banda islanders by the Dutch to protect their nutmeg trade. **1908**: Balinese royal family killed by Dutch soldiers. **1942–5**: Japanese occupation. **1949**: Independence from Holland after a protracted war. **1965**: Suharto coup and anti-communist witch-hunt/massacres. **1969**: Dutch New Guinea annexed as Irian Jaya (referendum cancelled). **1975**: Invasion of Portuguese East Timor. **1998**: In wake of South-East Asian economic crisis mass demonstrations and considerable rioting topple President Suharto. **1999**: East Timor's pro-independence vote followed by atrocities committed by rampaging pro-Indonesian militias. **2000** Maluku Christian-Islamic tensions flare into inter-communal fighting. **2002**: Autonomy agreement for Irian Jaya (now renamed West Papua) designed to take steam out of the Papuan independence movement. Terrorist bomb on Bali on 12 October.

Leader: President Megawati Sukarnoputri since July 2001, daughter of long ruling Sukarno. 'I can't see, she can't speak' quipped half-blind former president Abdurrahman Wahid before being ousted. 'Miss Megawati … makes George W Bush seem like an intellectual' sniped one newspaper.

Pressing political issues: Political instability, secessionist movement in Aceh, ethnic and religious discord in Maluku, Kalimantan, Sulawesi and Aceh. Rapid population growth, corruption, frail banking system.

Sanur. Local motorbike licences are available on passing a rudimentary test, bike rental is cheap.

NB Even though there are swarms of tourists in the south it's still surprisingly easy to get away from them in the smaller central villages.

Flores

A delightful, slow-moving garden island with nominally Christian villages which are full of over-friendly 'Hello Mister' kids. Komodo dragons roam the western tip as well as the Komodo/Rinca islands. Also worth seeing are the three differently-coloured lakes atop Mt Kelimutu and the brilliant rice terraces near Ruteng.

Java

In the fertile spaces between its fizzing volcanoes, Java houses more than half the Indonesian population, the capital (Jakarta), major cultural and industrial cities plus the fabulous ancient temple complexes of Borobudur and Prambanan – best visited from Yogyakarta ('Jogja'). Smoke-puffing Mt Bromo offers awesome sunrise views, across the 'sand sea' (access is via Problinggo; it's worth paying the slightly inflated room rates to stay in Cemoro Lawang village on the crater's edge).

Kalimantan

Vast tracts of mostly flat jungle, heavily logged in parts. Few towns are linked by roads. Hopper flights into the interior are typically cheaper and more frequent than longboats. Note that the inland Dayak culture is being rapidly eroded especially near the airstrips. As a result, classic longhouses and old women with dangle-lobed ears are increasingly hard to find. Banjarmasin has canals, floating markets and ludicrously massive hats, but calling it the 'Venice of the East' is an exaggeration. Camp Leaky is a great Orang Utang rehab centre reached via Pangkalanbun/Kumai.

Krakatoa

Its massive 1883 volcanic explosion killed 40,000 with tidal waves, shook clocks in Europe and blotted out the sun with ash. Today's hissing remains are fleetingly visible from boats going between Padang and Jakarta. For a better view take a charter boat from Labuhan (Java) (at least 10hrs return).

Lombok

There are some traditional villages in the far south and on the foothills of holy Mt Rinjani. The great beaches at Senggigi and especially on the Gili Islands are an increasingly popular beach alternative to Bali. Ferry connections include three a day from Labuhan (Lombok) to Poto Tano (Sumbawa); two a day from Lembar to Bali (six hours).

Madura

Most tourists bypass this island despite there being good beaches on the south coast. The main draw is to see the Kerapan Sapi Bull Races, traditionally held between August and October though now there are also 'show' versions.

Maluku (Moluccas)

The original Spice Islands and spur to colonialism are now desert island backwaters dotted with Dutch fortress ruins, great deserted beaches and picturesque volcanoes. At the time of research, the area is recovering from some horrific intercommunal fighting between the majority Christian population and Islamic immigrants. In 2001-2 Ambon, the main travel hub, was closed to tourists, but in October 2002 it was reported to be stable and 're-opened'. Check carefully before you go, eg using ⌨ www.websitesrcg.com/ambon/ or the Thorn Tree.

Nias

There are some stilt villages with traditional 'boat' houses in the south. Surf at Lagundi beach. Boat access is from Sibolga (Sumatra).

Nusa Tenggara

The collective name for the string of attractive islands east of Lombok notably Sumbawa, Sumba and Flores.

Siberut

Rewarding but time-consuming canoe boat expeditions into roadless forest villages. These are best undertaken with a guide/permit and can be arranged in Padang or Bukittinggi (Sumatra).

Sulawesi (Celebes)

Culturally varied (Muslim in the south, Animist in the centre and Protestant in the north) and geographically appealing with a jungle/mountain heart.

Tanah Toraja is a region of fabulous rice-terraced hills dotted with scenic 'boat' house villages where Christianity has animist safeguards (funeral sacrifices, voodoo-style *tau-tau* memorial figures in carved cliff niches). It's rather touristy unless you hike a good way beyond **Rantepao**, the traveller hub.

An easy five-day stroll between Gimpu (take a bemo from Palu) and quaint Tentena (beware of bilharzia in the lake) follows donkey tracks through lovely flower-filled, roadless villages passing the megaliths of the Bada valley. You can send your bags ahead by *bemo*.

Sweltering Makassar (Ujang Pandang) harbours many elegant Bugis schooners and there are cheap hotels around the fort.

There is great scuba diving in the north and from the Tongian Islands.

Be careful around Poso: there were some unpleasant attacks in late 2002.

Sumatra

Some tracts of jungle and mangrove still survive the onset of the oil business. In the mid-north some villages retain the attractive traditional architecture – notably around Samosir Island on **Lake Toba** (take a boat from Prapat) – while fortunately ditching cannibalism. **Ambarita** is Lake Toba's backpacker centre.

Brastagi also draws visitors for jungle exploration trips. **We Island** offers great snorkelling/dives and has cheap beach bungalows.

Medan is an overpoweringly massive city with traveller guesthouses ('Sugar', 'Zakia' etc) located around the grand 1906 mosque Masjid Raya. In

Pekanbaru – transit point for Singapore – head for Poppies' Guest House (☎ 33863). It's a two-hour river trip to Siak Palace.

Sumba

The island is mainly flat and barren. Classic 'Cattleman festivals' like mini staged wars are held at various places eg at Lamboya (February), Wanokaka (March) and in other villages (March–April); bring betel nuts.

Rende, Pau and other villages have big stone tombs. Waingapu (the main town) is accessible by relatively rare boats from Ende (Flores) and Bima (Sumbawa).

Sumbawa

A beautiful, rugged largely Muslim island. There are palaces in Sumbawa Besar and Bima and traditional villages around Donggo. Sape (an attractive port and many horse carts) has ferry links to Komodo (two a week). Poto Tano is the port for ferries from Lombok (three a day); Bima has services to Ende (Flores) and, two a month, to Makassar (Sulawesi).

West Papua (Papua Barat, formerly known as Irian Jaya)

The western half of New Guinea offers impenetrable jungle, snow-topped mountains, and undiscovered Stone Age tribes. West Papua tried to declare independence in 2000 and the separatist leader, Theys Eluay, died under suspicious circumstances in November 2001. Despite some new-found autonomy, the political/safety situation remains confused. Read carefully before you go.

Permits (*surat jalan*) are required to visit most areas; these are generally available from police stations in the regional centres. It's expensive and tough to get around without flying.

Pastoral Baliem Valley (fly to Wamena) is Papua's *Kathmandu Valley* with some tourism: many hikes are possible eg to Wolo, or Akima for the famous smoked mummies. The Paniai Lakes sound fantastic (fly into Enarotali). Sibil Valley is worth visiting for its stone-built villages and wildly adorned locals.

Reports at the time of research were conflicting as to whether you could now cross the less than cordial land border to Papua New Guinea. If you can you'll need to have an Indonesian as well as a PNG visa as the border is not valid on the 60-day tourist pass. There's an Indonesian consulate in the Beach Hotel in Vanimo and a PNG consulate at 28 Jl Percetakan, Jayapura; staff there should be able to tell you the latest details on exit formalities.

West Timor (Timor Barat)

Visit the *Lopo* beehive-shaped huts in hill villages around Soe. Kupang's twice-weekly flight to Darwin (Merpati Airlines) is the cheapest way to Australia. Check the safety situation before using the border with newly independent East Timor.

WHEN TO GO

Straddling the equator, coastal Indonesia is always hot though the mountain tops can be surprisingly cold at night and the peaks of central Papua have some of the world's more unexpected permanent snows. The seasonal variation is between wet and dry. But even the 'dry' is damp and humid.

The wet season generally starts later the further east you head: Sumatra (September to March), Java (October to April), Bali, Lombok and Nusa Tenggara (November to May). However, Maluku bucks the trend with heavy rain from April to August. The wet season brings dramatic downpours but these typically last only for a couple of hours each afternoon. Thus there is no reason to avoid visiting, except perhaps in the more remote islands where the mud roads become impassable (eg far West Flores).

FESTIVALS

In such a huge, multi-cultural nation there are an almost uncountable number of festivals; 🖥 www.expat.or.id/info/holidays.html has details of the different calendars, religious festivals and national holidays.

A free, annually-updated *Calendar of Events* booklet, listing around 300 events, is available from Indonesian tourist offices abroad. In Bali, every day is a festival.

Practical information

VISAS AND FORMALITIES

Most nationalities (though not Portuguese or South Africans) can travel to Indonesia without a visa if they enter and exit through certain specified 'visa waiver' gateways. The list of these gateways has expanded in recent years to include almost every sensible entry/exit point, although it still does not include land or air crossings from Papua New Guinea or East Timor (one-month visa, apply ahead). Israelis are generally refused entry altogether unless with special dispensation.

Theoretically you must be in possession of an onward or return ticket when you arrive in Indonesia. My tickets were checked at Kupang Airport arriving from Australia, though this seems to be rare. Those arriving by boat (eg from Singapore) are hardly ever asked. To be safe, you could buy a full price Medan–Penang ticket from any Garuda office. It is fully refundable within the next year, though you may have to return it to the original issuing office.

Visa extensions

Extensions to the two-month visa-free stay proved quite impossible despite numerous attempts. Leave and come back!! **Do not** overstay even by one day or you'll be in serious trouble.

MONEY

The US dollar is the most accepted currency but all major currencies, as well as travellers' cheques, are accepted in Bali, Java and the other main cities.

In bigger towns ATM machines are increasingly prevalent and convenient though limited in the number of bills that they can dispense at any one time, making it hard to withdraw more than $60 at a time. East of Martaram (Lombok) and in rural areas, especially at weekends, currency exchange becomes awkward.

Banks are open Monday to Friday, 8am–3pm, and very occasionally on Saturdays, 8–11am.

TRANSPORT [See map p31]
Air
Indonesia's airlines are recovering from brushes with bankruptcy in the late 1990s, and timetables seem to change fairly frequently. The flag carrier is Garuda whose increasingly competitive Citilink domestic service is challenging Merpati Nusantara and much smaller Bouraq and Mandala. Merpati also has border-hopping flights to Australia (Darwin), Brunei Darussalam and East Malaysia (Kuching). Air Philippines links Manado (Sulawesi) with Davao (Philippines) weekly (Wed, $70). Departure taxes are additional, generally $3–7.

The commercial website 💻 www.travelindo.com/search/flight/ is very useful for checking what flights exist and on what airline. To reserve online you must book at least 10 days prior to flying.

In remoter areas tiny seven-seater planes flown by missionaries drop supplies into remote valleys. If there is space you can sometimes hitch a lift. You pay only for the fuel that your extra weight requires but this still isn't a particularly cheap way to travel.

Train
Train services are available only in Java and in parts of Sumatra. Several trains run between Jakarta and Surabaya. The most comfortable are the air-conditioned sleepers *Bima* (via Yogyakarta and Solo) and *Mutiara* (via Semarang). The *Senja Utama* is an express service to Yogyakarta and Solo and it has reclining seats but no air-conditioning. The *Parahyangan* offers four services a day between Jakarta and Bandung, taking about three hours. Prices vary enormously between classes and the different trains.

Bus
Bus services are increasingly comprehensive even on immensely long journeys such as Bali–Banda Aceh, travelling both night and day. Long-distance buses on Java and Sumatra are generally air-conditioned and have reclining seats as well as TV with video programmes. Kalimantan and West Papua have few roads and none that penetrate deep into the interior. Western Flores, parts of Sulawesi and other rural areas have poor roads and slow, bone-rattling bus services which cruise the town centres touting for business before going to fill up with petrol and finally limping off. Earplugs and/or a broadened mind towards the worst twangs of 1970s pop music are often necessary.

Tourist bus There are well-developed bus/minibus links between various backpacker centres, especially within north/central Sumatra, eastern Java and Bali. You may pay 50–300% more than by local bus but will save time and a lot of hassle, generally travel on the scenic route sections during daylight, and will get dropped off at a guest house. Unfortunately, as tourist numbers have dwindled in the last few years many of these convenient services have faded.

❑ Muffed mufukat
Amidst vast ethnic and religious divisions, Indonesians' binding force has long been *mufakat* (consensus). Until 1998 the national manifestation of consensus was the much vaunted *Panca Sila* (five principles) of the Republic; nationalism, humanitarianism, religious plurality, justice and 'guided democracy'. In the latter, all opposition political parties were expected to pledge fundamental support for the Golkar government and villages were proud to declare themselves '100% Golkar'.

Things changed dramatically with the fall of Suharto, and Golkar's slide from power. Students discovered the exhilaration of street protest. And in 1999 the populous was astounded to hear that the East Timorese had actually voted for independence; propaganda had led most to believe in Indonesia's 'liberating' role there. Suddenly all the old certainties have been undermined. Indonesia is awaking to a new era of democratic confusion. Watch your step!

Bemo

These are covered pick-up trucks with bench-seats in the back; they're designed for 10 small passengers but are usually even more crowded and uncomfortable. They offer a cheap form of transport and are used as a shared taxi system within towns: generally if they're going your way they'll take you to your door but there'll be various side trips and detours en route to drop off other passengers.

Boat

PELNI, the state-owned shipping company, has modern ships serving dozens of ports from Banda Aceh to Sorong. The ships are air-conditioned and were built to accommodate 1000 to 1500 passengers in four classes. First-class cabins have attached bathrooms and TV. Economy-class accommodation (raised mats on a large communal floor) is much cheaper and perfectly acceptable except when the boat is completely full. Meals (typically fish-head soup) are included but blink and you'll miss them.

Most ships work on two-week loop schedules (a few on 4-week loops) with a two week refit-gap every year or so. Getting a current timetable is very important if you don't want to wait for days or weeks, especially in Maluku and West Papua. Timetables are available at most PELNI offices or download one from ⌨ www.pelni.co.id. This site is slow but a superb resource for route planning which also lets you check boat times from any port using a clickable map. If the site's English-language option is out of action, don't be put off. Select *Tanpa Intro* from the Indonesia bar. Point at *Jadwal Kapal* (schedule) then the *Jadawal Kapal Penumpang* option pops down. A map (sometimes annoyingly flashing) comes up. Click on the port from which you wish to leave and a list of departures comes up for dates in the near future on named boats (*kapal*). Click the destination (*tujuan*) for details of arrival times. The *tarif* option gives fares in each available class.

There are many small private boats on which you can negotiate a passage but the process is hit and miss. I waited a week in Palu (Sulawesi) looking for a ride to Kalimantan. Finding a fishing boat from Banjarmasin to Surabaya, on the other hand, proved easy – I left the same evening, though the chunder-wonder seas made the crossing anything but enjoyable.

Motorcycles

Motorcycles can be rented for about US$6–8/day, weekly rates work out slightly cheaper. Insurance is usually covered in the rate. Getting a temporary motorbike licence is easy but can take a day.

Other forms of transport

Taxis are available, though meters are commonplace only in Jakarta, Bandung, Semarang and Surabaya. A *bachach* is a miniature tricycle seating two passengers rather tightly with its driver in the front while a *bechak* is a bicycle rickshaw. A *suzuki* is a mini-bemo-style shared taxi. An *ojek* is a moto (motorbike hired with its rider). There are also *colts* (say 'coll') and jeepney-esque *opalets*. *Dokars* are horse-drawn buggies which are seen in Sumbawa and parts of Java (eg in Bogor, Yogyakarta, Solo and Surabaya) – less than US$1 per kilometre. Bicycles can often be rented (average cost $1.50/day).

ACCOMMODATION

Ubiquitous *wisma* and *losmen* are cheap guest houses offering a shared *mandi* (bucket shower) and adequate beds for $2–5 – expect to pay a little more in Kalimantan. The price rarely reflects the quality of a cheap place; a beautiful, clean beachside bungalow might cost the same as a flea-pit shack in a dreary town. A *penginapan* is even more basic. A Hotel/Otel is likely to be more expensive.

In very small villages if there is no formal hotel, seek out the *kepal desa* (village chief) and introduce yourself – in Bahasa Indonesia (or the local language if you're really clever). He will conjure up a family (probably his own) for you to stay with. Although initially sceptical about this, the four times I tried it, it worked unbelievably well – perhaps because the villages were so very remote. Though an offer of payment might be refused when offered verbally, it is appropriate to quietly leave behind a sum equivalent to a basic losmen charge. Carry a few envelopes so that you can do so tactfully.

FOOD AND DRINK

The staple food in most of Indonesia is rice. Spices are often used liberally and fish, chicken and coconut are common ingredients. *Nasi goreng* (fried rice), *bami goreng* (fried noodles) and *gado gado* (spicy peanut and tempeh salad) are found virtually everywhere.

If you eat meat you'll probably prefer flesh (*daging*) to innards (*babat*). However, in some rural areas of Nusa Tenggara the only food available in the evening was boiled rice and a diminutive dried fish. In Sumatra particularly, watch out for the searingly hot Padang-style food that burns its own ring of fire. The tandoori red appearance is a giveaway.

The cheapest places to eat are *warung* (street stalls).

Tea is the king of local drinks, but beer is available even in Islamic areas. Local *arak* moonshine served with lemon juice makes a great cheap alternative margarita.

STAYING IN TOUCH

International telephone code: +62. City codes: Jakarta: 21, Yogyakarta: 274, Medan: 61, Bandung: 22, Bali: 0361 (south), 0362 (north), Surabaya: 31.

Email is increasingly commonplace in traveller hubs, though typically cheapest through post offices. The letters I posted arrived reliably, the quickest taking only five days to the US.

ACTIVITIES
Hiking

Sulawesi is marvellous trekking country with a well-worn donkey track still used as a supply road (there are no vehicles) between Palu and Tentena where some Bada valley villages have megaliths. A grasp of Indonesian, or a dictionary, is essential as you have to stay in people's homes along the way. Also in Sulawesi, Tanah Torajah offers endless day walks amongst the stylish boat-shaped grain stores, grave cliffs and impressive rice terraces.

For $12 to $20 a day, Kalimantan Dayak tribesmen can take you on pig hunts or medicine-gathering walks into the deep Borneo jungles. My trip started by paddling and punting up gloriously canopied tributaries from Data Dawai, while the guide shot at hornbills with his blowpipe. Thence we walked for hours through leech-infested forest – beautiful trees but never a panorama. At night we camped on a hunter's raised wooden platform, covered by a tarpaulin, and surrounded by the echoes of a jungle night. Bring anti-mosquito protection.

Other hiking options include Siberut (be prepared for knee-deep mud) and various great volcano climbs. Leave early in the morning to see the sunrise over Kelimutu's three-coloured summit crater lakes (Flores). Sunrises at Mt Bromo (eastern Java) are easier if you join a jeep trip up and walk back. Mt Rinjani (Lombok) is a much tougher prospect taking three to four days to climb from Sapit; hiring a guide is advisable.

Scuba diving

Though there are good sites in north-west Bali (eg Malalayang Beach) and at Maluku, Sulawesi offers the best compromise between accessibility and natural wonder, notably the Togian Islands with their magnificent corals.

For useful links and ratings of Sulawesi dive operators see ▣ www.stormloader.com/divesulawesi/results.html.

Unfortunately the reefs at Maumere in Flores have been damaged by typhoons.

Surfing

Surf beaches in Bali include Nusa Dua and Sanur (October to March), Kuta (summer), Ulu Watu (for experts), with surf tours to otherwise inaccessible sites, organized by Bali operators. Nias Island off Sumatra is also well-known for surfing.

FURTHER INFORMATION

Bill Dalton's *Indonesia Handbook* (Moon Publications) is my favourite practical travel guide with a heartwarmingly genuine appreciation for the country. There are dozens of books on the constantly-evolving political situation, often easiest to find in Australia.

In each of the 27 provincial centres there are government tourist offices (DIPAR DA) which should have local maps. The **Central Department of Tourism** (☎ 21-383 8236, 🖹 386 7589, PO Box 1409, 17–19 Merdeka Barat, Jakarta) is helpful in answering direct questions. Beware that many Indonesia-travel websites are misleadingly out of date.

❑ Meeting the locals

● **The people** A very complex mixture of ethnic and religious groups. The Javanese are the most populous and enforce a political dominance. People are typically friendly, sometimes too much so, but in tourist areas there can be an air of money grabbing and pestering. Cries of 'Hello Mister' haunt travellers of either sex throughout the eastern islands.

● **Language** Bahasa Indonesia is a cinch – it's perhaps the world's easiest language. Just pick up a *kamus* (dictionary) and translate word for word what you want to say. It may not be stylish but it works. There is no difficult grammar, no weird script, and the pronunciation is very straightforward (note that 'c' is always pronounced 'ch' and 'e' is 'eh'). Plurals are formed by saying a word twice; orang (man), orang orang (men) though this is usually written orang2.

People often ask 'Where are you going?' This is not the Spanish Inquisition, they are just making pleasant conversation. Answer '*jalan jalan*' – just wandering about.

Some words in Bahasa Indonesia (like Malay, slightly simplified):
Thank you <u>very much</u> – *Terima kasih <u>banyak</u>*
Good morning – *Selamat pagi*
Good afternoon/evening – *Selamat sor-eh*
Good night – *Selamat malam*
How are you – *Apa kabar*
Response – *Kabar baik*
Sorry – *Ma-af*
It's delicious – *Enak saja*

Useful websites

🖳 www.itisnet.com/english/asia/indonesia/indonesiatop.htm has lots of useful stuff, with very thorough information on some destinations in Java, Bali, Lombok and Flores.

Sumatra is covered by 🖳 www.passplanet.com/Indonesia/index.htm.

For Sulawesi 🖳 www.sulawesi-info.com/ is opinionated, fact rich and regularly updated.

🖳 www.accomasia.com/indonesia.htm has many more well chosen and reviewed general links.

East Timor

The world's newest independent country had an unhappy few decades under Indonesian rule and is still recovering from the mass destruction of its infrastructure by pro-Indonesian militias – a violent reaction against the results of the pre-independence referendum. I admit I haven't been there yet but it's reportedly much more expensive than West Timor (or even Jakarta) thanks to the bubble economy around all the Australian and international ex-pats helping to rebuild the place. Baukau has colonial charm; lovely beaches and the Dili–Maubise road is said to be spectacular.

PRACTICAL INFORMATION

You don't need a **visa** for stays of 90 days or less. The new **currency** is the US$ – great fun was had importing all the necessary cents, nickels, quarters and dimes. There's an **ATM cash machine** at the ANZ bank in Dili which dispenses US dollars on Cirrus/MasterCard accounts.

There is at least one **internet café** in Dili, the telephone code is +670, plus 390 for Dili. Mobile phones work on the Australian Telstra network.

Dili can be reached by air four times a week from Denpasar on Merpati, or by Air North or Qantas (daily from Australia). The Batugede border crossing to West Timor is reported to be open but you need to get a visa to enter Indonesia here (available in Dili) and Australians should be particularly cautious: in West Timor, Australia is largely 'blamed' for the loss of the East. There are no PELNI boats from Indonesia.

Single-entry Indonesian visas cost $35 in Dili and take at least three days to issue.

You can read the latest East Timor news on 🖳 www.easttimor.com/.

Travel, hotel listings and much more are on 🖳 www.timoraid.org/timortoday/.

❏ **Geo-political information – East Timor (Timor Leste)**

Population: 750,000 (2000)

Area: 15,400 sq km.

Capital: Dili (50,000)

Other towns: Dare (18,000), Baucau, Maliana, Ermera (13,000), others under 7000.

GNP per capita: $2900 (2000 est), $880 (1994), $475 (1988).

Major exports/economy: Natural gas, coffee, fish, coconuts.

Ethnic mix: Tetum 33%, Mambai 12%, Makasai 10%, Kemak 8%, Galoli 8%, Tokodede 8%.

Religious mix: Catholic (91%), Protestant (2.5%), Muslim (0.5%),

Landmarks of national history: **1975**: Fretelin declared independence from Portugal but Indonesia promptly invaded (some claim with a tacit nod from Australia). **1999**: Pro-independence vote followed by atrocities by rampaging pro-Indonesian militias. **May 20th 2002**: Formal independence. See 🖳 http://news.bbc.co.uk/1/hi/world/asia-pacific/1504243.stm for a fuller timeline.

Leader: Xanana Gusmao, elected April 2002.

Pressing political issues: Rebuilding the destroyed infrastructure, relations with Indonesia, future gas revenues liable to distort the economy and price the farming majority into unemployability.

1 MARINDUQUE Easter Moriones festival ✪

2 ROMBLON ✴ ♨ ⬚ ✪

3 SIBUYAN forest, waterfalls

4 TABLAS Carmen on scenic bay

5 TICAO wild, few tourists

6 MALAPASCUA 'the new Boracay' ☼

7 CEBU Shipping centre, Pescadores coral garden, Mactan int'l airport

8 BOHOL Chocolate Hills ✪

9 SIQUIJOR island of witches!

10 CAMIGUIN ✪, ⬚ villages, 6 volcanoes

BABUYAN Isles

⚓ PAGUDPUD

LAOAG

APACALYPSE NOW? COAST

✷ VIGAN ⬚
CLASSIC SPANISH
COLONIAL TOWN

SAGADA – HANGING COFFINS

BONTOC   ✷ BANAUE ⬚
BRILLIANT
RICE TERRACES

'100 ISLANDS'

● BAGUIO
  CITY

● DAGUPAN
ALAMINOS

LUZON

Mt. PINATUBO   ● ANGELES
              ● SAN
         ● FERNANDO
        ● MANILA

MARIVELES

LUBANG   BATAN-GAS
☼ Binacas   ● DAET
                 LUCENA   NAGA ● NAGA   VIRAC
✷ SABANG ☼   BOAC ●①   Mt. MAYON   TABACO
✷ PUERTO   CALAPAN   LEGASPI
  GALERA ☼   MATNOG

● DAET   CATANDUANES ➤
"Land of howling winds"

MINDORO   ROXAS ●   ②   ⑤   SAMAR
         SAN   ④ ③   ⬚ W coast rd
         JOSE   LO   CARMEN ⬚   ALLEN   Sohotan NP
                      CATICLAN   MASBATE   CALBAYOG

BUSUANGAS   cattle

CULION ✪   ● CORON   BORACAY

⬚ EL NIDO   KALIBO ●   ⑥   ORMOC ● TACLOBATAN
                   PANAY   ROXAS ●   LEYTE
PORT   ✷ ♨   ● ILOILO   SILAY   BAY BAY
BARTON   CADIZ   ⑦   MA LILOAN   SIRAGAO
         TAYTAY ♨   BACO-   CEBU   ASIN   surfing
CUYO ✴ ✪   LOD   CITY   SURIGAO   BUCAS
                                          Lagoon
         NEGROS   TAMPI   ● TAGBI   ⑧   ⑩   BUTUAN
PUERTO   Sugar fields   ● BATO LARAN   NASIIT
PRINCESSA   DUMAGUETE ●   ⑨   BALINGOAN
                                   CAGAYAN
         DIPOLOG ●   ● DE ORO
PALAWAN   OZAMIS ●   ● ILIGAN
Picturesque diving centres   PAGADIAN ➤
                                   COTO   DAVAO ●
                                   BATO   APO
         ZAMBOANGA ●   LAKE
                           SEBU ●   GENERAL
         ● ISABELA   SANTOS
         ☼ JOLO?   BASILAN   MINDANAO?
              weavers   Hill Tribes
                        !! insurgency !!

Philippines

←—100 Km—→

🌋 ≈ IMPRESSIVE
    VOLCANO

SULU Archipelago
infamous for pirates

Philippines

The 7100 Philippine islands are dotted with great beaches, dramatic volcanoes and Spanish colonial remnants. Lively locals ride gaudy jeepneys in the cities, while the mountains are still inhabited by fascinating hill tribes.

A lack of regular boat services to neighbouring countries keeps the islands off the main trans-Asia route and contributes to the country's surprisingly under-exploited tourist potential. However, reaching the Philippines need not be drastically expensive thanks to the free stopovers in Manila (and sometimes Cebu) which are possible on certain discounted regional and trans-Pacific airline tickets.

HIGHLIGHTS

Head to north Luzon for 'sites' (old Vigan, the Banaue rice terraces, Sagada etc), for highland hikes and for encounters with various minority tribes.

South Luzon has some brilliantly photogenic volcanoes: Mayon is a perfect Fuji-esque cone (the best view is from the ruins of Cagasawa Church, accessed by jeepney from Legaspi), Mt Taal (a great cone-in-lake ensemble which can be viewed from Tagatay/People's Park), and Mt Pinatubo (fascinating lava flows from the 1991 eruption – take a jeepney to Sabang Bato from Rabbit bus terminal, Angeles, 2km to Target and then hike for 45 minutes).

For those who make it out there, the beaches, rock-scapes and diving opportunities combine to make North Palawan and Coron particularly enticing, but boats are rare (the best is the Friday service, get tickets from Superferry pier 4, Manila, more information is available from 🖥 www.diveright-coron.com/boat.htm).

The classic beach paradises are the miniscule Boracay and Malapascua islands – perfect white sand and still beguiling despite considerable development. As a

---

❏ **Country ratings – Philippines**

● **Expense $$$** Similar to Malaysia. Accommodation is typically more expensive than in Thailand, but scuba diving is generally cheaper.

● **Value for money ★★★☆☆** You get what you pay for.

● **Ease of transport ★★★★☆** Boats are frequent though not necessarily safe. Jeepneys and buses are also very frequent and convenient – once you work out where to find them.

● **English spoken ★★★★☆** English is the business language and much of the populous has at least a smattering of the language, though accents can be impossibly thick. Some Spanish is spoken.

● **Woman alone ★★★☆☆** A few minor hassles reported.

● **For vegetarians ★★☆☆☆** Surprisingly for an island nation meat is more popular than fish.

❑ **Essential information for travellers – Philippines**
- **Visa** A three-week visa-free stay is possible for most nationalities.
- **Currency** Peso. US$1=P50.10.
- **Time zone** 8 hours ahead of GMT (same as Malaysia and Bali).
- **Religious tone** Strongly Catholic, the only predominantly Christian country in Asia. Especially interesting at Easter.
- **Health factors** The tap water in cities is theoretically drinkable. The malaria risk is worst in Mindanao, Sulu Archipelago and Palawan.
- **Pulse of the country** Open-air Christian evangelical meetings; sharing food with friendly strangers on leaky inter-island boats; drinking a San Miguel on a beautiful tropical beach.
- **Special dangers** Smugglers/pirates in the Sulu Sea. On the southern island of Mindanao the Muslim separatist movement, the Moro Liberation Front (MLF), has agreed a ceasefire with the government, but some terrorist activity has continued courtesy of a small splinter group called the Moro Islamic Liberation Front (MILF). Exaggerated reports of tourist druggings and muggings – these are partly myth but Baguio has a particularly bad reputation.
- **Key tips** In Baguio and around Manila leave your valuables behind when exploring so that you don't need to fear, and can happily take up, invitations from genuinely hospitable locals. Many hostels have lockers.

transport centre Cebu is easy to reach yet it has some pretty nice beaches at either end and is handy for Bohol (the curious 'Chocolate Hills' – magical or just dull?). And don't discount Puerto Galera for beaches – despite its proximity to Manila (there are very frequent boats from Batangas direct or via Calapan) and its 'developed' image, I found the area really beautiful and surprisingly relaxing.

Mindanao is big and particularly friendly. You'll be 'on your own' as most tourists are scared off by the rumbles of insurgent separatist groups. These are not altogether unfounded fears, however, and you should take particular care in the south and south-west. Ironically that's exactly where you'll arrive when coming by boat from Malaysia or Indonesia (see notes on p30). Lovely, chilly Lake Sebu (access via Koronadal) is best on Saturdays for the hill-tribe market.

WHEN TO GO

The climate varies considerably between the islands. In general, monsoon rains fall in summer and especially on the west coasts a long dry season lasts from October to May. On east-facing coasts, however, there can be heavy downpours in the winter months, and rain is possible at pretty much any time.

The country is always hot and humid at lower elevations; in summer, rich Filipinos leave Manila en masse for the cool mountain air of Baguio.

There are dozens of festivals, with the most dramatic occurring at Easter time, notably in Marinduque and San Fernando (Luzon).

❏ Geo-political information – Philippines

Population: 82.8 million (2001), 76.1m (1997), 60.6m (1990).

Area: 300,000 sq km.

Capital: Manila 13.5 million (note this figure is for Metro Manila including Quezon City – 1.7m, Calocan – 700,000, Pasay – 300,000 and many more townships in a huge conurbation).

Other major cities: Davao (870,000), Cebu (750,000), Bacolod (440,000), Cagayan de Oro (425,000); Iloilo (380,000); Angeles (280,000); Baguio (260,000) and 26 other cities over 100,000.

GNP per capita: $3800 (2000).

Currency history: Peso/US$1 — April 2002: P50.10, Jan 2001: P50.97, Feb 1998: P42.5, Oct 1997: P33.2, July 1996: P26.20, Jan 1996: P26.23, Jan 1995: P24.44, Dec 1993: P27.65.

Exports/economy: A major source of foreign exchange is the remittances from Filipino workers abroad. Exports: textiles, pineapples, sugar cane, bananas, coconuts, electronics.

Ethnic mix/languages: Though Filipino (basically Tagalog) and English are the official lingos, there are 988 local languages and dialects. The five major ones are Tagalog (27.9%), Cebuano (24.3%), Ilocano (9.8%), Ilongo (9.3%), Bicol (5.8%). Approx 1.5% Chinese.

Religious mix: 83% Roman Catholic, 9% other Christian, 5% Muslim (mainly in Mindanao).

Landmarks of national history: **1521**: Magellan claimed the islands for Spain. **1762**: Manila briefly occupied by Britain. **1872**: Independence struggle began against Spanish rule. **1898**: Independence declared but regardless of this the USA bought the territory from Spain. **1942–5**: Japanese invasion, MacArthur swore he would return but in so doing Manila was bombed to smithereens. **July 1946**: Independence. **1965**: Ferdinand Marcos became president, his beauty queen wife began her infamous shoe collection. **1983**: Assassination of Benino Aquino (opposition leader returning from exile). **Feb 1986**: Marcos fled in the wake of a 'people's power' revolution and the world discovered his wife Imelda's shoe hoard. Benino Aquino's widow (Corazon) declared president. **2001**: Former actor turned president Joseph Estrada arrested on corruption charges – his supporters had needed so many low denomination peso notes to bribe electors that banks ran out of change!

Leader: President Gloria Macapagal-Arroyo, confirmed by election May 2001.

Pressing political issues: Continued insurgency in Mindanao, economic liberalization, Metro Manila power supply, corruption.

KEY REMINDER
Emphasising the positive:

THIS FONT = somewhere interesting

⊞ = atmospheric, quaint, charming...

★ = recommended

✸✸ = a must (a rare accolade indeed!)

Practical information

VISAS AND FORMALITIES

Tourists of most Western nationalities get 21 days visa free, but citizens of Hong Kong, Taiwan, the former Yugoslav republics (Croatia, Slovenia etc) and ex-Soviet states (Latvia, Russia etc) do need visas.

The 21 days can be extended allowing a total stay of up to 59 days if you visit an immigration office and pay around $20 – this is often faster in provincial cities than in Manila. Alternatively you can apply beforehand for such a visa. You're supposed to have a return ticket on arrival – mine wasn't checked but sometimes it can be.

MONEY

Exchange rates are better for cash (especially for high denomination US$ notes) than travellers' cheques which can be awkward to exchange. The black market offers little extra and the risk of loss from the many scams is high. Cash advances are possible but any use of credit cards typically incurs a 7% surcharge. About 300 ATMs are on the Cirrus system.

TRANSPORT

Given the plethora of air, bus and boat companies, a good travel agent can prove helpful. Try European-run Filipino Travel (☎ 528 4507, 🖹 528 4503, 🖳 travelct@skyinet.net) at 1555 Adriatico, 10 minutes' walk north of Malate Pension at Pedro Gil St, Manila.

Buses and jeepneys

The country is generally well served by long-distance **buses** but as there are no central bus stations, finding available options requires you to check out a plethora of different companies (Victory Liner and Rabbit are amongst the best known).

The alternative are **jeepneys**, long wheel-base jeep-style vehicles adorned to kitschy perfection with glitter, colour and mirrors. They cover most shorter-distance routes and are an ideal way to navigate Manila once you've learnt the general layout – destinations and routings are named rather than numbered.

Ferry

Since the islands are relatively close together there are frequent and cheap (if not especially seaworthy) shipping services all over the country. Also most islands are served by occasional direct boats from Manila.

For links to various ferry websites surf to 🖳 www.travelphil.com/.

Rail

Trains carry only freight in most of the country, though the Metrorail in Manila is handy.

Air

For reaching less well-connected islands (notably Palawan), it's worth considering a flight. There is a large selection of local airlines, most using Manila and Cebu as hubs: PAL (☎ 855-9999, 🖳 www.philippine air.com/ with online booking), Cebu Pacific (☎ 636-4938, 🖳 www.cebupacificair .com/), Asian Spirit (☎ 851-8888, 🖳 www.asianspir-it.com/FlytMain.htm), Air Soriano, Air Ads, Grand Air, Laoag International (☎ 551-9729), Mindanao Express and Pacific Airways.

Most domestic flights now have a 300P insurance surcharge. Note that baggage limits may be as little as 10kg.

Manila transport and how to escape

Using the raised MetroRail trains (single line) makes orientation easy, but jeepneys are often more convenient once you suss the right route. At Manila's NAIA airport the information office informed me that taxis (a coupon system) or an expensive bus into the city were the only options. In fact, if you walk five minutes out of the airport you'll come to a major road. Take any passing jeep-

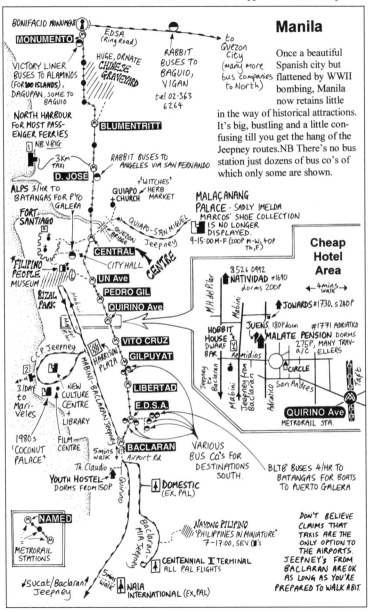

Manila

Once a beautiful Spanish city but flattened by WWII bombing, Manila now retains little in the way of historical attractions. It's big, bustling and a little confusing till you get the hang of the Jeepney routes. NB There's no bus station just dozens of bus co's of which only some are shown.

ney (heading to your right) which will drop you in Baclaran. From here you can walk through a market-crowded street to the MetroRail station near which another jeepney marked Mabini which will take you through the cheap hotel area.

ACCOMMODATION

The term 'youth hostel' simply denotes dorm room availability. Basic windowless rooms are available from about $4. Outside Manila and major resorts, $10–15 will generally get you a pretty decent double room with air-conditioning. It's worth travelling in couples as a double generally costs only 30% more than a single. Beach places often double their prices in season (usually December to May).

As in Indonesia, the mayor or village chief of small, out of the way places may be able to help find you a place to stay when there is no hotel.

In Manila, *Malate Pension* (☎ 523 8304/5/6; 💻 info@mpensionne.com.ph, www.mpensionne.com.ph) 1771 Adriatico, Manila, is a good place for meeting travellers (especially at breakfast in the downstairs restaurant) and its $6 air-conditioned dorms have trustworthy lockers.

FOOD AND DRINK

Many cheaper restaurants serve buffet-style food making choosing simpler. In case you have to ask, any meal cooked *adobo*-style is real Filipino food, *pancit* are noodles and *kanu* is rice. Eating *balut* (a boiled egg with a fully-formed foetus) is thought to be 'manhood enhancing'.

San Miguel Beer is drunk in great quantities and costs little more than soft drinks. Ask for wine and see what you get!

STAYING IN TOUCH

The **mail** service is relatively efficient. Poste restante goes by the American term 'General Delivery', and works OK in Manila.

The international **telephone** country code is +63. Manila: 2, Cebu City: 32, Davao: 82, Masbate: 56.

ACTIVITIES
Scuba diving/swimming

Popular year-round though the high season is from April to June. Diving is relatively inexpensive (the cheapest I found was only $13 for a boat dive including equipment), but much of the coral has been damaged by dynamite fishing. There are some stunning beaches: Boracay is, perhaps justifiably, the most famous but there are other less touristy alternatives, with Palawan increasingly featured in the top category.

Hiking

The mountains and rice terraces of north Luzon are a worthwhile alternative to the over-commercialized hill-tribe treks of northern Thailand.

FURTHER INFORMATION

Tourist information offices including the one at Manila's Aquino airport offer basic maps and help. Maps of the country are available in the stores in the Ermita (tourist) district of Manila, and from petrol stations.

There's a good library on the third floor of the grandiose modern **Cultural Center of the Philippines (CCP)** building (Roxas Blvd, Manila), which is open 9am–6pm, Tuesday to Friday.

❏ Meeting the locals

● **The people** Over breakfast at Manila's Malate Pension yet another group of travellers were discussing third-hand grapevine tales of backpackers being lured to drugged muggings by apparently friendly locals.

Later in the day, I walked nonchalantly towards Manila's surreal Chinese graveyard-city. Suddenly I was hailed raucously by a swaying gang of drunken Filipino men. 'Come here, come here!' they demanded loudly from the yard of a cramped little house. I shuffled on, trying not to notice. But they persisted. 'Here, Mister!!' As I slowed down, one chap scuttled out and grabbed me by the arm. I tried to stay calm and to remember what 'escape strategies' had been discussed in the morning. But there was no assault, just a San Miguel beer thrust into my hand. 'We celebrate, my friend marry!' said Fidel. I smiled wanly and gave a half-hearted promise to return later. Then I strode away relieved. However, after an hour or two inspired by the preposterous sight of graves furnished with postboxes and guest rooms, I decided it was time to live a little. I returned to the little party and decided to let events flow! Fidel and the gang were drunker than ever but seemed delighted to see me. Drink after dance after patently un-drugged drink, we became buddies. Fidel admitted to me that he'd invited in dozens of passing foreigners. Yet all except myself had ignored him and skulked past embarrassed. Fidel was genuinely perplexed: 'Surely everyone know Philippines is famous for hospitality'. We parted with a flurry of hugs, photos and address swapping. I stumbled off into the now dark streets, stopping and stooping into a little alcove shop to buy some rice. The smiling owners, crouched below a low wooden ceiling, gave me a discount and a jolly conversation in English. 'But aren't you afraid to be here after dark?' they asked. 'Should I be?' 'Well, no. Not really. It's just that every tourist seems to think they should!'.

● **Some phrases in Tagalog/Filipino**:

Greeting – *Mabuhay*	Delicious – *Masarap*
How are you? – *Kumusta*	How much is it? – *Magkano?*
Thank you – *Salamat*	

Useful websites

City net has a travel-related index at 🖳 www.city.net/countries /philippines/.

🖳 www.travelphil.com/internet_eng/index.html is the website of former LP author Jens Peters who now publishes a Philippines guide of his own.

Boots'n'all has a strong contingent of travel helpers to answer your questions via 🖳 www.bootsnall.com/cgi-bin/gt/insiders/asia/philippines.shtml.

🖳 www.webgate.net.ph/websites/travel.htm offers a long series of helpful links.

❏ OTHER GUIDES FROM TRAILBLAZER

Adventure Cycling Handbook	1st edn late 2003
Adventure Motorcycling Handbook	4th edn out now
Australia by Rail	4th edn out now
Azerbaijan	2nd edn out now
The Blues Highway – New Orleans to Chicago	1st edn out now
China by Rail	2nd edn late 2003
Coast to Coast (British Walking Guide)	1st edn late 2003
Cornwall Coast Path (British Walking Guide)	1st edn Mar 2003
Good Honeymoon Guide	2nd edn out now
Inca Trail, Cusco & Machu Picchu	2nd edn out now
Japan by Rail	1st edn out now
Kilimanjaro – treks and excursions	1st edn Jan 2003
The Med Guide	1st edn mid 2003
Nepal Mountaineering Guide	1st edn Oct 2003
Norway's Arctic Highway	1st edn mid 2003
Offa's Dyke Path (British Walking Guide)	1st edn May 2003
Pembrokeshire Coast Path (British Walking Guide)	1st edn Mar 2003
Pennine Way (British Walking Guide)	1st edn late 2003
Siberian BAM Guide – rail, rivers & road	2nd edn out now
Silk Route by Rail	2nd edn out now
The Silk Roads – a route and planning guide	1st end Apr 2003
Sahara Overland – a route & planning guide	1st edn out now
Sahara Abenteuerhandbuch (German edition)	1st edn late 2002
Ski Canada – where to ski and snowboard	1st edn out now
South Downs Way (British Walking Guide)	1st edn late 2003
Tibet Overland – mountain biking & jeep touring	1st edn out now
Trans-Canada Rail Guide	2nd edn out now
Trans-Siberian Handbook	5th edn out now
Trekking in the Annapurna Region	4th edn mid 2003
Trekking in the Everest Region	4th edn Jan 2003
Trekking in Corsica	1st edn out now
Trekking in the Dolomites	1st edn out now
Trekking in Ladakh	2nd edn out now
Trekking in Langtang, Gosainkund & Helambu	1st edn out now
Trekking in the Moroccan Atlas	1st edn out now
Trekking in the Pyrenees	2nd edn out now
Tuva and Southern Siberia	1st edn late 2003
Vietnam by Rail	1st edn out now
West Highland Way (British Walking Guide)	1st edn Jan 2003

For more information about Trailblazer and our expanding range of guides,
for where to find your nearest stockist, for guidebook updates
or for credit card mail order sales (post-free worldwide)
visit our Web site:

www.trailblazer-guides.com

ROUTE GUIDES FOR THE ADVENTUROUS TRAVELLER

Azerbaijan (with excursions to Georgia) Mark Elliott
2nd edition, 352pp, 182 maps, 30 colour photos
ISBN 1 873756 49 6, £12.99 Can$30.95, US$21.95
Fully revised second edition. What to see, where to go, how to get there, where to stay. By the author of South-East Asia – The Graphic Guide. 'Recommended' **The Independent on Sunday** '...meticulous research and evident affection for Azerbaijan..' **Daily News** 'Very comprehensive coverage' **Caspian Business News**

The Silk Roads – a route & planning guide
Paul Wilson & Dominic Streatfeild-James
1st edition, 320pp, 50 maps, 30 colour photos
ISBN 1 873756 53 4, £12.99, Can$29.95, US$18.95
The Silk Road was never a single thread but an intricate web of trade routes linking Asia and Europe. This new guide follows all the routes with sections on Turkey, Syria, Iran, Turkmenistan, Uzbekistan, Kyrgyzstan, Kazakhstan, Pakistan and China.

Tibet Overland – a route & planning guide for mountain bikers and other overlanders Kym McConnell
1st edition, 224pp 16pp colour maps
ISBN 1 873756 41 0, £12.99, Can$29.95, US$19.95,
Featuring 16pp of full colour mapping based on satellite photographs, this is a route and planning guide for mountain bikers and other road users in Tibet. Includes detailed information on over 9000km of overland routes across the world's highest and largest plateau. Includes Lhasa-Kathmandu route and the route to Everest North Base Camp. '..a wealth of advice...' **HH The Dalai Lama**

Trekking in the Everest Region Jamie McGuinness
4th edn, 304pp, 38 maps, 52 village plans, 30 colour photos
ISBN 1 873756 60 7, £10.99, Can$27.95, US$17.95
Popular guide to the world's most famous trekking region. Includes detailed walking maps, where to stay and where to eat along the way plus information on trek preparation and getting to Nepal. Written by a professional trek leader.
'The pick of the guides to the area' **Adventure Travel**

Trans-Siberian Handbook Bryn Thomas
5th edition, 432pp, 48 maps, 32 colour photos
ISBN 1 873756 42 9, £12.99, Can$28.95 US$19.95
First edition short-listed for the **Thomas Cook Guidebook Awards**. New fifth edition of the most popular guide to the world's longest rail journey. How to arrange a trip, plus a km-by-km guide to the routes. Updated and expanded to include extra information on travelling independently in Russia. New mapping.
'Definitive guide' **Condé Nast Traveler**

Vietnam by Rail Tess Read
1st edition, 320pp, 45 maps, 30 colour photos
ISBN 1 873756 44 5, £11.99, Can$28.95, US$18.95,
The 'Reunification Express' railway links the north and south and is the most popular way to travel the country. Includes a history of Vietnam's railways, and a detailed route guide with 13 strip maps. Plus comprehensive guides to 24 towns and cities. '...a timely and useful addition to the traveller's library...' **The Guardian**

INDEX

ACCOMMODATION

 has beds for under $6

 beds under $12

 most beds over $10+

 concentration of GH s

 worth the splurge

 expensive to stay but
worth a peep/drink at the bar

 GH that is an obvious backpacker choice
(info, bike hire, e-mail, travel services etc)

GH Guest House   *B+B* breakfast included

s/sng single room   *d/dbl* double

dorm dormitory   *sep* separate

H₂O water/bathroom   *a/c* air conditioning

pp per person   *rm* room

FOOD & DRINK

NB Lack of icons doesn't mean you'll
starve! It's generally **SO** easy to find
good, cheap fare that eateries are
usually marked only a) where
restaurants are also handy landmarks,
b) if there is a relative lack of dining
options, c) to show a place that has
special appeal/value/atmosphere.

X cheap food

⊠ somewhat nicer place to eat

⊠ swankier place, expat crowd?

 bar

 upmarket café

Key to symbols used in this guide

LINE TYPES

- Railway
- Metro/Suburban line station
- International border
- Crossing point open
- Crossing point closed
- Crossing point may open
- Road transport (bus, minibus etc)
- No public transport
- Roads
- = = = = Unpaved or pedestrianised road
- - - - - Walking path/Track
- Water/River
- Ferry
- Wall

TRANSPORT

- Main bus station ✈ Rail station
- Bus stand, stop or small station
- Airport Ⓜ Metro Station
- Jetty/Port Sleeper service
- moto Motorbike taxi
- Bicycle rental Motorbike rental
- p/u Pick up/bemo/songthaew/linega
- freq frequent/ sev several per day
- d/dep depart a./arr. arrive

DESCRIPTIONS

- PLACE 'Place' is interesting
- atmospheric, quaint, charming…
- ★ recommended ✦ must see!
- English spoken (where rare)
- [POX] 'Pox' is unprepossessing - don't make a special trip to visit!

PRICES

$ US$	S$ Singapore $		
M$ Malaysian Ringgit	฿ Thai Baht		
Đ Vietnamese Dong	K Lao Kip		
R/Rls Cambodian Rials	Ky Burmese Kyat		
Y/元 Chinese Yuan	P Philippine Pesos		
Rp Indonesian Rupiah	B$ Brunei $		

SHADING

- Park or green area
- Open area/car-park
- Market
- Enclosed market/shopping centre
- Travellers' area (GH s, bike rental, e-mail, cafés etc) or as described.
- Other 'area' (described)

RELIGIOUS BUILDINGS

- Temple/Pagoda Special temple
- Big Buddha reclining Buddha
- Indian temple Khmer Prasat
- Mosque Church

ATTRACTIONS

- Castle/Fort Palace
- Palace open as museum
- Classic Khmer temple
- Significant ruins
- Other ruins Museum
- Beach Cave
- Upmarket resort beach
- Scuba diving
- Attractive old houses
- Atmospheric (town, place etc)
- Backpacker centre
- Garden Viewpoint

AROUND TOWN

- Museum Bookshop
- Bike rental Motorbike rental
- Embassy/Consulate Cinema
- Bath-house/Hot spring Theatre
- Opera/Concert Hall TV Tower
- Post Office Telephone/Phone office
- E-mail/Internet café
- Info office (head here or to 'traveller area/GH' to get a map)
- Bank/Money changer
- Statue/Monument Gallery
- Stadium Hospital